130

Praise for Wah!

'*Wah!* is as poignant as it is hilarious, and that is saying something. Everyone with a mother should read this book.'
Louisa Young

'I have devoured *Wah!* the delicious memoir from Cynthia Rogerson. Perfect wet weather reading for anyone with a parent crumbling long distance or anyone who was far naughtier than said parent ever knew . . .' *Patrick Gale*

'A memoir about joy in the shadow of grief, *Wah!* is both moving and funny, with a wonderfully light touch – completely charming.'
Tim Dowling

'Wah! seems at first to be a tragicomic account of a dying mother who won't die. But gradually, with Rogerson's distinctive fusion of empathetic warmth and unrestrained frankness, it encompasses the entire scope of life from childhood to old age, and all the different kinds of love.' *Michel Faber*

'Cynthia Rogerson doesn't spare the horses of intimacy; she tells it like it is and she tells it all. *Wah* is witty, rich in revelation, and elegantly written. Her style owes something to Richard Brautigan – she's from California after all – and this only increases my delight.' *Chris Stewart*

'A selfie of a tearaway with a real writer in control of the chaos. A wonderful and courageous book.' *Bernard MacLaverty*

'Wah! Is witty, compassionate, playful, scarily honest and emotionally accurate. It does that rare, liberating thing, being funny about pain without diminishing either the humour or the hurt.'
Andrew Greig

'Novelist Cynthia Rogerson kept a few secrets from her late mother about her free-spirited past. In more ways than one, this sparkling memoir is a revelation.'
David Robinson

'A rich, lyrical text that will show the tears at the heart of things.'
Richard Holloway

'In this scintillating memoir, covering six decades and moving between California and the Scottish Highlands, Cynthia Rogerson delivers another wonderful book. Episodes from a conventional childhood, wilder adolescence and breakaway early twenties and her older self's commentary on them are laugh-aloud funny, poignant, rude, wicked, shallow and profound – sometimes all on the same page.'
James Robertson

'A marvellous read. It's searingly, almost wincingly honest yet at the same time teases the reader by embroidering over the line between memoir and fiction. Rogerson is especially good at portraying the tenderness and confusion of pain and loss, the complex tangle of feelings we have for our loved ones, and her wisecracks skewer even the bleakest moments.'
Lesley Glaister

Cynthia Rogerson (aka Addison Jones) grew up in California. She is the author of six novels and a collection of short stories. She won the V.S.Pritchett Prize in 2008, and her short stories have been widely broadcast and anthologised. *I Love You Goodbye* was shortlisted for Best Scottish Novel in 2011 and translated into five languages. She holds a Royal Literary Fund Fellowship.

Cynthia Rogerson

WAH!

Things I Never Told My Mother

SANDSTONE PRESS

First published in Great Britain in 2022 by
Sandstone Press Ltd
PO Box 41
Muir of Ord
IV6 7YX
Scotland

www.sandstonepress.com

ISBN: 9781913207731
ISBNe: 9781913207748

Sandstone Press is committed to a sustainable future.
This book is made from Forest Stewardship Council ® certified paper.

Cover design by Stuart Brill
Typeset by Biblichor Ltd, Edinburgh
Printed in the UK by CPI Group (UK) Ltd, Croydon CR0 4YY

In memory of my mother, Barbara Jones
1929–2018

Writing is really a matter of coming to terms
with your own squalor.
Frederic Raphael

When a writer is born into a family, the family is finished.
Czesław Miłosz

Contents

Warning

When my brother was born, we got a puppy. In my mind these were equal events and I had two brothers. A few years later, when it was my turn to Show and Tell at St Philomena's nursery, I brought a picture of our dog and said he could talk. That, in fact, we talked all the time.

Sister Rose sighed and shook her head.

'Show and Tell is not for fibbing, Cynthia. You have to tell the truth,' she said.

The other children sniggered. I blushed but didn't cry. Then I told a story in which my dog did not talk. He retrieved sticks, rolled over and scared burglars away. They were all lies – but good lies – and everyone clapped when I finished.

In my defence now, and by way of introducing this book, I would say this: maybe the dog talked.

Wah!

The summer my mother started dying in earnest, it stopped raining in Scotland. Our well ran dry and we took showers at my daughter's house. Wildfires broke out and no one knew what to do. All this distracted me from my mother's impending death in San Rafael, California – but it also seemed to emphasise it. Like her dying, it was both shocking and natural. What did we expect? Most people on the planet had already suffered because of climate change, but it was hard not to take personally. Tempting to see the drought as a result of Mom dying, as if in her death throes, her panic was drying up clouds. Or maybe the heatwave was California coming to me at last, summoned by decades of homesickness. Maybe it had missed me too, sought me everywhere till it finally found me hiding in the Scottish Highlands. I was tired and tended to read meaning into everything.

My first deathbed visit was in August.

'The end, it is here. You must come,' said her caregiver on the phone.

Ateca (pronounced Atetha) was a Fijian woman, sixty-four years old – the same age as me – and whenever she told me to do something, I did it. Her voice was gruff and staccato. When she watched football on television, she sat hunched forward, legs apart, and shouted like a man. *Run, run, run, you beauty!* Or more often: *No, no, no! What's the matter with you?*

I arrived to find my mother in a hospital bed next to her own bed. My sister explained that's what hospice means in California. Hospice comes to you.

'Mom, I'm here!'

'How did you get here?'

'Flew.'

'You flew! What do you mean?' This was a genuine question. She wasn't capable – had never been capable – of sarcasm. With dementia, she was even more literal-minded.

'I flew in an airplane to come and see you.'

'That is . . . charming!'

It turned out that at the end, not only did you lose your independence, you didn't even get to pick your own words. You just got what you got. My mother got charming, delightful, creepy, correct and wah! She used wah! a lot, by itself, with a capital letter and an exclamation mark. Basically her *Wah!* meant *I have no fucking idea what to say.* It was never said without a smile, so I think there was also an element of defiance. *I have no fucking idea what to say and I don't give a shit.* She never swore, but that didn't mean she didn't think in swears.

Her stock of phrases included *That's perfectly normal, Are you all right, He or she is an odd duck, Que sera sera,* and *So be it.* Oh, and *I love you,* of course. Now and then she'd come out with French words. *Moi?* covered all sorts of occasions, though was suspiciously close to *Wah!* which could be confusing. *C'est la vie!* came in handy sometimes. Lately she'd begun to ask the time a lot, enunciating every syllable. *Excuse me, can you please tell me the time?* As if she was late for an appointment and asking a stranger in a public place. She didn't learn any Fijian words, even though she heard Ateca on the phone all day. Not even *bula.* All of Ateca's conversations began and ended with *bula-bula*. Every time I heard that, an old Motown song would start up in my head. I didn't know which one, but that didn't matter. *She's my baby, bula-bula, bula-bula, bula-bula.*

I lowered my face to Mom's hospital bed and kissed her. She gave me three hard kisses back. I noted she still didn't smell like an old lady. She smelled of Clinique night cream and she looked pretty. Somehow, she'd skipped the unattractive side of old age and leapfrogged straight into the home run.

'See you in the morning, Mom. Goodnight.'

'God bless you,' she said, which was odd because we were the kind of Catholics who got embarrassed when people talked about God. Maybe Ateca, who was Pentecostal, had rubbed off on her.

It must have been confusing for my mother to see her own bed but not be in it. Or maybe sometimes she did see her old self in her old life, wearing that Lanz nightgown with the top button missing. Her husband not dead, but snoring next to her, making that loud popping noise like a rubber ball bouncing down the street.

'Hey, it's me,' she might have whispered to herself. 'Wake up. You won't believe what's going to happen to you.'

But then her own words would waken her, and she'd just be her old lady self in a hospital bed looking at her empty marital bed. She might notice it was much more neatly made than she'd ever managed and think: *Wah!*

The next day, when I popped into her bedroom to say good morning, her face lit up as if she hadn't seen me for a hundred years. Her famous red-lipstick smile, her teeth miraculously still white, still straight.

'Is it really you? All the way from Scotland?'

'Yup,' I said, feeling goofily happy.

'You're so beautiful! Come here, you.' She stretched her arms out towards me and we hugged.

4

Oh, I was going to miss this kind of appreciation. My mother loved me more than anyone loved me, even my father who'd set out to woo me and in large part succeeded. She loved me more than I loved her. I never loved my mother enough to tell her what was really going on in my life. In the early years, sometimes months went by when I didn't even bother sending a postcard. I used to tell myself I was protecting her, but the truth was less noble. I was a daddy's girl and kept her at a distance. I probably made my mother cry sometimes. Made the person who loved me more than anyone else in the world loved me, *cry*. So perhaps it wasn't ironic that at her deathbed I had an urge to record the truth of my past. As if the child who'd been careless with her abundance of motherly love was now insisting – *stamping her feet!* – on making up for lost time. Memories lurked everywhere I looked – had been lurking for decades – but they lurked no longer. They stepped into the light and said in a slightly patronising voice: *Yeah, you really did this and said that dumb thing, right here, in this exact spot.*

After breakfast with my mother and Ateca, I sat at my dead father's desk, opened my laptop and began to write. I began with my father throwing his glass of wine at me because I'd had sex with the boy down the street whom he'd expressly forbidden me to see. Had I really been that stupid? That bad? And then I remembered moving in with a man who lived inside his foam furniture factory. He'd picked me up hitch-hiking, which was the main way I met boys in those days. I studied my right thumb, recalling how I wriggled it at the side of the road fifty years ago. I'd loved not knowing which of the passing cars would stop, not knowing where I'd be in an hour. It seemed I could be my truest self with strangers.

Wah, wah, wah! I thought, sick of myself suddenly.

My *wah!* was not my mother's *wah!* It was more like the *wah* in *Peanuts*, when a grown-up tries to talk but all that Charlie

Brown hears is *wah-wah-wah*. And then, because my darling mother would soon be gone, I had a silent little sob for myself. Which was, I suppose, another kind of *wah*. But still not my mother's.

South Van Ness

Eighteen years old
California, 1971

I had a room in an old woman's basement that fall. I had to enter through the garage, and the room was dark and pine-panelled. There was a tiny bathroom but no kitchen. That was fine. I'd burned down the kitchen in the last place I'd rented a room. Clearly, I was not to be trusted in kitchens. There'd been Sufi dancers in that other place, and they'd refused to be angry with me even though the fire had destroyed all their vegan cooking equipment. I couldn't handle that. I needed punishment.

A few months ago, when I was still living at home in San Rafael, I'd slept with the new neighbour down the street whom my father had specifically told me to avoid. I'd knocked on his door and asked if he had any rolling papers. Within fifteen minutes, we were both naked and he was walking around the house with me pinioned on him, my legs around his back, arms around his neck. I was not petite so he must have been athletic. His beard exfoliated my face. I went back home, transparently fornicated, and my father's face got very red. Then he threw his wine at my face and said:

'Get out!'

I marched straight out of the house and hitch-hiked to a friend's house. The wine was white, and as soon as it dried there was no sign he'd even thrown it. Within a day, I'd found the Sufi house and moved out of my old bedroom. In front of my tearful

7

five-year-old sister and my envious sixteen-year-old brother, I walked out of my childhood home clutching a duffle bag full of clothes and shoes and books I considered good. I don't remember my mother in this. She may have been there. She was self-effacing and undemanding but loved us continually. She was probably there in the hall, watching me head off into the unknown. I have no idea what she felt. Perhaps she was asking herself if she was supposed to cling to me, beg me not to go. She was too shy to do anything so demonstrative, but she might have pictured it just the same. My father had removed himself proudly to the garage during my exit. *My house, my rules.* He had a point. I was a brat.

In my new life ten miles away, I started junior college and worked as a waitress in an old folks' home, and hitch-hiked everywhere. I got C minuses at college that first semester and I was a terrible waitress. Hitch-hiking was the only thing I was good at. I'd perfected it the previous summer in Europe, where I thumbed, occasionally on the wrong side of the road. It was a revelation I could go anywhere for free. Aside from being raped in the back of a van in France, it was fun and I made lots of friends. I met a man who called himself Morris the Minnow in Galway and camped with him on Inishmore. I formed a trio of hitchers with a Jewish woman from New York and a home counties boy called Julian, and we hitched from Paris, right across the Channel on a car ferry and up to his parents' ancestral pile in Hampshire. My address book was crammed with new addresses, where I was assured a place to sleep if I was in the area. I'd not made a success of high school, but I was quite good at standing by the road waggling my thumb at drivers. I'd finally found my gift.

One day, after my waitress shift, I was picked up by a tall man in a white van. I was on my way to San Francisco to sit in Café Trieste and feel soulful. It was a very big van, comfortable and clean. The back was full of chunks of foam.

'What's all the foam for?'

'I manufacture furniture,' he explained. When I stared blankly, he continued. 'I make furniture, beds and sofas mainly, using foam.'

He smiled with very white teeth and had a pretty face, like a woman. His blue eyes seemed honest and trustworthy. No beard – he looked like he might not be able to grow a decent one. His hair was strawberry blond and hung to his shoulders, not straight but not curly either. Fluffy. He looked old, maybe thirty.

'Cool,' I said. 'Do you have any rolling papers?' That was my only line.

We ended up at his factory on South Van Ness and 15th Street, which was near the freeway overpass. No houses on this block – just warehouses and flop houses. A fifteen-minute walk from Union Square, it was a side of the city I'd not seen. We entered and immediately there were stairs – steep and dark. I didn't hesitate a second but was aware this was a point at which caution would be appropriate. I kept taking my emotional temperature to see if I was frightened. At the top, he showed me where he slept – the factory was also his home. The walls of his bedroom were comprised entirely of yellow foam somehow attached to the structure of the building. The door was a wedge of foam that you had to fold back and then slide your body through. Inside was a piece of foam on the floor, made up into a bed. There were some clothes neatly folded in a corner on the floor, which was also foam. It was a padded cell with a single bulb hanging from the ceiling, but oddly cosy. Maybe it was the yellowness and the way it smelled of Johnson's baby powder. Outside the room was the kitchen. This was a wooden plank over two saw horses, on which sat a can opener and dozens of cans of tuna and sweetcorn, a few plates, bowls and cups. Cutlery stuck out of an empty sweetcorn can. There was also a jumbo-size box of Corn Flakes and some boxes of powdered milk.

'No stove?'

'Raw food is better for you.'

'No sink?'

'There's one in the bathroom,' he said and smiled kindly, as if it was a silly question. Why would any house need more than one sink?

All this time, he was kind of dancing around me on the balls of his feet, his long skinny legs propelling him in a bouncy way. He seemed delighted I was there, albeit bewildered. Nothing he did set off alarms. I liked his minimalism. For foreplay, he showed me the factory beyond his bedroom. There was a rough-hewn balcony which we stood on, and below on the ground floor was a veritable swimming pool of foam. Then he climbed over the railing and leapt down. I followed. Falling on so much foam was like falling into cake. It made me giggle. The sex wasn't memorable, but I was still so immature. It was like smoking a joint but not knowing how to inhale, which I'd done for years. Later, he dropped me off at an onramp for 101 north and I was back in my pine-panelled basement room within an hour.

I kept failing at college. Maybe my mother was wrong and I wasn't a genius. I was always too tired to study and my salary wasn't stretching as far as I thought it would. I was working full-time and I didn't see how I could make more money. I liked the idea of a philosophy or an English degree but wasn't prepared to make many sacrifices to get one.

I didn't have a boyfriend. I wasn't sure Foam Man would describe himself as my boyfriend, though we'd met up three more times. There was a boy I met at college who showed me how to give a blow job one day. We did it in my pine-panelled room. It was hard to keep quiet, but we had to try because the old lady upstairs could throw me out. I hid how disgusted I was, because he didn't seem to think it was disgusting at all. Besides, it seemed a useful life skill to acquire.

'Move your hand like this, just at the base,' he whispered.

'Like this?' I whispered back.

'Yeah. But you're not sucking. You're slurping. Suck.'

'Like this?'

'Ouch! Goddammit.'

I gagged at one point. I was C minus at blow jobs too. I kept clearing dirty tables, daydreaming in classes, and hitching home regularly to see my family. The tension had evaporated within days of my leaving, and now they were always glad to see me. Even my father. We enjoyed each other's conversation too much to stay alienated. I was waiting for my life to begin, I guess. I was making lots of mistakes and not having as much fun as most people my age seemed to be having. Life was generally a little flat. I was waiting to know who I would be, but mainly I think I was waiting for someone to love.

One night in my narrow bed, I was listening to the radio and the new Harry Nilsson song came on. It was called 'Without You' and was on the radio all the time that fall. His reedy voice was perfect for a song about being left. A curious thing happened as I listened. My chest filled up and I wasn't tired any more. I pictured myself as both the sad-eyed leaver and the broken-hearted one left behind. The song was corny, but also painful because it seemed to be saying something true. Lovers some-times lacked the power to hang on to loved ones, and worse – sometimes loved ones left, even when they knew they were loved.

Harry Nilsson kept crooning that he couldn't live, if living was without someone. Had I ever loved anyone that much? Had I ever been loved that much? No, I had not. Did I want to? Yes, it turned out I did. But who to pour this love into, and who to be the beloved of? Why, Foam Man of course! He wasn't perfect, but he was the only one I could think of. I fixed on his face, his shoulders, his bouncy way of walking. I got up, got dressed and left the house. It was late, maybe 10.30pm. I was exploding with resolution. It felt great to be following an impulse and not analysing anything. Thinking, I decided, was overrated. I walked to the onramp for 101 south and stuck out my thumb. I wore my usual outfit – hip-hugging bell-bottoms, a peasant blouse (no bra), and a corduroy jacket that had belonged to my father.

I quickly got a lift to the city, and then stuck out my thumb again on Lombard. The air was cool and the foghorn was mourning away. Standing at a bus stop with my thumb out, I felt vestiges of fear while watching a group of men loiter outside a corner bar. One of the men kept hawking and spitting, and another kept laughing like a hyena. Finally, a car pulled over and the driver rolled down his window:

'Hey, you working?'

'Working? No,' I said, puzzled, and got in his car.

He turned and stared at me, and I waited for him to say something else.

'Are you going up to Van Ness?' I finally asked. 'I need a lift to 15th and South Van Ness.'

'Oh, what the hell,' he suddenly said, and pulled out into traffic.

My swollen heart had waned a little but when I heard his footsteps coming down, it began to flutter again. I'd never experienced emotion as a physical object, like a thick liquid in my upper chest. Was this love? I decided it was, and also that I wouldn't require more than this chance to love someone. Being a beloved would be the icing on the cake.

'Jesus! What are you doing here? It's past midnight.'

'Yeah, well. I just suddenly wanted to see you.' There was an awkward pause, so I added, 'I was in the neighbourhood.'

I couldn't articulate the romance of my impulse. It would sound impossibly juvenile in spoken words. But surely he'd recognise the dramatic gesture for what it was? He was so much older – he must know all about dramatic gestures.

'Huh. Well, come on up and get warm. I've got some peppermint tea. Then I've got some paperwork to do.'

Peppermint tea? Where was the wordless embrace? The sense of rightness?

But within a month, I'd moved out of the pine-panelled basement and into the foam factory. I dropped out of college, but still hitched to the old folks' home to waitress till I had enough money to fly back to Europe. If I wasn't going to get a degree or a career or a beloved, I might as well travel. From the beginning, when I moved in with Foam Man, it was understood. He offered no mushy talk and neither did I. My midnight visit was never referred to. This was my base camp while I saved up to travel. A temporary base. He didn't ask for money and I didn't offer it. I didn't even pay for my share of our daily tuna fish. We never drank, though sometimes shared a joint at bedtime. He had such a long lanky body, it was nice to feel entirely wrapped in it. We tended to read in bed, more than anything else.

Then the day came.

'I've got my ticket.'

'Yeah?'

'I leave next weekend.'

'Wonderful. You must be excited.'

This was exactly how he was supposed to behave, but my heart sank. The preferred response, I realised with sickening clarity, was: *Please don't go.* I willed Foam Man to say those words, or any version of that sentiment. My throat became sore with unshed tears as the time of departure grew near. It was all tragic and unnecessary. I felt my life teeter between completely different paths: the known and the unknown. But it wasn't really teetering. It was timidly waiting for choice to be removed. All he had to say was *please stay*, and I would stay. Like the lyrics that had propelled me out of my bed six months earlier and sent me to his door, I now had the eyes

13

with hidden sorrow, and I was leaving. If he would only notice and burst into song. *I can't live, if living is without you*.

But he didn't, and I left.

Cashmere

The days passed, hot cloudless days, and my mother kept not dying. I never forgot my purpose in being there, but I was easily distracted and lacked the attention span required for sustained anxiety. I wanted to be practical, so I cleared out the hall closets. Old sleeping bags, Christmas wrapping paper, my sister's dollhouse furniture seemed unimportant now so I gave them away. Early in the mornings when it was cooler, I took long walks to the levee or China Camp. I read a book of my dead father's – his bookplate still glued in place. Sometimes I sat in Andy's café and phoned my sister. All these activities felt like deathbed commercial breaks. Satisfying in their way, but also heightened because they were sandwiched between my mother's dying moments.

I had many roles at home in Scotland. Here, I was just the daughter of a dying woman. A woman I'd never bothered getting to know, mostly because I thought I knew her already. She'd made me, but who the hell was she? I began a list.

Things I Learned from My Mother:

- Ants are okay. If your See's candy box is invaded by them, just wipe the ants off and give it as a gift.
- If you get tired of that long line of ants snaking across your kitchen counter, spray them with Windex.

- If your husband accuses you of being paranoid when you suspect him of infidelity, then he is certainly messing around with another woman.
- If your husband is handsome, sexy, funny and a hedonist, be certain he will not be kind, patient or loyal.
- Cider vinegar diluted in warm water makes your hair shiny.

Every morning I crept to her bedroom and peeked to see if her chest was still rising and falling. She had so many things wrong with her: bladder cancer, multiple sclerosis, an under-active thyroid, vascular dementia. The hospice doctor had said it was only a matter of days, maybe hours, but true to form, my mother was doing her own thing. She napped on and off all day, and every evening cleaned her dinner plate with gusto. If she'd noticed Death loitering around the foot of her bed, she'd probably have said: *You're creepy. Scoot!*

It was her eighty-seventh birthday in a few days. What to give someone who had everything but time? See's candy was an obvious choice, but I wanted to buy something luxurious and beautiful – after all, it was her last birthday. As I perused the racks of cashmeres, I dithered. Was it dumb to spend $200 on something she might never wear, or if she did, might end up covered in drooled fruit juice? In the end I bought a cheap fleece, machine washable and soft. When I got home after being away an hour, her face lit up like it always did.

'Is it really you? It's you!'

'Yup, it's me,' I said, noting the curious happiness her smile always gave me – a kind of happiness so predictable, I'd not always recognised it as such. Had even, at times, felt repulsed by it. I may not have told her much about my life, nevertheless she'd witnessed a multitude of my childish humiliations. My dearth of dates in high school was a particular sore spot. How could I respect someone who had such poor taste as to love me?

'All the way from Scotland. *Scotland*!' She said this as if Scotland was the moon.

'Yup. Scotland.'

That night, after I'd watched *The Sound of Music* with Mom, I began a story about my first marriage ending. We'd been as amateur at divorce as we'd been at courting. I hadn't laughed much at the time, but now we seemed hilarious. It made me wonder what else I was taking years to see in the correct perspective. Maybe everything. It was fun to tell the truth for a change in my writing. But the truth about truth, I discovered, was there was always more than one version. First I felt one way about that marriage, and the next hour I remembered it differently. Maybe numbers were the only things you couldn't mess with. Calendar dates, amounts of money, phone numbers.

On the morning of Mom's birthday, without thinking very hard, I took the cheap fleece back to the store and exchanged it for a cashmere sweater. I was a wreck. I needed to give this deathbed birthday the best shot I could, no matter how unlikely my effort would be appreciated. And in case that makes me sound generous, a small voice was whispering the cashmere would be mine soon anyway.

Keys

Fifty years old
Scotland, 2003

After my first husband moved out, keys stopped working for me. They wouldn't turn in locks. They wouldn't go in locks in the first place. Even the checkout lady at Tesco found her key stuck in the till while serving me. I was always losing keys, but this felt a different level of dysfunction.

It'd begun as a healthy break-up. After twenty years, we told ourselves we no longer loved each other. Not properly. We'd gone to Amsterdam to save our marriage, but all we did was discuss how exciting life would be once we'd parted. We were so proud of ourselves. We got drunk in a tiny bar near the train station. Over three nights, it had become our place. We sat in the same chairs by the window, ordered the same drinks and watched the cyclists almost get hit by cars over and over. Sometimes cyclists would have to steady themselves by holding on to the roof of a passing car after a previous car had caused them to wobble. Sometimes drivers would speed up to zoom around a cyclist, narrowly miss a pedestrian, then slam on their brakes to avoid a head-on collision with another car. No cyclist wore a helmet. It was riveting.

'What will we tell the kids?' I asked.

'The truth.'

'Okay. But which truth?' He hadn't shaved in a few days, and it was quite annoying how nice he looked.

'Is there more than one?'

'Of course.' I was thinking of ways I could come out of this looking all right.

'What do you think we should tell them?'

'I don't know. We could sit them all down and tell them we love them, that it's nothing to do with them, but we're going to live apart for a while.'

'For a while?'

'Sure. It will be forever, but we could let them figure that out in time. Not hit them with the whole shebang right away.'

'You always sentimentalise things.'

'I do not.' I was deeply insulted.

'But you do. Your writing too.'

'Like you've ever read anything I've written.'

'There you go. Painting me as a selfish moron because it makes a good story.'

I huffed and drank in silence for a minute or two. He bought more drinks, and by the time he got back to our table I wasn't angry.

'I've got an idea,' he said.

'What about?'

'We could tell them you're a lesbian.'

Pause while it sank in.

'You genius!' I admitted. We toasted the idea, which struck us as hilarious because it was so naughty to lie to our darlings. Not to mention hijacking gayness to let me off the hook. I'd been so ashamed of my behaviour, but suddenly, sitting in that bar with the suicidal cyclists outside and naked women behind picture windows lining the street, it seemed a mere peccadillo. You couldn't even call it an affair – it was more of an accident. No one seeing us would suspect we were planning our divorce. And that was funny too. We nearly peed ourselves laughing. Then we went back to the hotel, crawled under the sheets and had sex for the first time in ages.

Once we were back home, we got on with the business of parting. We wrote lists of things to do, but we did them in the wrong order. My husband gleefully began his single life while still living with me. He joined several dating sites. Well, why not? We were being so sensible, so open. But we forgot to tell the kids.

'Hey, Dad,' said our eldest one day, when he ran into his father downtown. 'You off somewhere nice?'

'Yep. Got a date, actually.'

'A date?' He thought it was a joke, but not very funny.

'Yeah.'

'With who?'

'Oh, you don't know yet, do you? Me and your mum, we've split up.'

'What?'

'Yup. Sorry about that. Got to dash.'

The other three found out the next evening, when we were all eating dinner. I'd made macaroni and cheese, a huge bowlful because it was everyone's favourite. We had a guest, the son of a friend in California who'd sent him to live with us because he'd dropped out of high school and she didn't know what to do with him. He wore his jeans rapper style, with the crotch at his knees and the crack of his bum clearly visible. He also wore mirror sunglasses while sitting at the kitchen table. It was not great timing, having a house guest as we were breaking up, but it also seemed entirely normal. On the surface it was a typical family dinner – bickering, spilled milk, giggling, eating.

'Is *Inspector Morse* on tonight?' I asked my husband. He always remembered these things.

'Yes. But I won't be here.'

'Oh. Okay.' It was hard to swallow my macaroni, but I pretended I didn't care.

'Can you pass the salad? And also iron my blue shirt?' he asked.

'For tonight?' We were talking in lowered voices.

'Yeah.'

'Seeing her again already?' I couldn't help myself.

He gave me a look I'd never seen on his face before. Joyful guilt. It was disorienting. What had I created?

'No, no. I'm seeing someone else tonight. Siobhan from Clachnaharry.'

There was something about the way he stretched out those syllables, and the way the dog was under the table licking the floor, and the cat was scratching the sofa again, and the way the younger two were flinging bits of bread at each other. I'd begun pouring juice from the jug into glasses, but I found myself throwing the jug-full in his face. There was a moment's silence at the table. The kids' faces were probably frightened, but I didn't notice. I wasn't very good at being angry – I lacked practice. Come to think of it, I wasn't very good at breaking up for the same reason. This was my first.

'Are you insane?' he asked, standing up with juice dripping from his face. His voice sounded young and tearful.

'*You're* insane!' I threw back, like a five-year-old. 'And I am not going to iron your fucking blue shirt.'

Then it dissolved into slapstick. I told him to leave and he didn't. I pushed him out the door and locked it. He shouted to open it and I refused. He appeared at all the windows, banging and shouting. No one let him in. Sometime during the commotion, while we were all racing to barricade the windows and doors, I explained to the kids we were splitting up, so it wasn't exactly wrong that their dad was going on a date. The fact of our impending divorce was now a rider on the much bigger drama of Daddy trying to break into his own house. Our guest rushed enthusiastically to every door and window my husband appeared in, shouting in a silly voice: *No, no, you can't come in! Not by the hair of my chinny chin chin!* My kids thought this was hysterical, but I suspect they also knew something terrible was afoot. And all along, under everything, was a sense of déjà vu. Of course! Hadn't he shoved me out of the house when he'd discovered my peccadillo six months ago? Oh, we were terrible parents, playing out our wars in front of the children. But when did other parents conduct these things? Our children were omnipresent.

Later that night, of course, he was allowed in and we pretended all was normal. He must have cancelled his date because he watched *Inspector Morse* with me. I remember not being able to follow the plot. Two days passed, in which I pretended nothing irreversible had happened yet and soon this exhausting game would be over.

Then he left. Or, to be precise, he moved a few feet away.

I came home from Tesco to find he'd taken our camping stove and set up camp in our extension. He'd nailed up the connecting door. It was glass, so for privacy and soundproofing, he'd piled up photo albums against it. Also old encyclopaedias, pillows and sleeping bags. There was an outside door and he kept his bit of the house locked, even when he was in it sometimes. Things were not panning out as I'd thought they would. He was supposed to disappear into his new life, and keep paying for me and the kids to stay in our home. I was supposed to be fighting off gorgeous men knocking on my door day and night.

The reality was hearing the clickety-clack of high heels on the other side of the wall. I didn't own heels. I was already taller than him, and didn't like to make him feel small. Or I didn't like to feel tall. I never figured that one out. The reality was sneaking a look at his profiles on dating sites, and raging because he pretended to read literature. It was watching him go to salsa classes when he'd never danced in my presence, even when I was dancing like a mad thing in front of him. It was watching him lose weight and wear fashionable clothes, noticing he now had contact lenses and his grey hair had become brown. Without me, he had become the very man I'd wanted him to be.

KEYS

I was cutting up onions for spaghetti sauce one day, when suddenly there he was, walking past the kitchen window, chatting happily with some big-boobed woman. Chatting! I used to yearn for some easy small talk, some banter. And yes, as a small-boobed woman, I took the big boobs personally. Taunted by tits.

But I had not wanted this man, I reminded myself. I'd plotted to lose him. So why was I furious? I couldn't shake off the notion he was mine, even if I had no use for him. Logic wasn't helpful. I even missed our fights – the ones we had over and over because we couldn't resolve them. Like the car key fight. I'd once (maybe twice, but certainly not more than four times) locked the kids in the car with the keys still in the ignition. It was distressing, especially if it was a hot day. I would smile like a maniac through the window, pretending Mommy was just playing a silly game until the nice policeman opened the door. Their Daddy never left the keys in the car or the car unlocked, which would be all right if we were not in the car at the same time. Travelling as a family – to the beach for a picnic, for example – could be disastrous, especially if I was driving. The first time we were locked out of our car, we called a locksmith – but after that we learned how to break in with a coat hanger, usually borrowed from a nearby house. It happened at least three times a year. We got to be very good and briefly considered a career of car thieving. Our usual routine:

'The car's locked,' I would tell him. 'Where are the keys?'

'You drove.'

'I know. But the doors are locked.'

'I know. I locked them.'

'We're in the middle of nowhere.' This said slowly, with contempt. 'You really think there's thieves in the area?'

'You left the keys in the car again, didn't you.' Not a question.

Near the end, I locked the keys in the car on purpose. I wanted to live through our weird ritual one more time. But it

23

wasn't as much fun as I'd hoped, as if that part of my life was already sealed off from me. Ironically, now I was the only adult in charge, I never left the keys in the car and I always locked it. I ceased relaxing on a deep level – I was shocked to realise how much I'd depended on my husband to keep us all safe. And if I was driving alone, I developed a habit of pulling into certain lay-bys for a scheduled weep. I looked forward to it. A lament for my lost imperfect life, though I wasn't sure if I was pining for him or the family unit.

The fracture of his leaving opened the door to all sorts of other fractures, like a spreading fault line. My beautiful sixteen-year-old daughter began telling me to fuck off regularly, as in:

'Good morning, honey, you look nice today.'

'Fuck off.'

One day I had enough and told her to move next door with her dad. It seemed reasonable, but she refused. I tried to phys-ically move her, but she clung to the door frame. The other kids ran to get their dad. Maybe pushing people out of the house had become a family tradition, and they felt he wouldn't want to miss out. Boy oh boy, would our daughter cramp his bachelor style.

'Dad, Dad! Tell her she can't do this,' cried our daughter.

'Of course I can,' I said, trying to unpeel her fingers from the door frame.

'You're quite right,' he told her, standing on the other side of the door. 'You are *not* moving in with me.'

I could tell she was a little hurt by the way he put it. Though in fact, later that day, she did move next door with her dad. No one went to bed that night. It was too odd, her not being there. Then she marched back in to take her television, which was our only television. We all watched her unplug it. What next? Oh, extreme situations needed extreme responses. At midnight I piled everyone, including my defecting daughter, into the car and drove to the new twenty-four-hour Tesco, where I bought our first flat screen television. Then we went home and watched

Jurassic Park. I may have made pancakes. If I didn't, I regret that.

Noticing parents out together with their kids was hard. Watching *Finding Nemo* with my nine-year-old was torture. It seemed the basic theme of every Pixar film was family togetherness. Christmas that year, predictably, was its own very special hell. Why, oh why, had I inflicted divorce on my children, and why had I told myself they were fine? He'd been right. I did sentimentalise everything. I'd been so absorbed in my selfish discontent that I'd deprived them of the basic entitlement of childhood – their own selfishness. The ways I'd justified myself were pathetic. Telling myself they were now more robust, better equipped for independence. Mentally editing the events till they became humorous anecdotes. Nonsense! Divorce was pivotal in anyone's childhood. Presumably they told themselves their own stories about it, which were different from the stories they told me. My own stories wouldn't stay still either. They kept wriggling about, so what seemed true about our break-up one day, was something else entirely the next.

I remember laughing with my women friends and my also newly single sister. I had a break-up song, an Eva Cassidy version of Buddy Holly's 'It Doesn't Matter Anymore'. I played it continually in the car, driving the kids crazy. Everything was heightened, I felt alive – but overall those times were not fun, and they were only funny in retrospect. I felt exposed, vulnerable, and couldn't wait to scurry into the protection (however false, I didn't care) of a new relationship. And then keys stopped behaving. I broke my car keys – both sets. One in the ignition, the other by slamming a door on it. I couldn't find the house door keys. I began to look at all keys with suspicion.

Twenty-one years earlier, on our wedding day, I'd been seven months pregnant. I wore a dress I made myself and my nearly-husband took the afternoon off work. When his secretary found

25

out why, she wanted to come too. She was one of the witnesses, along with a tall Liverpudlian I'd never met. He sounded exactly like a Beatle, and because of this I had a short fantasy of kissing him even though it was my wedding day. Pregnancy had sedated me and I'd become dreamy, inclined to silly thoughts. We were living in Toronto by then – his work had taken us there – which was why none of our friends or family were present. Our world had just us in it. I was so lonely that I tried to befriend our almost-non-English-speaking mail lady, to the point of finding out when her birthday was and giving her presents. I was fairly certain my nearly-husband was not lonely. He was the most solitary but least lonely person I'd ever known. I was given some red roses on our wedding day – or had I bought them? – which I left behind at the pub where we had fish and chips afterwards. I never saw our witnesses again. In hindsight, the day was romantic in a bleak and original way. At the time, it felt like something that needed to be done.

Wait a minute, that's not quite true. I'm trying to sound tough. No one makes her own wedding dress for a wedding that's a chore. It took me a long time to make. Why hadn't I bought a wedding dress – or a frock, as my boyfriend kept calling it? Surely I could've found one that accommodated a seven-month bump. Or why didn't I wear my old rose print dress, which was loose and would be fine if I ironed it? Because, despite the marriage proposal being a conversation about health insurance while walking down Spadina after seeing *Harold and Maude* (which I adored and he did not, a sign I tried to ignore), I'd secretly decided the wedding was a real wedding and I was going to damn well mark the occasion. I told my parents I was getting married in a letter. My mother wrote a sweet letter back, saying congratulations, and how nice since we were going to be parents. My father didn't write anything. It would be years before I realised they might have welcomed an invitation. They might have even paid for a wedding. Later both my siblings had big traditional church weddings, which my parents contributed to. After my sister got married, my mother started randomly giving me household items from Gump's – a crystal single rose vase, a Portmeirion salad bowl – saying she wanted to make up for not giving us wedding presents. Such was my self-absorption, I hadn't even noticed the dearth of wedding gifts.

When the dress was finally finished, I ironed it and hung it up in the closet. For days I kept opening the closet to glance at it, dreading I'd find fault and feeling vast relief when I didn't. On our wedding day morning my boyfriend went to work as usual and I gave myself an egg yolk facial and placed cucumber slices on my eyes. Then I took a long bath with bath oils. I took inordinate pride in my lack of stretch marks. My stomach was a smooth pale melon, and under the skin I could clearly see – and feel – my baby kicking, wriggling, a bit of gentle punching. No room for somersaults any more. I was going to miss this, I thought. Just being on my own, but not. I liked the idea of our hearts beating – not in unison, because the baby's heart needed to pump faster – but in close proximity, keeping each other company.

When I was dressed in my finery and ready to go, I walked to the bus stop on Davenport. It was late November, freezing but dry. I wore a long coat and no one saw how lovely my dress was, but I felt lovely. On my feet were a pair of red leather shoes with tiny gold stars. They were beautiful, but too small and my feet were already hurting. I thought my feet too big, so was always making the mistake of squeezing them into too-small shoes.

Well, here I am on my way to my own wedding and about to be a mother, I told myself, as the bus rolled across Yonge and Bloor. *Aren't I clever?*

Yes, indeed, I replied.

Yippee, I'm normal!

You think?

Our wedding was to take place in the Toronto Young Offender's Court, as there'd been a problem – maybe a flood – at the Courthouse. I didn't mind. It added to the colour of the day and seemed fitting. Nothing good or lasting ever began smoothly, right? We were given pieces of paper from which to read our vows, which we did without stumbling. Then my boyfriend slid a ring on my finger, and it didn't matter one bit that it was the ring my first boyfriend had given me on the hillside above Camp We Ch Me, and which I'd only removed from my finger thirty minutes earlier. I was proud to be a cheap date, even on my wedding day.

Seven weeks later, on a January afternoon, I went into labour. I'd been having Braxton Hicks contractions for days, but this was different. My husband ran for the bathroom. After a while I shouted through the door:

'Don't worry, it's absolutely normal to get the runs when your wife goes into labour. It's in all the pregnancy books.'

'Okay. Thanks.'

'You done yet?'

'Yeah. No.'

It was hard to be patient, but eventually we were off to Toronto General. By dawn, in a dimmed overheated room, while it blizzarded outside and cars skidded in the parking lot, I was presented with a frowning red-faced baby. His head was slightly misshapen from being squeezed. I remember thinking: *Is that you? Is that really you?* He stared back at me, serious and almost accusing. *Of course it's me. I have come to change your life forever.*

'Look at him,' I whispered to my husband. He looked tired and fifteen years old.

'It's a boy,' he whispered back.

'I know.'

'I thought you said it would be a girl.'

'Yeah. But it's a boy.'

Pause.

'Okay. That means you get to name it.'

That had been our deal, since we couldn't agree on names. It was an odd thing to talk about now, but I got it. He was taking a while to catch up, and this conversation was a way back into the moment. I felt the same. It was at least a day before I felt attached to my life again, that I wasn't observing it from a distance.

All babies stayed in the hospital nursery for five days. Every four hours a nurse would wheel a long steel trolley into the maternity ward. Each trolley contained six swaddled infants, wedged into their space. She would shout out the surname of each baby, and we would raise our hands and shout back:

'Here! That's my baby, bring him here!'

Then she would more or less lob them like footballs, trusting us to catch our babies.

Sometimes when he was in the nursery, I would lay in bed and make myself remember his face. It was hard because he was changing by the minute, but each time I saw him, I always knew it was him. And I began to see all the other babies in the ward as inferior because they were not him.

Time went on. More babies. Moving countries, changing jobs. Again and again, nothing turned out the way I thought it would. I'd begun by making a decision – I would be a mother by hook or by crook! – but then I was pulled willy-nilly through my days and I didn't know where it would lead. I'd no idea that one day keys would cease to work for me. Nor did I know that sometime after that, I would stop bothering with keys at all. Eventually I lost all my keys, except for the car key. I'd been a lapsed Catholic for many years, but I remembered what faith felt like. Not locking doors was a bit like that. I knew thieves existed, but I chose to live as if they didn't. Like those cyclists in Amsterdam, riding pell-mell through a sea of moving metal as if death didn't exist and helmets were beside the point. It was curiously easy, when I got used to it.

Three Kisses

In that first summer of my mother's deathbed, I felt close to her. Or as close as possible, given her dementia, our history of non-closeness and my substantial ignorance of her inner life.

One afternoon – one of those afternoons that lasted days, with flies buzzing loudly and every car on San Pedro Road making much the same aimless droning sound – I kissed her soft cheeks on impulse. The way I'd sometimes grab my kids when they were little and kiss them for the hell of it. We'd just finished eating bear claws and her skin tasted of sugar from the pastry. I stroked her hair – slightly greasy because she hated being showered these days, but still thick, still lovely – and kissed her again, this time on the top of her head. She pulled my hand to her mouth and kissed it hard, three times, as she always did. Ateca thought this was normal, that she'd always kissed people three times, often on the hand. The first time I'd seen it was ten years ago, on her last visit to Scotland. The second day of the trip, she fell in the bathroom in the middle of the night. Managed to hobble back to bed and there she lay until I came home from London the next afternoon. At least fifteen hours.

'Oh, your mother – I bet she's broken her hip again,' my father had said, half apologising, half cranky. He'd just had lunch with a friend of mine in a pub and left his wife with a probable broken hip? I didn't want to think about that yet. In any case, my mother kept saying things like: *Thank God, your father knew exactly what to do.* The message being: *You mustn't blame him.* But I did. Oh, I really did.

She was still in her nightgown, her hair messy, her face shiny, and there was a distinct smell of urine. She'd *hate* the ambulance men seeing her like this. At first she protested when I began taking off her nightgown, but she quietened when I used a warm washcloth to freshen all the parts of her body that needed freshening. I spent considerable time on her feet because it made her giggle. It was the first time in memory I'd seen her naked. Bodies in general are not as old-looking as faces, and there was something soothing in the act of washing my mother. By the time the ambulance pulled up, I was applying red lipstick to her mouth and just had time to give her a quick puff of Chanel.

The ambulance men were young and handsome. On the count of three, they lifted her and laid her on the stretcher, all the while making her smile. Even I was entranced. Knights in shining armour! As she was carried out to the ambulance, she called to my father:

'George! George!'

'What is it, honey?'

'Three kisses! Three kisses!'

They kissed each other loudly three times.

'See you at the hospital,' he said happily, as if he going to meet her at a nice restaurant later.

That was the first appearance for me of the three kisses. Maybe it was one of their private rituals. *Here's a kiss. I want another. Here's one more. I want three kisses! Oh, all right, but you are so demanding!* Or the source of the three kisses might have been something less cute. A defence mechanism brought into play when she felt frightened. Kisses as weapons or protective shields. Because no one will be mean to you while you're kissing them, right?

31

Ten years later, she was kissing everyone in sight three times. The mailman, the UPS man, the doctor, the carer, the neighbours, the checkout girls at United Market. No hello was complete without three kisses, often on the hand. People generally liked it, or pretended to. One man said she was the only woman who had kissed him in decades. He seemed grateful.

After she kissed me three times with her bear-claw-sweet lips, she fell asleep mid-sentence, as was her way now, and I went back to my laptop. I'd begun a story about being derailed from my academic ambitions by a crush on a boy. I'd liked his English accent and his cowboy boots. When he asked me hitch to Mexico halfway through my first semester, I hesitated two minutes before saying yes, why not. It was one of the least sensible acts in my life.

For years, I thought going home was not good for my mental health. I couldn't say exactly why, but it had become a lot more pleasant. 122 Oak Drive had always been a nice house, unpretentious, and the neighbourhood still had the higgledy-piggledy road down to the beach with all the houses looking as different from each other as the people they housed. I felt at home. I may not have known them all, but these were my people. Already, I had invitations to dinner parties and other outings planned – going to a movie in town or to Point Reyes for a picnic. In fact, visiting my mother's deathbed was uncannily like being on holiday. Was it wrong to enjoy myself while she lay dying? I was aware it could be seen that way, but I looked forward to those outings and knew I wouldn't be cancelling any of them to linger by her deathbed. All my life she'd been telling me – and us all – *I'm fine! Go ahead and have fun!*

And so it was, ten years after the crime had been committed and five years after he'd died, I finally forgave my father. He would have hesitated, considered cancelling that pub lunch – but my mother would have played down her hip injury. *Damn,*

damn, damn! she would have been thinking, lying in bed and willing her bones to mend. They'd been looking forward to this trip for months, as excited as little kids, and now look! Guilt and embarrassment and frustration and rage and physical pain – she would've felt all those things, but she would have smiled her fabulous smile and told my father: *Don't worry about me, honey. I'll be just fine here. You go!*

I Don't Know You

Twenty-five years old
California and Mexico, 1978

I was trying to be a different person. A better person. I made colourful salads for dinner, cutting up carrots, celery, cucumber, whatever cheap vegetable I could find, and then I'd sprinkle seeds and apricots on top. For lunch, I often just ate plain yoghurt, slowly and appreciatively. I exercised, didn't drink, and only occasionally smoked joints. I rode an old bike to class or walked, my bookbag on my back, and I frequently thought to myself: *Well, will you look at me now. A college student! Me!* It had taken a year of community college classes to be eligible for UC Berkeley, but here the hell I was. At my father's university, finally. Walking in his GI Bill footsteps. Better late than never, right, Dad? Goddammit.

I was living in a small room in a house full of boys, like Wendy in Never-Never Land. They seemed happy about my presence, but not in a flirty way. Maybe I made them feel safe and that we'd never run out of toilet paper or fresh milk. It was a Victorian house on College Avenue, and it was filthy. The kitchen sink was filled with pots and pans soaking in cold greasy water. The tiles of the shower were spotted with a furry black growth. I had to walk through a boy's room to get to my room, which was really a converted upstairs porch. My windows looked over rooftops and beyond to the Berkeley hills. Sometimes the rooftops were gilded at sunset, and I'd have to stop what I was doing and stare, or take photographs with my mother's old Kodak Brownie. This was a step up from my previous room, which for a year had been my brother's bedroom closet in a big purple hippie house in San Rafael. On the plus side, that closet had given me a lot of experience tip-toeing past boys sleeping and otherwise engaged.

I was older than most of my peers by four years. A late bloomer, but I'd assumed not too late to experience a typical student life. I was wrong. I'd not relied on my parents for years and this made me feel superior. I couldn't stop thinking of my fellow students as juvenile and spoiled. Maybe that explained my relative lack of popularity, though this idea is in hindsight. At the time I was too busy sneering and writing to my British friends to notice I had few college friends. I was working part-time as a file clerk at the Snoopy factory in San Francisco. The air was full of fluff that made my chest hurt. I loved Charlie Brown. I identified with him, but filing took up too much thinking time. How could I daydream and still remember the order of the alphabet? It drove me crazy because it was a menial job, a five-year-old could do it, and I was bad at it. I worried I'd never be good at any job. *Good grief!*

I loved to read, so studying literature made sense. Maybe I'd be an English teacher or a journalist. But I was often cranky during lectures. A typical class:

'Lawrence used the snake to represent evil, and here we see it again, in the stanza that begins . . .' intoned Professor Spencer from the podium.

I watched my hand shoot up.

'Yes? A question from the back?'

I always sat in the back row, a strange preference considering I was prone to actions like this.

'How do you know Lawrence meant snakes to mean evil?'

Pause while he looked at me. I was, he seemed to be saying, an idiot.

'It is widely understood by Lawrence academics to be the case.'

'But how do they *know*? Did he say? Write it down somewhere?'

I'd had a great English teacher in Marin Catholic High School. Father Pettingill never presumed to know what a writer intended by anything – he was much more interested in evoking our responses. There was no right or wrong interpretation of, say, 'The Love Song of J. Alfred Prufrock' in Father Pettingill's classroom. Once, when caught picking his nose while he thought we were reading, he just laughed, proffered his snot-bearing finger and said:

'Hors d'oeuvres, anyone?'

How could anyone not like a man who had the quick-mindedness, the sheer shamelessness, to do that? The English professors at Berkeley were boring and pretentious by comparison. But still, there I was, a university student with T.S. Eliot and Faulkner in my bag. I'd started in the second semester, just after Christmas. Not the traditional time to start, but it seemed appropriate, given the ethos of New Year's. My new life! Within weeks of moving to Berkeley, I had a routine. I gave a wide berth to Car Wanker, the man who liked to masturbate in his Ford Granada by People's Park. I loved saying hello to Bubble Lady, the smiling round woman dressed in black who blew bubbles into my path. I learned to avoid eye contact with Hate Man, randomly cursing strangers at the corner of Telegraph and Bancroft. Polka Dot Man wasn't scary, but I avoided eye contact with him too. Mostly I sat in Café Med on Telegraph, smoking Sobranies and making notes for my first novel. I drank so many espressos my periods stopped and I was, conceivably, unable to conceive. Or maybe it was the fact I'd gone off the pill after too many years and my ovaries had forgotten what to do. I wasn't worried yet. In any case, I was busy being celibate.

I bought an old Remington typewriter with ivory keys and sat at my desk in my porch-room with grand ideas about my

literary future. I'd not kissed anyone for a while, or not memor-
ably. Almost two years ago in Scotland, I'd fallen in love with
Christopher Parker, a man from Cape Town I could never think
of in terms of a first name. He'd maddeningly refused to have
sex with me because he was a Buddhist – though kissing and
cuddling was allowed. I only knew him three days. A short while
later he fell from a scaffold on an oil rig and died, thus guaran-
teeing his kisses would become the kisses against which all other
kisses would henceforth be found wanting. I thought about
those kisses a lot. Maybe not having sex was the sexiest thing in
the world. And maybe something about this new knowledge
altered how I looked because boys had stopped climbing into my
bed. I couldn't understand it. In the past, it had been so easy to
be easy. Or maybe infertile females sent out a subliminal signal.
No good shopping here! I was lonely of course, but it was a nice
loneliness. Heaven, to live in a state of *want*. To imagine all my
woes were simply due to the lack of a decent kisser, and yet not
have to deal with the messy reality of anyone. Christopher
Parker would never disappoint me or get on my nerves.
Meanwhile, I was busy writing my great novel about unconsummated love.

My mother was still writing me letters three or four times a
week. Even though we were only across the bay from each
other, neither of us drove and I didn't have a phone. Stinky the
Rapist was getting a lot of press coverage, and sometimes there
was a newspaper clipping about him in her letters because he
preyed on girls like me, hitch-hiking in the Bay Area. Mostly
her letters were short and newsy, about my sister and father and
the dog's bad behaviour. Many exclamation marks and capital
letters.

One day I got a letter from Cowboy. That wasn't his name,
but in my head I always called him Cowboy because he wore
cowboy boots and sometimes a cowboy hat. He was the only
one from my London days who sometimes said things like *I'll*

come visit you in California one day. I'd always replied *Cool*, but I never believed him. It cost too much, it was too far, too daunting. Then his letter arrived. *Arriving Feb 28th at 2.30 TWA. See you then.*

I had no time for a visitor! I was a serious celibate student – look at me, cycling to the library with a pensive face and a heart pumped by ten espressos. I bought him a postcard of Jack Kerouac and scribbled *Happy Trails* on the back. I'd discovered the phrase on a Quicksilver album. It was vague enough to cover almost any occasion, with just the right vintage tone. Phrases, music and clothes from the thirties and forties were in fashion again. The fifties were too recent for a revival. I did not refer to his arrival details, which I hoped precluded any commitment on my part. Then I forgot about it.

One afternoon I arrived home to find him sitting on the front steps looking unhappy. It was the first time someone from my British life had visited, and worlds collided in my stomach. I felt carsick. Who would I be now? My subdued and pseudo-British self? Or my California self, confident and utterly American? As I began to speak, I found my voice modulating itself, softening. Ah, so it was the pseudo-British self.

'Good to see you.' I tried to hug him, but he was having none of it.

'I've been waiting ages. Where've you been?' He reminded me of my ten-year-old sister when she was pretending she wasn't about to cry.

'What do you mean? I was at class.' Voice louder, back to American-me.

Then he looked a little embarrassed.

'Sorry,' he mumbled.

'That's okay. You okay?'

'Not really. Booked the wrong flight, didn't I. Flew to Los Angeles. Why didn't you tell me L.A. was so far from San Francisco? I thought they were right next to each other, and the

L.A. flight was cheaper. Had to get another bloody flight. Cost me bloody half of what I have, just to get here and I haven't slept in . . .' He paused to think. 'A long time.'

I led him inside and put the kettle on. Noticed he was still handsome, but in California he was quite short. Also, he seemed a little dim. I hadn't noticed that before either. Maybe he was just jet-lagged. I recognised his cowboy boots, but not his brown suede jacket with fringes. I couldn't decide if it was a step too far. David Crosby wore one, so maybe it was all right.

'Why did you think I was going to meet your plane? I don't have a car. I never said I would meet you.' I tried to say this gently, but I was remembering that no one had ever met my flight in Heathrow. Not once.

'What's this?'

'It's tea.'

'You're joking.'

Again, I could hear tears in his voice, but what could I do? He'd accommodated my California self easily enough, or at least without comment. Maybe he was too upset to notice I was different here. I was getting away with something, but I wasn't sure what. Impersonating myself?

Then, without much ado, he moved in. I carried on my student life with him ensconced on the floor near my bed in his sleeping bag. We'd never flirted, maybe because when we'd met he'd been my boyfriend's friend. We were comfortable enough to dress and undress in front of each other, which was handy. I was able to work on my novel and essays while he listened to my albums on headphones. Sometimes we both sat on the bed, smoked joints and listened to music. We'd just discovered Dire Straits and George Benson, and I introduced him to Dan Hicks. I slept as well as I ever did, despite the fact I now had to step over his body when I got out of bed before I tiptoed past the sleeping boy in the next room.

*

'I'm going to Mexico tomorrow,' he announced one morning over granola. He'd been talking about it since his arrival, but still – I was surprised.

'Good.'

'You're coming too, right?'

'What? No. I've got exams in a week.'

'But you have to come. You're the reason I've been wanting to go. All those stories about Baja with your brother.'

'Huh.'

'Freight trains and hitching,' he said, to jog my memory.

Jesus, I thought. What had I created? That trip with my brother had grown into a series of anecdotes which I'd unfolded six thousand miles away. It was difficult to remember what had happened and what I'd invented.

'Look,' he said.

'What?'

He seemed bursting with words – eyebrows raised, eyes intense – but all he said next was: 'Come.'

'No. It would be counter-productive in the extreme, to take off just now. This is my first semester.'

He laughed even though it was obvious I was annoying him.

'Coun. Ter. Pro. Duc. Tive? Too many syllables for me, college girl.'

Maybe he was teasing me because he didn't know how else to treat my new ambition. None of my British friends had gone to college, though some – like him – came from middle-class families. Maybe he felt threatened, though his mother was a physics teacher, so more likely he just felt confused. Was it, or was it not, cool to care about education and careers?

'I'm not coming. Send me a postcard, Cowboy.'

'Please.'

'Nope.'

But then I felt the same mounting tension in my chest I felt when I was about to contradict my professor or sneeze. It was physical, an involuntary impulse. I couldn't eat any more granola.

'Oh, all right, I'll come with you!' I heard myself say, and sighed angrily. 'I have to be back for my finals. They're in a week. So we basically turn around as soon as we get there.'

'Yeah, yeah,' he agreed, happy as a puppy.

We found a lift to Los Angeles that day on the KFOG ride-share slot. All we had to do was chip in on the gas and meet the driver at the bottom of University Avenue. We waited at the bus stop because there was a bench. I was in a bad mood, mad at myself. Cars and trucks whooshed past, each time buffeting us with exhaust. Twenty minutes crept by and cars kept whooshing past, everyone in a hurry to get home and open a beer, turn on the box. It was getting cold. We ran out of conversation. I began to wonder if Cowboy's entire stock consisted of puns and Grateful Dead lyrics. Should we go home again? Finally, as the sun hit the bay, our driver pulled up in an old Chevy Bel Air. The licence plate was tied to the bumper with string.

'You the ride-share guys? Sorry I'm late. My damn kids.'

I got in the front, Cowboy got in the back, and off we went. I remembered that all trips began with false starts and doubts. There would be a particular rhythm to this trip like there was with every trip. I settled down to wait for it. The driver put on a tape, Gerry Rafferty's 'Baker Street'. I'd heard it on the radio a thousand times. As soon as 'Baker Street' ended, the driver rewound the tape and played it again.

'Hope you don't mind. I fucking love this song.'

I knew he had the words wrong – it was *trying*, not *crying* – but I didn't say anything because he seemed so happy belting it out. It was hard to tell how old he was. He'd mentioned his ex-wife in Oakland and the kids he'd just been visiting. He might have been in his forties, or he might have been younger than me. He wore a green overall, like a mechanic. The freeway went straight down the valley. It was dark now, but I could sense the expanse on either side. The winter fields, the mountains rising up between us and the Pacific. The sky was clear and the stars were so bright they looked like they'd cut you if you touched them.

'We should come back on Highway One. Much prettier to go up the coast than the valley,' I said.

Cowboy didn't reply. I turned around. He was asleep across the back seat, his hand tucked between his knees and his mouth slightly open. Well, that was fine. I would be the boss of the trip. I had a sudden nostalgia for my brother because he always took the lead when we travelled. Always sat in the front seat. I would have to talk to the driver. Not continually, but often enough to keep him awake. Small talk exhausted me, so I skipped it.

'So, is life turning out the way you thought it would?'

'What? Huh. Not really, I guess,' he said slowly.

'No? Is it better or worse?'

'You know what? I can't remember what I used to imagine. But it feels worse, anyway. Even though I can't remember what it was I expected. Like I'm still waiting for it all to begin, you know?'

'Yeah. Yeah.'

'I mean, this can't be it, can it? Just this?'

A couple of times we stopped for gas and the bathroom. Fluorescent-lit places, with nothing for sale but junk food and fizzy drinks. At one station, just north of Santa Barbara, there was a large group of men smoking and spitting. I scurried to the bathroom and locked the door.

When I thought the driver was beginning to doze, I asked him more questions: *So, what do you think happens when we die? What's your biggest regret? Do you believe in love at first sight? If you won the lottery, what would you do?* I was tired, but I wasn't bored. Why couldn't I ask Cowboy these kinds of questions? Maybe his reticence infected me. I'd always been susceptible to the personalities of others. Or maybe I wasn't keen on real intimacy, only the kind I could establish in a transitory way. Much easier to ask a stranger the big questions.

Sleep caught me somewhere north of Los Angeles. When I woke it was dawn and we were parked on the edge of a busy road. My teeth felt furry.

'Sorry, but this is as far as I can take you. Downtown is half an hour in that direction.'

We got out and stretched, pulled our packs on. The driver held his hand out the open window and I shook it.

'Good luck! It's been real nice talking to you, real nice,' he said, and for a second I thought he was going to ask us to get back in the car. Then he started up the engine and drove off.

I began forgetting what he looked like almost immediately but remembered how he sang along to 'Baker Street' with the wrong words. And how he thought that after we die, we go to a kind of room where we get to see other dead people. It's like a party, with everyone saying things like *Oh my God, is that really you? It is! It's you!*

We shook ourselves to get warm, looked for a café and couldn't find one. There were freeway overpasses everywhere. A few women in very short dresses strolled by, looking cold. I unwrapped a bar of chocolate and we shared it in silence as the streetlights clicked off. We stuck out our thumbs again. I sang a Beatles song begging the drivers not to pass me by or make me cry, while wriggling my thumb in what I hoped was an engaging way. I was irresistible, we were irresistible, but it was local commute traffic and they resisted us for hours. It was late afternoon by the time we were through San Diego and over the border, into the snarl of Tijuana. Signs everywhere, gaudy and in English, enticing us to buy tattoos, weddings, divorces, massages. We kept hitching and were dropped off in Ensenada an hour later. It never occurred to us to consider a hotel as a place to sleep. Between us we had less than fifty dollars. Eventually we found a building site with steel girders rising to the starry sky. A large hotel almost completed. No windows or doors. After looking in every room to make sure it was empty, we laid our sleeping bags on the concrete floor and slipped inside them. Cowboy had bought a bottle of mescal earlier and we drank some now. Speculated about the worm in the bottom of the bottle. Was it plastic or real? If real, was it dead? If dead, why wasn't it rotting? We finished the bottle and I was a little drunk but too nervous to sleep. Being in charge was nerve-wracking. I imagined guard dogs. Drunks or junkies looking for a dark corner to hide in, then stumbling on us. I'd done this before, but I didn't think it was a smart thing to do. I suffered another wave of homesickness for my brother. Had I really imagined I could repeat that Baja adventure without him? Then I fell into a fudge-like sleep.

The first thing I saw in the morning were the humped shapes of other bodies on the floor, mostly wrapped in colourful but dirty blankets. Snores came from at least three directions. I lay still and tried to figure it out. Sleeping men were not a danger, but still. I was pondering various contingency plans when they drifted into dreams. When I next woke, it was to the sight of boots. Half a dozen Mexican construction workers were milling around our sleeping bags as if we weren't there. Some were already working, measuring up planks and leisurely sawing. Once they noticed we were awake, they stopped working and wanted to talk about who we were and where we were going. All I wanted was to find a place to pee, but I chatted for a few minutes, pulling my jeans on inside my bag. A few of the men weren't needed on the site and indicated we could ride in the back of their pickup. So we rode out into the rosy chill dawn, the mescal still in our blood, wedged up against some bags of tools. I think we smiled at each other.

We found a café in downtown Ensenada, ordered refried beans and tortilla de patatas. Our Nescafé came with condensed milk. We ate everything on our plates and didn't talk, aside from *pass the salt*. Mexican voices came from the kitchen, and the sound of frying. 'Stayin' Alive' by the Bee Gees was played twice on the jukebox by an unshaven man who danced to it, clapping his hands rapidly and stamping his feet, all the while puffing on a cigarette, ash flying everywhere. Maybe this was still night to him. Both times he finished, half the café applauded. A cloudy bottle of hot sauce sat in the middle, with a small bowl of chillies I kept swatting the flies off. Waitresses were bare-legged in short skirts and low tops, and they moved lazily, good-naturedly. Much jewellery was evident on everyone, even the cook with his shirt half unbuttoned. Mostly gold crucifixes, hearts, skulls and skeletons. Everything was familiar but also exotic. Even the air tasted different. I was getting used to it, but that first sniff had not been pleasant. Meat going off, male sweat, cheap aftershave. People were friendly, often speaking in English, but it was hard to tell if they liked us. Why should they? In the bathroom, filthy and small, I washed my armpits with hand-wash, rubbed cold water on my face, smeared on some moisturiser and scrubbed my hands. Brushed my teeth and took a multivitamin because I always did.

Our road south was a quiet two lanes, unspooling over a thousand miles down the Baja peninsula to Cabo San Lucas. A lot of the time, we walked along the roadside because it was less boring than standing with our thumbs out. Sometimes no cars came for fifteen minutes. Mostly we didn't talk much. Or sang snatches of songs from beloved albums. We tried to sing them in the same order the tracks were on the album, and took turns choosing the album.

'You have a terrible voice,' he said at one point, politely.

'I know.'

'No, really. I've never heard anything like it.'

I liked that he could be this honest with me. He could insult and not sound mean.

'First side of the first New Riders of the Purple Sage album,' I commanded.

He immediately began singing 'I Don't Know You'. But then he got some of the lyrics wrong.

'You're just testing me, right?'

'Yeah, yeah, just a test,' he said.

'Liar. You really forgot the words.'

'Didn't.'

'Obviously did.'

But it was too hot to argue properly. I wanted to tell him, as the song said, that I didn't know him. Not well enough for the kind of fights I had with my brother sometimes.

I kept thinking about trips with my brother, because so far this trip seemed a pale comparison. Not as funny or scary or vivid in any sense. But maybe I only treasured events when they were in the past. Perhaps in about a year, this trip with Cowboy would seem even more wonderful than the trip with my brother. What else might I be deluding myself about? Maybe I'd look back one day and realise I had a huge crush on Cowboy. Good grief!

The next night, a driver picked us up at dusk and offered us a place to sleep. It was a large, corrugated iron shack in the middle of nowhere. He told us he was a poacher of *tortugas*. Giant tortoises, which he kept alive to increase their market value. Lots of people around there did the same thing. *Todos hacen lo mismo.* He kept them in a sectioned-off bit of the shack. Being *tortugas*, the barrier didn't need to be tall, and we could see them. They looked dead, but I didn't say. He cooked up some canned stew and corn tortillas, using a one-burner kerosene stove. His teeth were mostly black, with an occasional gold cap, and his arms and neck were covered with religious tattoos. For all I knew, only his face was free of God. If he turned up on my doorstep in Berkeley, would I open my house to him as he'd welcomed us? I felt a hypocrite, so I gave him my address, using my high school Spanish to explain.

'Mi casa esta su casa. Verdad!'

He smiled, but not as if he believed me. Later he indicated where we were to sleep on the floor.

'Buenas noches,' he said. 'Dios te ama.'

Then he left, smiling his black and gold smile, and we never saw him again. I didn't sleep well. All night long those tortoises shuffled and breathed and made strange noises. I lay there imagining how heavy they must feel. How gravity must be so hard for them.

Travelling with someone could tell you things about a person that even living with them couldn't. It could make or break a relationship. Maybe people getting married should be required to hitch to Mexico on $50 before the wedding. Cowboy turned out to be all right to travel with. He wasn't fussy about food or hygiene, not overly talkative, not paranoid. In fact, he seemed quietly enthralled even when nothing at all was happening. He was a light person, in the best possible way. I decided he was not in the least dim, merely British. That explained the puns and childish teasing, the modesty, the disinclination to engage in serious conversation. Back in London he had a routine which I always fell for, even when I told myself not to. We'd be visiting a friend and get in a pee-stinky lift, then when the door opened, I'd get out but he would not. The door would close on his cackling face. I'd been fooled again, stuck on the wrong floor. This made him happy each time. He also liked water pistols. He'd jump out from shadowy places and squirt water at me, saying *Aha!* then run away like a kid, giggling. Aside from his first day in California, I'd never seen him angry or moody. Good person to travel with, and who knew what else. Though darkness, I felt, would probably creep out for me eventually, and then what would happen? I couldn't imagine having a serious conversation with him, but already I wanted to. Or told myself I did.

'So, it's Wednesday,' he said the next afternoon.

'Is it?'

It was early morning. We were sitting on a kerb, eating hunks of white bread and drinking Mexican Coca Cola, which didn't taste the same as American Coca Cola. We'd ceased commenting on things like this.

'Yeah. So, like, when do we need to turn around?'

I noticed his accent. Was he becoming American?

'Oh, I don't know,' I said. 'I guess yesterday. Shit.'

The end of the adventure was hot on the heels of the proper beginning, which felt unpleasantly familiar. Oh, where the hell was I? In a foreign country again, miles from the library where I was supposed to be. We were just silly tourists, making ourselves miserable for no reason. We walked a mile north. Traffic was sporadic. One or two cars every half hour. If we were lucky we'd be in San Diego by dinner, but it was much more likely we'd get short lifts and take days to get there. We were surrounded by desert on one side and the Pacific Ocean on the other, turkey vultures wheeling overhead. I had a sudden case of the runs. *El chorro*. My stomach bacteria had been happy enough when it seemed I was going to remain in Baja, but not now we were heading north. I found a cactus to squat behind and buried my favourite pair of underpants in the sand. I was down to three pairs now. None were clean – I'd already begun turning them inside out. I travelled light and was ridiculously proud of this.

'Let's stay one more night. I need to not eat for a while.'

'Yeah, okay,' he said. 'How about that beach we passed a while ago?'

Cowboy remained in excellent health. He walked to a store that sold diarrhoea medicine, and I was so grateful I almost kissed him. We got a lift to the beach with a Londoner, which was disorienting. A man in his thirties, very tanned.

'How long have you been here?' I asked.

'About ten years. Never going back to Britain. Blimey. Tried it once and look at me now.'

He indicated his left leg, flopped sideways. 'Went completely dead on me, middle of bloody Shaftesbury Avenue. Docs can't figure it out. But I know.'

'What?'

'Know why I'm crippled. My body's smart. It was saying *get me the fuck out of here*. Get me back to bloody beautiful Baja!'

Then he laughed loudly, and we laughed too, to keep him company. But it didn't seem very funny. It seemed sad.

We met two Australian boys on the beach. A tall skinny one called Stretch and a short sunburned one called Dart. They invited us to drink some beers. It was relaxing speaking English to someone other than Cowboy. I went swimming in my underpants and a T-shirt. The sea was cool for a second, then I got used to it and it was warm. I floated, then swam, then floated again. I hadn't eaten since last night and was feeling light-headed and slightly euphoric. At one point I looked back to the beach and saw the Australian boys and Cowboy. The beach looked like a postcard, almost too pretty to be pretty. White sand, palm trees, half a dozen palm-covered beach huts. The sea was a gelatinous turquoise. I told myself I was happy, and to remember this moment. Then I asked myself how long I could stay right where I was. As long as I want, I answered. But a little breeze came up, and with it, fear. I thought about how much water was below me. About how I might look to a shark, and how jellyfish could sting me and not even know it. Just float past me, thinking jellyfish thoughts. The beach began to seem dangerously far – had a current taken me further out? I swam back to shore and was glad when I reached it.

The next day, we headed north again. I ate a banana wrapped in a fresh corn tortilla and thankfully it did not lead to another ruined pair of underpants. But the blue sky had fled and it began to rain. The kind of rain that meant business. We got a lift in an old truck, both sitting in the cab, the rain hammering on the roof.

'Qué pasa?' the driver asked with a cocked eyebrow. 'De dónde?'

'Soy de San Francisco,' I said. 'Él esta de London.'

'Aha! Gringo y Limey! Muy simpatico,' he said quickly.

He was very short with a hard-looking beer belly, a luxuriant moustache and bad teeth. I noted none of these prevented him from being handsome. What made a man handsome? Nothing obvious, as far as I could tell. After a few hours, we stopped. The road had disappeared and a river was there instead. We were fifth in the line of stopped cars and trucks. Other vehicles soon pulled up behind us, and after a while, we all got out and wandered around in the rain, which was like taking a warm shower in your clothes. I was glad to be stranded. I wanted choice to be taken from me, and besides, extreme weather was always exciting. It laughed at my final exam deadline. Cowboy seemed as tickled as I was. The truck driver shrugged as if this was normal, and indicated he was going to have a siesta.

'Cuando vamos?' I asked.

'No sé,' he replied. 'Anoche? Mañana? No sé.'

The sun came out. Steam rose, and people shared their food and water. Little groups formed and disbanded. Campfires were lit, frisbees thrown. Kids and dogs ran in little packs. It seemed everyone was used to flash floods in the desert. Our truck driver was visible in his cab, hat still covering his face.

'Think I'll take a little wander,' said Cowboy. 'Back in a tick.' I noted he sounded English again. Good, I thought. People should stay who they were. It seemed the only chance anyone had of staying believable. There was a huge flat stone not far from the road, and I lay down on it, my face covered with my cap because the sun was still bright. I was sleepy but I didn't sleep. The air was heavy and moist. I listened to people. Quite near, a couple were fighting in English.

'You always did, and you always will. I get no respect,' said the woman in an about-to-cry voice.

'Oh, right, so it's all my fault again,' said the man.

Then there were car doors opening and slamming and their voices got louder.

'Well, fuck off then,' he snarled.

'What the fuck do you think I'm doing, you wank-stain?'

I lifted my cap. A chubby woman in shorts and spaghetti string top took off her shoes and waded across the thigh-high river. The husband, if that's what he was, honked the horn a few times and shouted:

'Get the fuck back here! I'm sorry! I won't do it again. I love you, you sad bitch.'

But she kept walking. I slid my cap over my face again and decided it was like *Lord of the Flies*. One little fluke of nature and anarchy descended. This thought produced a perverse little worm of happiness in my belly.

Then I heard Cowboy's voice: 'I'm back.'

'Hey,' I said from under my cap.

'Here's an idea,' he said nervously.

'What.'

'Marry me.'

I was flooded with a silly pleasure. No one had ever asked me to marry them. Not unless you counted marriage of convenience proposals.

'Fuck off.'

His laughter was as gratifying as the proposal. The water receded in the evening, and after much discussion, people shook hands, hugged, and started up their cars. We were off again. I watched the moving road out the front window, which was filthy with smeared bugs. No one talked. It could have been midnight, or nearly dawn. There was something soporific about driving on roads not in good repair. The wheels rolled over heat cracks, potholes, gravel. I dozed on and off, and all the time the words *Marry me* hummed and swelled. Our friends were having babies, but none of them were married. Marriage was deemed unfashionable, square. What had made him, as he approached my figure, face under cap, ask? If his proposal had been sincere, it made no sense. We hadn't even kissed. If it was a kind of British joke, I didn't get it.

The road north was washed out again further up, and the detour involved a ferry from Santa Rosalia to Guaymas on the mainland, and from there we'd head to Mexicali. The morning had come and another day began passing. There was a clear sky now, very blue and sharp, but I felt blurry. I ached to lie down someplace. I'd stopped thinking about my exams, but I was worried about money. We had some but not enough for a ferry, and where would we spend the night when we got to Mexicali? So far, we'd re-traced the trip I'd taken with my brother. To step outside this particular known felt risky. The driver paid for our ferry tickets. He didn't even ask for money.

Mexicali was like Tijuana, only smaller and less American. It was evening again, and our driver careened down dark streets at high speed till we came to Juanita's Taverna. It was big, with a stage and two bars. He strode in and we followed him like two gobsmacked children.

'Qué deseás?' the bartender asked.

'Tres cervezas y una chica bonita, por favor.'

Three beers and a pretty girl? Three beers appeared, and a second later a girl tapped our driver on the shoulder, smiled shyly and said:

'Hola. Mi llama es Teresa.'

The evening passed. We drank beer and watched them dance. She smiled constantly. No matter how closely I looked, her smile seemed genuine. I was drunk. It was the best phase of being drunk. Everything was clear and I loved not just my own life, but life itself. I had a vague recollection of having eaten street tacos earlier, but nothing since. The band played 'Mexicali Blues' and we sang along. We were squeezed in a cubicle of vinyl seats, the lights were low and there were no candles. It was hard to talk, the band loud. Some of the songs were in Spanish, but most were covers of American and British rock. Beach Boys, Beatles, Elvis Costello's 'Alison'. Our driver was either kissing Teresa or dancing. He hadn't done much talking but now had the look of someone who understood everything. Then he shouted something to us.

'Quieres llegar alto?'

We didn't know what he meant. He smiled and shook his head. When the band stopped for a break, he went up to the guitarist and they talked. Exchanged something.

'Aqui,' he said back at our table, pressing something into my hand. A small paper bag of marijuana and a pack of rolling papers. I showed Cowboy.

'Gracias,' I said. 'Muchas gracias.'

'Yeah,' said Cowboy. 'What she said. Thanks, man.'

Then the night was swallowed up the way nights are when you've had a lot to drink and then smoke a few joints. It ended in a hotel room presumably paid for by our driver.

'Buenas noches, amigos, y adios!' he said, smiling broadly and saluting us. And then he strolled away with Teresa clinging to his arm, just like the movies. Our room was tiny and looked down into a huge, darkened factory, which contained row after row of sewing machines. Or maybe I had double vision.

'Shit. I think I left my cap in his truck,' I slurred. 'I love that cap.'

'Bummer.'

'What if we never see him again? Do you think we'll ever see him again?'

But I fell asleep before an answer came.

The next day we spent our last pennies on a bus to Tijuana and slept all the way. From Tijuana, we hitch-hiked. An American man driving his alcoholic wife back from a Mexican rehabilitation centre dropped us off at Bakersfield at dawn and we hitched to Highway One, just north of Los Angeles. It was briefly strange to be back in the United States. A period of about thirty minutes when I didn't feel I was in either place, then – whoomph! I was fully in California. Our rides took us past artichoke fields, wild empty beaches, rows of apricot trees and almond trees. We never waited more than ten minutes for a ride. Once, the same song was still playing on the radio in our next ride.

We stopped at Santa Cruz to stay with my friend who could dance like a whirling dervish. Berkeley was only sixty-five miles further north, but I was reluctant for the trip to end. Maybe I didn't want to face up to another academic failure. We had a shower, and after dinner were given the two living room sofas to sleep on. I liked sleeping near him. I was used to it now. It was comforting hearing his particular way of breathing, with a hiccupy sound now and then. When I woke in the night and noticed he wasn't there, I heard giggles from down the hall. My friend's housemate, a petite girl with brown eyes and curly hair, had stolen my cowboy!

'Think I'll hang on here a few days,' he said the next morning, looking sly but also happy. 'You can get on with your studying better without me around.'

'Yeah, no problem,' I said.

I seethed and then slumped inside, realising I'd been waiting. For what, I wasn't sure. Another proposal so I could say yes? And then I began to doubt myself. I'd misheard him and he'd never said *Marry me* at all. He'd been asking me something about Larry, one of my roommates. Or asking me to carry something. In any case, it was too late now. I stored my dubious and probably groundless regret in a mental safe reserved for moments of masochism in the future.

I missed my exams, but they let me take them anyway in a room by myself. By the skin of my teeth I passed them, even the poetry exam. For the questions concerning *Gawain and the Green Knight* and for *The Canterbury Tales*, I had to leave my blue book blank. On the first page, I scribbled *Poetry from olden days not my forte*, and such were the liberal times, I got a C minus for honesty. Cowboy came to say goodbye on his way to the airport. He looked used up.

'So long. Keep in touch,' I said.

'Good luck with university. And thanks for everything.'

It was on the tip of my tongue to say thanks for the memories – it was how I felt – but we didn't have that kind of relationship. I still didn't know him that well. Though I supposed there might not be a cure for that. If I lived with him the rest of my life, maybe I'd not know him any better. Maybe a marriage could depend on that kind of friendly distance. The more I thought about it, it began to seem that a certain amount of ignorance might be essential to a happy marriage. In which case, maybe I preferred knowing someone to not. I might miss arguing.

And then I dived back into reading and writing, and not being touched by anyone but my kid sister and a roommate's mongrel dog called Berk.

By spring I'd finished my novel about unconsummated love. It was 32,000 words, which I imagined was quite long enough, and painstakingly corrected with Tipp-Ex. On impulse, I crawled under my desk and wrote with a ballpoint pen on the underside. I pressed hard, so the words were engraved in ink: *Love makes you stupid*. I felt clever, and I was thrilled to think someone might read my words one day. They would have no idea who wrote them, and I liked that too. Then I sat at my desk and wondered if the words were true. Did love make you stupid? What the hell did I know about love? I'd let three days of kissing a stranger lead to two years of celibacy. In seventh grade Sister Angelina had said that none of us knew ourselves as well as God knew us, and reprimanded me for insisting that *I know myself very well, thank you very much*. But the older I got, the more I understood her. It seemed to be in excruciatingly slow motion, this getting to know oneself business. In fact, it seemed to be going backwards. I knew myself less and less. Maybe I just did what I wanted to do, then found a way to justify it. Told myself a story that made me feel all right. But being a good person, according to Sister Angelina (and Socrates, Plato, Pope Paul and a zillion other enquiring humans), involved a daily task of personal scrutiny. It was work. Now it occurred to me I'd been sedated by those pivotal kisses of Christopher Parker. It hadn't been unconsummated love, just unconsummated sex. And warping, in some hugely time-wasting way. They'd certainly made me stupid because here I was, at my sexual prime and alone. I wished I'd written *Sex makes you stupid*. Because love must make you smart, right? Bright and big and beautiful. Love was what kept rescuing me from the mess that sex – consummated or not – got me into. Even when love was not attached to anyone in particular, but just a willingness to say yes.

Except, apparently, when a boy I fancied proposed to me.

At Easter I went to a homeopathic doctor about my absent period and was told to give up coffee and ChapStick. After a week of no espressos and chapped lips, it arrived. I toasted my prodigal ovulation alone, as I'd not told anyone it had stopped in the first place.

Cowboy wrote in June, a postcard from London telling me he'd been to a Grateful Dead concert. After a week I bought him a postcard of a cowboy. It was a black-and-white photograph, and even though the cowboy's face was almost invisible under his hat, you could tell he was a handsome man. Something in the set of his shoulders, the shadow of his jaw. There were tumble-weeds on the flat prairie around him. A romantic image. Alive in his moment, maybe thinking: *Who the dickens is the guy with the camera?* On the back it said the photograph was taken in 1895 near Whiskey Town – but there he was, fresh in his present, which probably seemed like it was going to go on for-ever, like it always does.

It took me a while to think what to write. In the end, I forced myself to quickly scribble something, so it would look as if I'd given it no thought at all. *What a long, strange trip it was*, I wrote. It was a reference to a Grateful Dead lyric he'd under-stand. Maybe I knew him after all.

Something Fishy

I'd been pacing myself for the death climax, but my return date to Scotland came round and my mother was still right as rain. Maybe she was a zombie. Or maybe not remembering she was mortal halted the process. Did Death require acknowledgement? I took one final walk down to the levee, packed my suitcase and stood by her wheelchair in the living room.

'I've got to go, Mom, but I'll be back soon.'

'You better,' she said, in her mock-scolding voice, then she pulled my face down to her red lipstick mouth and gave me three loud kisses. 'Is it bear claw time yet?' she whispered in my ear.

'Sure,' I said. It was always bear claw time as far as I was concerned.

Then Ateca said: 'Hurry up, you must go now. *Now.*'

She followed me out to my brother's waiting car, then stood there like a sentinel in the driveway as we drove off. Her hands were pressed together as if she was praying, while tears washed down her face.

'What's that about,' asked my brother. 'Crying, for Christ's sake.'

'Don't know. Channelling Mom?'

'Don't be stupid. Mom never cries.'

'As far as we know,' I said. 'She might be a private crier. Some women are.'

I'd convinced myself that my brother relied on me to enlighten him about female ways. Any empathy he'd achieved with girl-friends, and later his wife, must be down to smug me.

'Huh,' was all he said.

As we drove down 3ʳᵈ Street towards 101, I felt a wave of affection for San Rafael – the town that had made me. It'd seen all my childish illusions and adolescent embarrassments. Probably the least picturesque town in Marin, and for decades I'd held it in contempt – so conventional and way too affluent for a hippie girl to approve of. But now even the sight of Thrifty's at Montecito shopping centre made my throat hurt. That was where I'd lost my father when I was six years old. I was working on a story about it, so it was fresh in my mind. My earliest strong memory kept offering up insights, almost as if I'd cleverly stored it all those years ago with this future plundering in mind. But that, of course, is a nonsense. I remembered it because it was nightmarish. Easy times slide right off the memory, only the scary times stick.

I turned to my brother and said: 'Or maybe not. Mom never cries. Ateca cries at everything, anyway. She watches those Hallmark movies and cries her head off all the way through. Come to think of it, she cries when she's happy too. Maybe she's glad I'm leaving.'

'Wow. Crying is so complicated,' he said in a monotone, as if he was only half listening, and then he signalled to merge onto the freeway.

I got home to Scotland, three minutes passed, and then the phone rang:

'You must come now,' Ateca said. 'It is the end.'

'Again?'

'Yes! Death, it is here!'

'Okay, okay.' I was standing in my cold kitchen, which immed-iately seemed unreal and grey. It hadn't really been three minutes. It was, by now, late October. When I arrived back in San Rafael – sombre-faced, expecting a corpse – there she was, looking exactly like a corpse. It was horrific but also weirdly gratifying – people on deathbeds *should* look like they're dying. Her breathing was shallow and raspy, her cheeks were unnaturally pink. She seemed so tiny! I noticed her luxuriant facial hair. My first impulse was to look away, as if I'd caught a glimpse of her on the toilet. She was always vigilant about facial hair – and being Italian, removing it had been a lifelong project. The sight of it now proved either she was an imposter or this, at last, was Death. The reality was somehow less real than the imagined death throes. I'd cried, doing that, but now all I felt was a nervous numbness. I kissed her forehead, which was feverish and dry, and said I loved her.

'I love you too,' she wheezed, and tried to kiss me back three times but only got to two.

Then I went to bed in my dead father's office, where I didn't sleep till dawn thinking of everything that must come next.

When I woke late the next morning, groggy and jet-lagged, I found her sitting in her wheelchair at the table, eating breakfast. *The Sound of Music* was playing.

When she saw me, her face lit up.

'What are you doing here?'

'I'm here to see you,' I said.

'You are? Really?'

'Yes!'

'You are beautiful!'

'Thank you. I get that from my mother.'

Pause.

'Wah!' she said, smiling, hands raised and upturned.

It was a relief she wasn't dead, or at least I knew relief would be appropriate – but I couldn't shake a sense that, as my mother would say, something fishy was going on. I was there under false pretences! By this time, I'd spent hundreds of hours imagining her death. My weeping and brave eulogising, all of us packing up her house, telling funny stories about our naughty father and our spacey mother. I'd gone through all the stages of grief, but here she still was, singing along to Julie Andrews and munching bacon.

'You said she was dying,' I whispered to Ateca, trying not to sound accusing.

'I know. God is good!' She rolled her eyes up and pointed upwards. 'God is good!' she said again. Then she asked if I wanted a blueberry scone, which would be out of the oven in ten minutes.

'Sure,' I said, and felt my old San Rafael life drift up and wrap its tentacles round me again. Did I struggle against it? My real life was not here. I had a husband at home, children and grandchildren, good friends. A house I'd lived in for thirty-five years and a job I loved. I loved that life, damnit, and I wanted to miss it.

'You want coffee too? Your Peet's is still in the freezer.'

No, no, no! I will not be seduced! But all that came out was: 'That would be fantastic.'

And I meant it. Because I was a fickle shallow thing.

Right on cue, Captain von Trapp began singing 'Edelweiss'. Like him, I also blessed my homeland.

Monsters

*Six years old
California, 1959*

I was shopping in Thrifty's with my father. He had a list from my mother, maybe some film for her Brownie box camera and Breck shampoo, both of which featured big on her list of essentials. It was hot and the gum on the sidewalks was sticky again, but inside Thrifty's the air was cool. I was wearing pink shorts and a white T-shirt. My dad was wearing a white T-shirt too, and I liked that, looking the same. I may even have put on the T-shirt to match his. We weren't talking, just walking, and I was content because my brother and mother were not there. I had a sudden urge to hold his hand, but the hand I grabbed did not belong to my father. Right shirt, wrong man. The wrong man with the wrong eyes, the wrong skin and the wrong smell. I looked around, but there was no one else in the aisle. The man's mouth was overloaded with teeth. Teeth were coming down over his lower lip, and his arms were too hairy.

'Guess you thought I was someone else. Your dad?' he said gently.

It felt like a trick question. I said nothing and leaned away from him.

'Your big brother?'

I shook my head impatiently. My brother was younger than me! This proved it was a trick question or he was just stupid.

'Don't cry. No need to cry,' he said.

Was I crying? I wasn't.

'What's your name?'

I kept my mouth shut. More tricks.

He tried to take my hand and smiled. 'Come on then.'

But I would not take his hand again. I'd been following him for a while – walking right next to him – and he'd let me. I began to howl for my father, in between sobs that shook my body. I was alarmed to be crying. Ashamed of acting like a baby, but unable to stop. It was like losing control of my bladder during story time, watching the puddle seep out from my skirt.

Then a nice lady who worked at the ice cream counter gave me a triple scoop cone. She told me not to cry too, but I didn't mind her saying it. The toothy man was gone. Maybe she sent him away.

'Everything's going to be all right,' she said. 'I promise. We'll find your daddy.'

I told her my name and my dad's name.

'Mr Jones, please come to the ice cream counter. We have a lost child here,' she said into a box. Her voice boomed around Thrifty's and I felt reassured.

I listened, hiccupping and sniffing, liking the way something was happening, however futile. She was older than my mother and had a crumpled face, like a week-old balloon. I wasn't sure everything was going to be all right – how could it? I'd seen my father replaced by a stranger, a hairy-armed monster, with my own eyes. Strangely, as if my taste buds had not been informed of the crisis, the ice cream tasted delicious.

In the time it took for my father to appear, I figured out a future for myself as a fatherless child. I was unclear whether I needed my mother more than she needed me, but I decided I would hug her very hard if she cried. And I would be a good girl for her, help her take care of my brother. I'd hold him when she gave him his inhaler. More time passed without my father, and the ice cream lady talked into the box again. He must have left Thrifty's and been hit by a truck. Or been kidnapped, stolen by a father-stealer. Then, just as I finished my ice cream cone, along he came. He had a sheepish look that broke into a wide smile when he saw me.

'Well, there you are!' he said. 'I was looking everywhere for you. All the other stores in the mall, and here you were all along.'

My relief was a tidal wave, but I pretended I'd always known he'd appear. I didn't tell him I'd written him off, nor did I mention I'd been crying. I was many things, but I was not a sissy. No sirree.

And that was it. We didn't tell anyone. Not my mother, not my brother.

It was the time of milk cartons displaying missing children. I'd eat my Wheaties and study the face of the latest missing child. We lived almost rurally – no sidewalks or streetlights in a road that ran higgledy-piggledy down to San Francisco Bay. The houses were former summer cabins from the 1890s and a few newly built bungalows like ours. My brother was too young, but I was allowed to run free with a gang of neighbourhood children, about eight of us ranging from five to ten years old. In the long summer weeks we only returned at dusk for food, like animals. If my parents were concerned about the milk carton children, they didn't show it. But I took the milk carton children seriously. I worried about them. I got to know them because the same child appeared for weeks sometimes. Their smiling face, their name, their age, what they were wearing when last seen. I was especially interested in the girls my age. What had happened to them? Whatever it was, it couldn't happen to me because I was prepared. If a strange man tricked me into his car, I'd wait till he seemed unsure, maybe admitting he was lost or worried about a place to stay. I'd lie. Tell him it was all right, I could help him. He wouldn't believe me at first, so I'd pretend I didn't care, just like you would if you were not pretending. I'd yawn, stare out the window and say:

'Okay, I don't care. My, isn't it a nice day?'

Eventually he'd trust me and I'd direct him to a safe place – but it would really be the police station, or my grandmother's house. It was such an obvious ploy, so easy, I couldn't understand why the milk carton children hadn't thought of it. Or maybe they had, but they were not good liars.

I had a bad dream the night of the Thrifty's drug store incident. Like most bad dreams, it was set in a familiar place. I was at our neighbourhood beach, and the small island just offshore rose up out of the water and revealed itself to be the humped back of a monster. Being an island had been a disguise, and its true self was strange and menacing. As I ran home in my dream, I couldn't run fast enough, so I swung my body through my arms like a chimpanzee. Still not fast enough, so I took to the air and flew. Flying was like swimming, or how I imagined swimming would be. I wasn't a swimmer yet, but felt I'd get the knack of it any day now. All my friends could swim, even my little brother could float. Being able to swim was something you couldn't lie about. You had to know how to do it, or you'd drown, and then you'd not be alive again, ever. I escaped the island monster from the bay, and the dream ended with me dog-paddling through the air, homeward bound.

I went down to the beach the next day with the dog, as I often did, and there was the island. It looked entirely like its old self – humped and treeless and green, except for the bits stained white with guano. I stared at it and it didn't move an inch. I marked out its relation to the San Rafael Richmond Bridge, so I could check it again later. See if it moved. Then I walked back home. I knew all these houses almost as well as I knew my own, and today they were all marked by some past tragedy or aberration. I didn't dwell on this in a morbid way – it was just how things were and today I was noting them. There was a chicken farm at the end of the road, just a small one, and I stopped there for a while to think about things. It made my dog happy, but not the chickens.

The days went on, and I kept thinking about losing my father in Thrifty's. I couldn't leave it alone, like picking a scab or a bit of sunburned skin. Each terrifying segment needed to be replayed. The moment I looked up expecting my father and it wasn't him. The strangeness of the stranger. His arm hair and surfeit of teeth. The ice cream counter, the triple scoop. How it felt when I saw my dad walk up with his funny smile, the one he had when he was over the moon but acting like it was no big deal. I knew that expression so well. I admired everything about him, so I admired this too.

'Well, there you are!' he'd said, as if we'd been playing hide-and-seek.

'There you are!' I'd said back, hopped off my stool and walked to him. Not run.

Nothing bad had happened, but I couldn't shake a feeling that something had. The molecules of the world had altered and I'd accepted a new order.

Last Rites

The priest came to give her the Last Rites. He was a tall middle-aged man. My mother had always enjoyed the company of men. Women were fine of course, but they couldn't perk her up like men could. He held her hand in greeting, and she pulled it to her mouth for three kisses. It was the first time he'd met her and his initial response was to resist – but he lost the tug of war and she had her way.

'How are you, Barbara?' To my mind, an insane question.

'I just thank God I'm not worse,' she replied. Mom could put a good spin on anything. And then, as if extracting a file from her perfect hostess past, she asked: 'Are you staying for lunch? Please do.'

When he anointed her forehead in the sign of the cross, she closed her eyes and raised her mouth as if he was about to kiss her.

'Through this holy anointing, may the Lord in his love and mercy help you with the grace of the Holy Spirit.'

'Delightful,' she whispered.

'Do you have any sins to confess, Barbara?'

He said this in a very low voice, and not as if he expected a reply. She looked at him sharply, lips parted, as though she understood something was expected of her and wasn't going to let anyone down. Then she smiled proudly, almost flirtatiously, and said:

'You go first.'

I guess she thought it could be the correct response, or if not correct – well, it covered all sorts of scenarios. When in doubt, ask a man to talk about himself. He frowned and opened his mouth, maybe to say something defensive or patronising, but Ateca swooped in with:

'You're a smart cookie, Barbarajones.'

She often said my mother's names as if they were one word. Her broad arm dropped protectively around Mom's shoulders. And there they were. A tableau of love.

Mom had always done her best. In fact, it was one of her phrases while I was growing up. Difficult exams, lack of a prom date, falling out with my best friend? *Just do your best and then don't worry about it!* The implication being that doing your best may not reap rewards, but at least you'd have no regrets. By rights, she should have had a faithful husband, an immunity to MS, daughters who never moved far away. And she deserved the kind of deathbed you see in movies, with loving children holding vigil day and night. But the truth is, some horrible parents get the family send-off, while some excellent parents die in the company of recent acquaintances paid to be there. As close as I felt to her now, the only person my mother felt truly close to – the only person she *loved* in an active sense – was Ateca. In many ways, she was a better husband than Dad had been. She was always there, for one thing. Not away in Timbuktu on business or in the garage. *I'm busy, Barbara! I've got to fix the goddamn some-thing or other again.*

Mom used to wake at night, shouting *Let the darn dog out!* The dog being dead, Ateca figured she'd get more sleep if she slept with Mom, so until the advent of the hospital bed, that's what she did. A few visits ago, I'd found Ateca face down on the bed with Mom massaging her back.

'I love you, Barbarajones.'

'I love you more,' my mother had replied, omitting to mention any name at all.

They were like an old married couple without the tension or bickering. Days were full of rituals. Bacon and egg at 11am, followed by Mom napping in her wheelchair by the desk, followed by *General Hospital* at 1pm, followed by *The Sound of Music* and Svenhard's bear claws, followed by dinner at six, followed by bed once again. Her dementia may have meant Ateca's name and gender wouldn't stick, but it couldn't touch her affection. I observed this with a mixture of gratitude and envy. It should have been me, seeing my mother out.

The priest packed up his gear – holy water, a candle, his missal – and submitted to my mother kissing his hand again.

'God bless you, Barbara.'

'Que sera sera,' she replied.

The next afternoon in front of the television, while my mom kissed my hand over and over with her whiskery lips, it occurred to me that for a daddy's girl, I was pretty hard on my father. I'd loved him enormously, continually, but never blindly. I hadn't even liked him much sometimes. Nor had I always been a good daughter to him. In a slightly queasy mood, almost cringing, I decided to write a story about my father and me which would reveal the full extent of my own unlikableness. A dog crime story that would never deserve forgiveness.

Meanwhile, me and Ateca were still laughing about the priest. Every time we remembered his face when Mom told him *You go first*, we laughed hysterically. Was anything funnier than a vain man having his bluff called by a dying innocent?

'You know God loves your mother,' Ateca said gruffly, suddenly not laughing.

'Well! That's good news,' I said, not knowing what else to say.

'Oh yeah. He loves Barbarajones, all right.'

Then she punched the air as if she was watching her favourite team on television and the quarterback had just slid through the goalposts, football tucked into his chest.

I Miss You

Sixty years old
California, 2013

I committed a great crime once. It began with an act of love. My father was in the hospital, dying. A stroke, I'd been told. I'd only been back in Scotland a month and my first reaction was crankiness. I didn't have time for this now. Whose idea was it to let Dad die now, damnit?

'If you want to say your goodbyes, you better come back now,' said my brother, calling from the hospital. His voice had more than a touch of weariness. Was he enjoying the drama a tiny bit? Underneath the crankiness, I certainly was – even as I loathed myself for doing so. I still didn't believe my parents would actually die. These medical emergencies were just feints at death, a game or joke to scare us. They would stay alive because, heavens, *they must, they must*. My brother regaled me with the hellish process leading to this denouement. Most of which involved his efforts and time. Not our sister's and not mine. Just his. All by himself. When he was so busy already with work and family, and he wasn't feeling great either.

Our father may have loved us equally, but he didn't treat us equally. An example: my brother liked our dad's Alfa Romeo but had never been allowed to drive it. Even when he'd passed his test, even when he was older with a good driving record. After he was married and had children, and again later when he was the CEO of an international transportation consultancy,

71

he asked if he could take the Alfa for a spin and the answer was still *NO*. Me and my sister had no interest in driving the Alfa, but were confident all we'd have to do is ask for the keys. When my sister got married, Dad insisted they take the Alfa to the church. Earlier this year when he stopped driving, Dad finally offered the Alfa keys to his son.

Here you go, he said gallantly. *No use to me now. She's all yours.*

He probably imagined gratitude, but my brother tossed the keys back at him. The gesture was decades too late.

'The doctor promised he's dying,' my brother said to me now.

'Literally promised?'

'Okay. Maybe I read that into his tone.'

'You're going to cry if he recovers, aren't you?' I accused.

'Ah, just come, will you?'

'Okay, okay, I'm coming.'

I asked him to prop his phone by our father's ear.

'He's not conscious.'

'Do it anyway.' I was still the big sister, damn it.

I pressed the phone hard to my ear and heard soft bleeps, presumably the machine monitoring – perhaps enabling – my father's continued existence. Then I just listened to him breathe. The breaths were recognisably his and therefore dear, even intimate. I'd heard him breathe the day I was born, and under those breaths was his still-beating heart. *Don't stop*, I willed his heart. *Do not stop.*

'Sis? You there?'

'Was that you breathing? Christ.'

'Yeah. My deepest apologies for being alive.'

'Jesus. I said to put the phone next to his ear, okay?'

'Whatever.'

Sigh.

'Dad. *Dad.*'

'Dad.'

'Dad, I'm coming home.'

Then I used my coaxing flirty voice.

'Wait for me, Dad. You got to wait for me, okay? Oh, and here's some good news. There's a new Ian Rankin novel out this month.'

I heard a popping, a snorting. Then his voice erupted into my ear, and it sounded as if someone was pinching his nose.

'Nmmumm. Ph.'

'Good! That's settled then. See you in a few days.'

I cancelled all the things that needed cancelling and went back to California. One of the first things I did was hire Ateca. She told me about previous octogenarians she'd taken care of, but she had no qualifications or references. I hired her because she told me to.

'You need someone to live here. Now is the time for live-in,' Ateca told me. Her tone was low but insistent.

'True. But we can't afford it.'

'I will live here. I will be cheap. What can you afford to pay a week for daytime help?'

I told her and she said: 'I will live here for less than that.'

'But, then what about . . .'

'Good. My boxes are already in the garage. I'll sleep on the sofa.'

I was sleeping in my old bedroom, which was the only other bedroom. I guessed she'd already figured all this out. She'd have my bed after I left.

'Okay,' I said, after a minute.

Ateca began marking her territory by cleaning and cooking. She also badgered Mom into washing more often, which was a miracle. *Come on, Barbarajones, time for your shower.* My main task was to drive Mom to the hospital to visit Dad every day. He'd become convinced he was involved in a movie production.

The doctor is such a good actor, you'd think he really was a doctor. It's so clever – look around you – all the cameras are hidden! Between his delusion and Mom's dementia, conversations were interesting. When it was time to leave, I always made sure they kissed. Three kisses and a promise. *See you tomorrow.* I had no idea I was about to commit a great crime. A crime that would give me insight into murder and possibly suicide. But most definitely guilt.

Dad had a dog he loved more than he loved Mom or us children. Beau was the same breed he'd had as a boy, an Australian shepherd, one eye blue and one eye black. Over his lifetime he'd had six other dogs, all golden retrievers, all sweet and dumb, loving anyone who stroked them. Beau was smart and liked no one but Dad. He followed him everywhere, his toenails clicking on the hardwood floor. Wherever my father sat down, Beau would sit too and commence licking his master's bare legs. In his eighth decade, my father had taken to wearing pairs of baggy L.L.Bean shorts every day. They all had stains at the back, which I tried not to look at. It was hard to see the king deposed, shuffling down the hall with stains on the back of his shorts.

Beau was not liked by anyone else because he was a terrible dog. A bad dog in every sense. He stank. He growled with real menace and in the car he barked continually like a heavy smoker coughing. He bit people, seemingly just for the fun of it. He never did what he was told. He pooped in neighbour's driveways and attacked their pets. They gossiped about Beau, or maybe just when they saw me, hoping I could do something about it. I couldn't. I was afraid of that dog. Walking Beau when Dad was in the hospital were the worst minutes of the day. Twice Beau's back hips collapsed on the beach, and I had to lift his stinking haunch back up while at the same time protect myself from his snapping teeth. I was afraid of him, but that's no excuse for what I did.

My father recovered from his stroke sufficiently to be discharged after two weeks. I was almost disappointed. It was so peaceful, just me and my dozing mother and Ateca. The house was cleaner than it had ever been and I was already dependent on Ateca's blueberry scones. I went alone to fetch him.

'Good news, Dad. You're going home.'

His face lit up and he said:

'Fairfax?'

'No Dad. Not the place you grew up. The house you've lived in for sixty years with Mom.'

His face fell, then he looked at me blankly.

'Your wife. Barbara,' I prompted. Still the blankness, so I said: 'Beau will be over the moon to see you.'

'Oh good,' he said, happiness returning.

My father was not senile, so this mental lapse may have been due to the effects of institutionalisation plus the stroke. Or maybe near the end, the concept of home changed, acquired existential dimensions. Maybe the self we were at six or seven – when our personality began to solidify – was who we dwindled back to. Childhood homes were the real homes. Subsequent homes were just houses we got used to.

He was so frail I had to help him go to bed that evening. My mother was still watching television because *Masterpiece Theatre* was about to begin, and she never missed that. She was a bit peeved with him.

'You're going to bed now? Are you nuts?'

'Gdumpht,' Dad had said, shunting his new Zimmer frame down the hall. I followed, bracing myself to catch him. The hospital had loaned us a wheelchair, but he resisted sitting in it, as if to do so would be to set out on a road of no return. Beau followed and kept tripping me. His growling seemed to say: *Get out of the way, he's MY person, not yours!* Dad was mellow, biddable, very unlike himself. I tucked him in, kissed him goodnight, then watched television with my mother. Beau remained with Dad, on his ancient beanbag next to his side of the bed.

That first night of his homecoming, which was also the night of the great crime, we were all in our beds and probably asleep by 11.30pm. Beau began barking about 12.30. My mother shouted:

'George! Let the dog out. Let. The. Dog. Out.'

I got out of bed, but not before I heard Mom fall down.

'Gosh darn it! Darn darn darn it!'

She never swore, even when no one could hear her. And she often fell out of bed. She'd had multiple sclerosis almost forty years and was a pro at soft falling. Ateca was lying on the living room floor, rolled up in her red blanket like a sausage. She didn't sleep on the sofa because the floor was better, she said. It was an open-plan house, and she saw me slipping down the hall to my parents' bedroom.

'You want me, Sister?' she whispered. She always called me Sister. She called all women she liked Sister. I liked it.

'No, I've got it. You go back to sleep.'

'Okay.'

I helped Mom back into bed, let the dog out, let the dog in, pulled the quilt over Dad, and went back to bed again. I fell asleep but in what felt like two seconds, I was awoken by Beau barking again and my mother shouting *Let the dog out!* Then I heard her fall for the second time. Ateca again offered to help, but I refused. I repeated my previous actions and got us all settled again. My eyes were itchy and I recognised a certain tingle in my muscles, a fizziness in my head, the way I used to feel when one of my children was sick and not sleeping. Anxiety plus exhaustion equalling a kind of insanity. I suddenly remembered the sedatives the vet had prescribed ages ago, when Dad had mentioned – in a jokey, proud manner – Beau's anti-social behaviour. To my knowledge, he'd never used them because nothing Beau did was wrong. I found the bottle, stuck a pill in a piece of Monterey Jack and fed it to Beau. I went back to sleep feeling smug.

Barking wrenched me from sleep a third time, and without pausing a second or worrying about Ateca witnessing, I plunged two sedatives into more cheese, fed the dog, replaced my mother into her bed, covered Dad with the quilt, and went back to sleep. Again and again, I don't know how many times, the pattern repeated. I kept dosing Beau until his legs stopped working – presumably due to an overdose of barbiturates. Now he was unable to move from his smelly beanbag, a foot from my father. He just lay there, making drunken barking noises. Dad finally woke up. He raised up his pale old man self – which I was still getting used to, my real dad was handsome and healthy – and said:

'Lethdogout.'

'Yeah, okay, Dad,' I said, thinking *The damn dog can't move!* Then suddenly he spoke in a perfectly clear voice.

'Did anyone buy more brandy? I meant to get some at BevMo! but it was shut.'

'What?'

In the hospital, the enforced sobriety must have been a profound shock to his system. I should have had a drink with him earlier, allowed a smidgen of his old reality back in, despite the doctor's orders of no alcohol. I was about to say this, when his eyes closed and he slumped back onto his pillow, mumbling 'Schuffelgy . . .'

'Yeah, yeah, you go back to sleep, Dad,' I said, over the barking.

'What on earth are you doing?' demanded my mother, sitting up now and staring at me, and I knew without looking that her left eyebrow was cocked.

'Nothing, Mom. Go back to sleep.'

'Cut it out. Whatever you're doing, just knock it off,' she said sternly, then she too slumped back into sleep as if a stun gun had just shot her. I'd noticed that about old age. Sleep could ambush you anytime. You'd be doing something routine, even something fun, and wham! Only last month, my parents had been bickering over the remote control. Bickering was the norm, so I ignored it till the room became silent, then looked up from my book to find them both slumped in their chairs, snoring.

I got on my hands and knees and started dragging Beau's beanbag out of the room. It was hard work. His teeth were bared as he started making half-hearted lunges towards me, barking even harder. By now, I was delirious. All I wanted on God's earth was for this dog to shut up. I finally pulled him into my dad's office and shut the door. The barking contin- ued and I realised in some small foggy part of my brain, the humane thing to do now was finish him off. I fed him the rest of the pills in a piece of salami, which he ate up in grateful- seeming gulps.

'I'm so sorry,' I whispered, out of my mind.

'Ruff! Ruff! Ruff!'

Since they were his final barks, I figured I should stay with him. It was the least I could do. Even bad dogs shouldn't have to die alone. After a while, I found myself looking around and not thinking about Beau at all. The walls were covered with sailboat photographs and paintings. There was a huge one, a framed black-and-white photograph of Dad's 27-foot sloop keeling hard over near Angel Island on the bay. I noticed the little figures on the deck. There he was, my father, probably aged forty-five, with the ponytailed teenage son who kept defy- ing him. They were leaning back so far they were almost standing up. They wouldn't have been aware of someone taking their picture. They would have been completely inside that moment, salt spray in their faces, the hull slapping hard on the surface of the bay with each wave, the sails flapping, the hal- yards twanging, their hearts pounding. Me and my sister had not enjoyed sailing, and it occurred to me for the first time that my father and brother *did* have something good between them after all. Those adrenalin-charged times which never needed to be discussed later, or if referred to, would be re-created as intense danger overcome with nonchalant courage. And all along I'd thought we sisters had the better end of the dad deal. But we hadn't shared his happiest times. Those unarticulated saltwater adventures were completely beyond our ken.

One final *Ruff!* and Beau was silent. Thank Christ. I went to bed, vaguely conscious that what I'd just done constituted murder. Maybe this was how most heinous crimes were committed. Not with foresight, not with much thought at all, but simply a response to the drip drip drip of annoyance and tiredness. The unacceptable became not only acceptable but imperative, in small increments. I'd killed Dad's dog.

In the morning, the dog was not dead.

I texted my siblings. *Think I OD'd Beau. He's alive but not moving. Help!*

My sister texted: *Oh well. No problem. You up for a drink later? xxx*

My brother texted: *Call vet. Have him put down.*

I sat on the floor with Beau a while, willing him to decide for me. If he got up or showed an inclination to get up, I wouldn't call the vet. He did neither, he just tried to bite me, so I called the vet. Then I texted my brother.

Vet booked. Can you help me dig a hole?

What for?

Dead dog.

Get vet to take dog.

Seriously?

All our dogs were buried in the back yard. No one disposed of their dog like a bag of garbage, did they? We certainly were not that kind of family, at least when our parents were in charge.

Seriously, he texted back.

I briefly considered putting Beau's corpse in our dried-up fish pond, then shovelling garden dirt over it. But then I kept picturing the heyday all the racoons would have, digging it up.

The vet arrived with his black bag, just like the vet in All Creatures Great and Small, a PBS show my parents loved. He was a middle-aged man with a sad tired face, and I immediately wanted to confess my crime. I opened my mouth.

'Oh, I think I should tell you . . .'

'Looks like a stroke,' he said, examining Beau, who was looking as if he'd given up being the worst dog in the world and was now in the throes of depression.

'That's what my dad just had. How interesting.' I was so tired, I actually forgot for a moment that the dog had not had a stroke.

'Common for these things to happen.'

'Is it?'

'Oh yes, you'd be surprised. When a beloved master is sick or dies, the pet often follows suit.'

This narrative was much more appealing than the truth, and I lost the urge to confess.

'How old is he?' He checked his notes and answered himself. 'Ah. Almost fifteen. Good innings.'

'Good innings,' he repeated when I didn't join in with a comment.

Then he sat at the kitchen table with us all. My parents were in their robes eating grapefruits, while Ateca hovered behind them, wiping chins and pouring coffee. Once I thought I saw her look at me in a strange way, as if saying *I know what you did, you dog-killer*. But when I looked again, the look was replaced by *Good for you, you got rid of the bad dog*.

The vet slowly explained the situation and his intentions, then he said:

'It's the kindest thing to do. Would you like a moment to say goodbye to him?'

There was a pause.

'No,' said my dad with a peculiar look on his face. Bewildered, but also like he was drunk and trying to act sober. His speech was clearer, but there was a new nasal tone to it. 'You go right ahead.'

'Did you just say you are going to kill our dog?' my mother asked with a sweet smile, like she couldn't believe her luck.

The vet smiled slightly and replied: 'Essentially, yes. He won't know. He'll just go to sleep and not wake up.'

'Delightful,' she said.

I went with the vet back to my father's office where Beau lay, panting on his beanbag. He massaged the skin around Beau's lower front leg. The needle went in and I watched as my dad's love object faded. It took less than a minute, and then Beau was just a dead dog. To my surprise, I cried. I cried for that dog as if I'd liked him. As if I hadn't just killed him. Then my dad shuffled into the room, let go of his Zimmer and began lowering himself to the floor. His face was oddly mottled. Purple, pink, white. His eyes were watering and I could tell he didn't give a shit what he looked like or what we thought.

Later my siblings came over and we took Dad out to breakfast downtown. Mom stayed at home as usual. We'd invited her but hadn't expected her to say yes, and anyway she had Ateca now. I'd had an idea we siblings would rally around our bereaved father, but they proved to be harder-hearted than I thought. I suppose it's easy to be soft when you live six thousand miles away.

'Let's drink to Beau,' I said, hopeful, raising my glass of orange juice.

'Do we have to?' asked my sister.

'Oh, Jesus. Okay,' said my brother. 'Here's to the worst dog ever. May he enjoy biting other dogs in dog heaven. Amen.'

I kept sneaking glances at our father. I felt responsible for him. Just getting him into the car and then out again had been challenging. He was looking out the window vacantly and I noticed his eyeballs seemed to be shrinking. I could see an open slit between his eyeball and the rim of skin below. It was pink and sore-looking.

'You don't want your French toast, Dad?'

'Nah. You have it,' he said, pushing his plate towards me.

'You want more coffee?'

'Why not,' he said, sighing. 'Can you please pass me a napkin?' And then he blew his nose on it.

The days passed and he seemed to be getting better, but he was listless. He continued being polite and saying nice things, even to Ateca, whom he had yet to acknowledge by name or correct gender. Like Mom, he saw her as a man, and referred to her as Fiji Man. He accepted her presence as just one more surreal thing in his new world. He needed help in the bathroom and was probably relieved he didn't have to rely on me.

'Please tell Fiji Man I need to go.'

'Go where, Dad?'

'Just tell him. I need to *go*.'

'Oh.'

He was probably missing the two things that had given him more pleasure than anything else. What was the point without a dog licking your legs and a dry martini running down your throat? On top of that, he was bowing out before his wife, which meant she won. *Damn her.* Some of this was my fault. What could I do? I needed to do something. I ordered a toy dog on Amazon, which bore a resemblance to Beau. When it arrived, I worried Dad would think it insulting and silly, but he didn't. He stroked that toy dog and slept with it. When it fell, as it often did when he catnapped in the living room, he panicked when he woke and didn't see it immediately. I got into the habit of picking it up as soon as it dropped and replacing it under his arm. This attachment was the final proof I needed that my dad of yore had left the building. He'd have thrown the toy in the garbage immediately, after yelling at me for killing his dog. *Goddammit! I can't believe you were so stupid!*

The last time I saw my father, he was sitting in a wheelchair next to my mother, who was also in a wheelchair. I'd parked them close together, which may have been presumptuous. Normally Mom sat by the desk with a good view of the television, while Dad's seat was the wicker armchair on the other side of the room where he could read his book and ignore the television if he wanted. They might have both been seething, as I set them next to each other. *This is torture!* I asked Ateca to take a photograph of the three of us with my phone. She took six photos and all of them were blurred, not in an artistic way. I didn't ask her to take more. Such was my superstitious state, I felt it was a sign and mustn't be tampered with. I kissed them both soundly several times on their cheeks and then on the top of their heads – equal amounts of kisses, as if they were my children and I was proving I had no favourites. This was, of course, a lie. I had a favourite child too, but it changed every day, sometimes every hour. Probably, over time, they'd all been my favourite child roughly an equal number of days. My dad had been my favourite parent since I was about seven, but that was about to change.

'See you soon!' I assured them in a jolly voice.

My mother fell mid-kiss into one of her naps, but my father was staring at me, suddenly sharp as a tack. He looked the way he used to look when I'd disappointed him. He tilted his head, opened his mouth, and I braced myself for a tirade, maybe even an accusation of canine-cide. But all he said was, slightly nasally:

'I miss you.'

'I'll miss you too,' I said, no longer jolly.

'No, no. *I miss you,*' he repeated, as if I'd misheard the first time. I had, but I was still mystified. Did he miss me in the present tense because one of us was essentially gone already? Or maybe he missed my child self, our uncomplicated love. I missed that too, suddenly. Those were good days.

'I know.'

Then, having killed his dog and deprived him of alcohol, I jumped his ship just as it was entering the first storm it would not weather.

All the way home, I kept remembering Beau's deathbed. The smelly beanbag, the vet standing up after giving the lethal injection, my hypocritical tears. Dad lowering himself to the floor. I'd tried to help him. His skin was so loose on his skeleton, it took a while to get a good enough grip before he stopped slipping under my fingers.

'Wanna pet him. Wanna say bye.'

Then the man who'd ruled our house like a ship's captain, who'd withheld coveted car keys from his only son, whose chair no one else was allowed to sit in, curled up around his dog and cried like a baby.

George is Dead

Once I realised my mother wasn't going to die again, I relaxed. I even had a little daydream in which I found a job and a place to live nearby and let Scotland slip my mind. The way I'd let California slip my mind over the last forty-odd years. As well as reconnecting with old friends, I made friends with some of the newbies in the neighbourhood. Knowing the history of their houses was a great social lubricant and soon I had a half dozen houses to drink wine in anytime I liked. I resumed my routines. Walk, write, watch *The Sound of Music*, eat, hold my mother's hand and let her kiss mine three times. Go out for a glass of wine with some of my re-discovered friends. They were so much fun I decided I liked them better than my friends back home. Whoever the hell they were. Every day was cool and sunny, and I was very happy to not be an orphan yet. Which was strange, because in my youth I'd almost wanted to be an orphan. I remembered the time me and my brother hopped a freight train because we'd decided to visit Mexico. Thirty-five bucks between us, plenty of danger, yet it never occurred to us to phone our parents for help – or indeed, to even tell them we'd gone to Mexico. I began a story about that trip in the morning, while the house was still cool enough to think.

Ateca was excellent company. She told great stories about her past when I coaxed her – being bought in marriage for two whale teeth, her husband being killed in a land dispute – stories which made my own past seem pedestrian. But left to her own devices her main topic was my mother's bowel movements. Sometimes she had to use her fingers to coax a lazy turd along and was keen I knew all the details. Even when I was in Scotland, she kept me abreast of the latest.

'Cynthia. I have good news,' in the hushed tone one might announce winning an election or discovering a cure for cancer.

'It's three in the morning.'

'Your mother had a BM today. First time since Sunday. Very big BM.'

'Good.'

'God did this.'

Mom had few expectations of conversation, and as long as Julie Andrews never stopped singing, she probably wouldn't notice if none of us talked at all. She didn't like to leave the house, but once I got her outside she was euphoric. I took her for drives out to China Camp, where I parked and we silently watched the beach as if it were a television programme. One day I pushed Mom in her wheelchair to our neighbourhood beach.

'Oh! Look! Look! What are those things?'

'Waves, Mom.'

'Oh yes, waves. Look at the waves!'

She squeezed my hand hard, forcing me to see the waves as she did. Not merely beautiful, but *incredible*. Was this an upside to dementia? A second chance to experience the world for the first time? At any rate, it was infectious. With Mom nearby, the world became shinier and my confusing past rearranged itself. It was still confusing, but it made sense that it didn't make sense. The world itself was a confusing ongoing saga, and how unlikely, how lucky, to be inserted into it for a while. The facts were these: *I hadn't always been here, and I wouldn't always be here*. It was so simple, so indisputable, so bleak – and yet with Mom squeezing my hand, I watched those waves and a sweetness filled my chest as if I'd inhaled bear claws.

My mother's dementia was vascular. The doctor said she'd have bad days and good days. This meant nothing to me. Everyone had good days and bad days, right? It'd been a slow decline and she rarely seemed aware of her mental state. Only now and then did she notice.

'I don't understand,' she said. We were in the living room and one of the hospice volunteers had just left. Sixty-year-old Marcia from Peacock Gap, who'd wanted Mom to colour with her. It had been a tedious hour, with Mom pretending she liked crayons. Her dementia never touched her good manners.

'What don't you understand, Mom?'

'I don't understand why . . . why am I still here?' She was agitated, angry and lost-looking. Both eyebrows were down, her face darkening.

'You mean here, in this house?'

'I don't know.' Then she turned to me, pleading. 'Aren't I supposed to be . . . to be somewhere else now?'

'Well, do you mean like an old folks' home?' I was thinking: *Or a coffin?*

'I don't know!' she burst out. 'But something's fishy.'

I agreed and put on *The Sound of Music* to calm her. I held her hand and watched Maria run through that mountain meadow again, trying not to imagine her constant sense of waiting and not knowing what it was she was waiting for.

Another time, the phone rang and she woke from her hundredth nap of the day.

'George! The telephone is ringing! George!' Then she ordered me: 'Go get your father, I think he's in the garage.'

Ateca answered the phone and I reminded Mom why Dad couldn't be in the garage.

'Oh! I knew that!' Then after a few minutes, she said: 'Did you know my husband George is dead?'

'That's sad,' I said.

'Poor George. Having to be dead,' she said, with real regret, and sighed. Maybe she was remembering the time she forgot to buy soy sauce for his teriyaki marinade. Or maybe the sigh had nothing to do with Dad at all.

'Yeah. Poor Dad.'

There was a pause. Perhaps she was wondering why I'd called her husband Dad.

'Excuse me, can you please tell me the time?'

'It's almost 3.35.'

'Thank you so much for that.'

'Do you want a bear claw and some juice?' I asked.

'Yes! Yes! Yes!' as if I'd asked the million-dollar question.

When it was time to go back to Scotland, I told myself I'd never see my mother alive again. I tried hard to summon up belief in this so I wouldn't waste the last sight of her. I'd store it up so I could replay it later. But nothing happened and I couldn't fake it. It just felt like a normal goodbye.

'Bye, Mom, I love you.' I kissed her and stroked her head.

'Are you going? When will I see you again?'

'Soon,' I said. And then I left.

Going to Mexico

Twenty-one years old
California, 1974

'Come on. Let's go.'

'Coffee,' my brother groaned. 'Go where?'

'Mexico, remember?' I kicked his bed. It'd been his idea, damn it. I'd just hitched all the way to Santa Cruz from San Francisco so we could leave today.

'Oh yeah. Cigarette,' he rasped.

He had asthma, shouldn't smoke. I hated it when he wheezed, but I threw him one anyway.

'I'll make coffee, you get dressed.'

As the water boiled, I shouted from the kitchen:

'How much money you got?'

'Fifteen bucks, I think.'

'I got twenty. So, we've got maybe forty-five bucks together. That should last a while.'

'You mean thirty-five.'

'Jesus.'

He was always correcting me. I hated it. There came the sound of radio music from his bedroom. I started a little shuffle on the kitchen floor, while spooning coffee into cups and looking for food to take. Sardines. A bag of peanut M&Ms. A red pepper. The water boiled and I took him a cup.

'What'd your boss say?' I asked him.

'He said I might have a job when I get back.' He sat up in bed, scratched his long wiry hair and yawned. One side of his face had sheet marks on it. Some dirty socks and underpants were draped over his bedside light, and on the floor a Hornby train set was just visible below the usual mountain of used Kleenex. Nothing in sight to indicate he'd one day be the CEO of his own international consultancy.

'Come on, get your stuff ready,' I said. 'Goddammit.'

It was often like this. He'd have an idea, convince me, then drift off from it. I was always nudging him back to his own plan. I turned up the radio because Lou Reed's 'Walk on the Wild Side' was on. It was played every half hour, but I wasn't sick of it yet.

Finally, we were headed to the freeway entrance. It was the sixth hot day in a row, and the sky was no longer blue, but burnt white. No clouds, just a shimmering glare. The only sign it was February and not July was the green lawns. My brother remembered things he'd forgotten to pack, which reminded me of things I'd forgotten. He'd forgotten socks, I'd forgotten my toothbrush, and neither of us had brought soap. We stuck out our thumbs and talked about replacing our forgotten items, till a car stopped. It was going to Watsonville, about twenty miles away. It was a bad town to hitch out of and it was nearly afternoon, but we took the lift. We had almost six hundred miles to go. We were dropped off on the north side of town and had to walk through to hitch on the other side. It was a long walk. The town was full of Mexicans, and being lunchtime, the smell of tortillas and corn and beans was overpowering. I felt discouraged.

We stopped at a panateria and bought half a dozen donuts and coffee, sat on the kerb outside and ate all the donuts and drank the coffee from plastic cups. The donuts were greasy and soft and delicious. After that, we leaned against our packs and closed our eyes and smoked. The whole town was having a siesta, so we didn't feel out of place.

'Well, let's go home now,' he said, and stretched.

I was happy. Sugar and laziness always improved my spirits. He liked donuts too, but I suspect he ate mainly to keep me company.

A young fellow with a laundry bag for a backpack and a battered Stetson sauntered up to us.

'Where you guys headed?'

'Mexico,' said my brother. He was nearly always the spokesman, though I talked more when we were alone.

'You catching the express?'

'Huh? We're hitch-hiking.'

'What? You'll never make it tonight. You ought to catch the train. The express. Leaves at midnight. Goes all the way to L.A. without stopping. You'd be there by sunrise.'

My brother sat up. He loved riding freight trains. 'Where's the yards?'

'That's where I'm going.'

We followed him past the canning factories, through Brussels sprout fields. Ten sets of tracks ran parallel for half a mile in the middle of the yards. A couple of brakemen smoking in front of a corrugated iron hut on the far side looked at us without interest. It was still hot, and under a cluster of trees a group of Mexicans were camped. A few men I thought of as hobos – pale, rough-looking men – were less hidden, loitering near the tracks. I felt conspicuously female. I tucked my hair into a ponytail and pulled my corduroy cap down low.

Our guide said: 'They call me Stibo, by the way. I'll be round.' And he wandered off.

We spent a long time waiting in the shadow of a derelict boxcar. At first, we felt a little nervous of the guards and the men waiting to catch the train. Then we argued about who should carry our money and passports. I won and we didn't speak again for a while, but relaxed enough to feel bored. Then we talked about relationships, one of our favourite topics for passing time. It was getting dark and the yards were coming alive. Boxcars were being shifted, rolling silently like black monsters, then bang! They'd hit another boxcar and a brakeman would run up to make sure they'd joined properly. The smell of diesel was strong. There were stars and a three-quarter moon on the horizon. We were sitting on some disused tracks, legs loosely crossed, smoking. It was a little dull, huddling in the dusk – as if we'd been there forever – and I was proud of my non-excitement. We'd hopped freight trains before, but never as far as Mexico, and never from a yard this big. I think this was the time we both liked – to feel at home after hours in a train yard. And all along, the sound of those boxcars rolling, then banging into each other. Yardmen's footsteps crunching on the gravel and their shouts to each other as they checked the boxcars hooked up. They used flashlights, and sometimes we saw their faces. Mysterious and dirty-looking, their hats pulled down and their clothes smudged black. Their voices in the dark were gruff and slightly menacing. They said things like:

'She fixed all right?'

'Sure.'

'Okay. If you say so.'

'I say so.'

My brother sighed and said:

'Kind of romantic, isn't it?'

What a waste, we agreed, and laughed. It was occasionally funny to us that we'd seen each other grow up, and now at nine-teen and twenty-one, we were still playing together. Like the afternoons when we'd been little kids and bounced on all the living room furniture playing at cowboys while Copland's *Billy the Kid* blasted out of the speakers. That had been risky fun, in its way, and this was too. He was two years younger, but I couldn't remember a time I felt older than him. We learned to ride bikes the same summer and both learned to swim the following summer. By the time I was fifteen, he'd overtaken me in height, and now there were six inches between us. When I had my first date, he'd already had four. Riding freight trains was entirely his idea. He showed me how to do it. I'd gone to Europe before him, but no doubt he'd go soon and venture further than tame English-speaking places.

A figure walked towards us from the tracks.

'Want some wine?' Stibo said.

He sat down and passed a bottle around. It was cheap fruity wine and went down easily. We talked small talk. The yard, past trips, past troubles. I knew it was a game, but I loved being a hobo sometimes.

'Spare some of that vino? I'm fucking dry,' said a man, stumbling up to us. He was followed by two others.

'Don't you be cussing now, there's a lady present,' slurred another.

'I'll fucking cuss if I want to cuss, so fuck the fuck off, cunt.'

It felt like a black-and-white Depression-era film, but I wasn't alarmed till I saw a knife flash. The third man, who hadn't spoken, said, 'Watch it!' and wrested the knife off the other man, pocketing it as calmly as if he'd taken a toy from a kid.

'Sorry,' he mumbled, tipped his hat, and then they stumbled back off into the dark.

Before we had time to absorb it, Stibo shouted:

'Hey, there's an open one!' and pointed to a boxcar gliding on the rails without a sound. It hit another boxcar with a deafening crash.

'Come on, that one's sure to be hooked up to the express.'

We followed Stibo to the boxcar. He leapt on, then my brother did. I tried but couldn't. Too many donuts.

'Here, quick.'

My brother gave me his hand and pulled me up. We could hear the footsteps of a brakeman coming.

'Bulls round here give you hell,' muttered Stibo.

We cowered in a dark corner and didn't make a sound. A flashlight beamed in and almost touched us. I stopped breathing but nothing happened, and the footsteps went away.

We sat in the boxcar for almost an hour, sometimes violently jolted by other boxcars. It was clean and dry inside, with some grain scattered. We smoked and finished Stibo's wine. I was wide awake, my ears keening to every sound, bent on hearing the express when it came, or the sound of brakemen. I arranged my gear so we could take off quickly. Finally, at what we reckoned was around 1.30 in the morning, we heard a distant whistle. Was there anything as sweet and sad as a train whistle in the middle of the night? We all whooped, even Stibo, who was presumably used to this moment. We crept to the open door and watched the express come round the bend into the yards. It had four engines and a mile of cars. We agreed – it was a beautiful train.

Then our smiles froze.

'Oh, shit,' said Stibo softly.

The express was hooking up to a different set of cars. We waited till it calmed down and was stationary. It sat purring some distance away. We jumped off the boxcar and ran hard, indifferent to getting caught. All that mattered was getting on that train. The ground was chunky gravel, awkward to run on and very noisy. Stibo ran the fastest, having less gear. My brother was close behind him, propelled by his long skinny legs. I ran as hard as I could, my pack bouncing on my back, and was quickly left behind. I watched the two figures disappear. Sweat was running down my face and body, and my eyes were watering. Finally, I saw them. They'd reached the caboose and were walking. I caught up and no one said anything. My body was pulsating, the blood pounding. We walked at a fast pace, looking for open boxcars. There weren't any, as far as we could make out in the moonlight. The train whistled in a way that said: *Time to go!* There was a flatcar next to us, with diesel truck cabs chained to it. We pulled ourselves onto it and lay on our stomachs behind enormous wheels. I felt the train slowly move beneath me, and we looked at each other in wonder. Stibo wrapped himself in a blanket. The train was gathering speed, and everything was flapping and threatening to blow off.

We left Watsonville and headed towards the coast to follow a route no roads took. Maybe because we were headed south, I felt we were rolling downhill. Gravity, not diesel fuel, sent us hurtling. It was incredibly noisy and cold. My brother sneezed and shouted something. All I could hear was: *Eep!* Sleep? I crawled to one of the chains that secured a wheel and wrapped my arms around it. I saw a clear night, the moon shining on dark mountain ridges. I looked over to my brother. He was a humped shadow behind another wheel, unreachable. The vibrations were too violent to lay my head down. I pulled a sweatshirt from my pack and made a pillow. Tucking my jacket down as far as I could, I hugged the chain again and settled down. Then I saw the Pacific Ocean, with the oblong moon mirrored on its turbulence. The vibrations, the noise, the dark, the cold, my fatigue – all my senses were being obliterated. I felt a rising inward surge as if I was being tickled from the inside, and I teetered towards some nameless thing. Maybe this was how people felt before they succumbed to death or orgasm or heroin – only one of which I had experience of. I didn't know much. All I knew was that I should have been miserable and was not. The umbilical cord of my memories stretched and stretched, then quietly snapped. I was a tiny breathing thing curled around a chain. That's all I was. Then the undertow of sleep tugged me down. I observed my slip into oblivion as if I wasn't in my own skin. It was *so delicious* to be me.

In the morning, my eyelashes were glued together and I heard my brother before I saw him. He was shouting.

'Wake up! Get up!'

My body ached. My skin was gritty and my hair knotted. I noticed there was another white sky, but this time it was tinged yellow.

'Are we in Los Angeles?'

The train was going slowly and we were rolling into a yard with dozens of tracks and empty boxcars.

'Yeah. The outskirts. Come on. We've got to get off.'

'But it's moving.'

'Too risky getting off in the central yard.'

I sat up. I'd not taken off my shoes, and my jacket was still on. I looked around for Stibo, but he was gone. I watched my brother throw his pack off, then jump down. He landed heavily on the embankment. I thought he was going to fall, but his legs kept moving and he stayed upright. Then he ran alongside the flatcar, coaxing me.

'Hit the ground running! Run in mid-air first.' He demonstrated with his hands.

I understood, but only vaguely. I had to pee and was very thirsty, but understood it was important to be quick and agile. Not think about anything else. It was about six feet to the moving ground and I didn't let myself think – I jumped, landed clumsily and rolled a few times. I tore my jacket and bloodied my hands, but I was fine. Proud of myself in fact. My brother ran up and I braced myself for admiration.

'Where's your pack?' he shouted. His face looked strange. He was rarely anxious, and I hardly recognised the expression.

I pointed to the disappearing flatcar. My pack looked so familiar – so like a piece of me – I wanted to cry. It had our passports and all our money. I had ruined everything. He didn't speak. He ran after the train. I watched as he pounded over the rough ground and lunged for our flatcar. It took a few leaps, a few grabs, but he got a hold of it. He swung from it for a second, his skinny legs flailing in the air inches from the wheels. Then he pulled himself up, crawled to my pack and tossed it to the ground. By this time, the flatcar was so distant I could only see the shape of him. The train should have been slowing, but it was going faster. He would be out of sight in a minute, and then what? I would be alone on the outskirts of a Los Angeles freight yard, and he would be alone on a speeding train with no money, no clothes. I saw him leap. It seemed impossible, because by then the embankment was a steep ravine of chunky gravel on a hillside. He leapt and hit the ground and I watched him roll, his arms and legs cartwheeling. Then he disappeared and very soon the train did too.

This was eerily familiar. I'd had a nightmare about killing my brother when I was about eight. In my dream, we were standing on the back steps and I pushed him. It was only three steps down to the grass, but he kept rolling and rolling, faster and faster. It was one of the worst dreams of my childhood, and now I'd done it for real. I had killed my brother. He was lying dead in a ditch full of dirty water, and I would have to find someone and tell them. Get help, somehow. I tried to move and a part of me noted that legs-like-jelly was not just a cliché. Another part of me understood that I would never forgive myself, that my life was over. He was my little brother, not my equal. It had been my job all along to protect him and I'd failed. I think I whimpered. I probably prayed, as I was a relatively new lapsed Catholic. I certainly swore. Then I began to run. Probably all of this took two seconds. Pray, rant, run. The gravel was a nightmarish quicksand. My lungs burned and I made loud animal noises with each exhalation. And finally, there he was. Face up, completely still, covered in dust. As I got closer, I could see blood on his hands and face. I instructed myself to feel for his pulse. What were the steps of artificial resuscitation? He was dead, but I would try anyway. And I couldn't stop myself consoling him. I stroked his shoulder and crooned as if he were five years old and fallen off his bike.

'Hey, hey. It's okay. You're going to be fine.'

He opened one eye and croaked:

'Stop. Touching. Me. There.'

I couldn't take in the fact of his aliveness quickly enough, and he had to remove my hand himself.

'Think it's broken. Or dislocated, or something,' he said.

He sat up, groaning. I knew I should be relieved, but the momentum of grief had already taken hold. I was heavy with it and kept crooning inanities.

'You're going to be all right, everything's going to be all right.'

'Shut. The fuck. Up.'

He stood slowly and felt his bones, and I surveyed him too. His chest was very sore, and he guessed some ribs were cracked. His right leg, which had taken the brunt of his fall, was not right. He couldn't put much weight on it. I fetched our packs, found some water for him to drink, and we both ate an apple. Then he said it was time to go. We distributed some of his stuff into my pack, so it was as heavy as his. Then I walked and he hobbled towards the highway.

'I'm sorry,' I said. 'I wasn't awake. I wasn't thinking.'

'That's okay,' he said.

'That's big of you.'

'I know.'

'You can carry our money and passports from now on, okay?'

'Damn tooting.'

I laughed and began to believe he was alive. I'd tried helium before, at a party. It was like that. My chest felt light, felt full of light, and we were on our way to Mexico.

My brother was a hero. I promised myself that from that day forward, all the way down the long years of our lives – and I was predicting a myriad of bickering spells, of giddy laughter and hedonism, of lazy beer-buzzed afternoons – I'd never forget how he caught up with that flatcar. He wouldn't have had time to think about it, to gauge the risks. He just ran and lunged towards the thing he needed.

Death, It is Here!

In December, I was summoned to my mother's deathbed again. This time she had pneumonia. She'd stopped breathing several times and was not responding to antibiotics. Ateca called me, wailing:

'Death, it is here! You must come!'

I cancelled a dozen plans and bought another ticket to San Francisco. In the past, I'd look at fellow passengers and wonder what secret sadness and fears they had tucked inside: cancer diagnoses, children with impending prison sentences, loved ones dying or dead. Now that was me, but I was hollowed out. The journey itself – about twenty hours, door to door – was numbing. Now and then I veered into the sad realities and experienced a short flash, a spasm almost, of sorrow. Throat swollen, chest tightening, a heaviness to my body. But I couldn't sustain it and my mind would wander to free sprays of duty-free Chanel or the new shoes I was wearing.

In the departure lounge of Heathrow's Terminal Five, I resumed list-making.

Things I Learned from My Mother:
- Vegetables and fruit are not necessary for survival. But candy bars and white bread and fizzy drinks are WRONG.

- Naps are a good thing.
- It is normal for things to go wrong. Say to yourself: *Que sera sera* or *So be it!*
- If you are caught in a fib or doing something silly, or in any situation in which you appear foolish, giggle charmingly and pretend you don't care.
- It's okay to not always like the people you love. Otherwise you end up thinking you don't love them any more.
- If you do little things to annoy your husband, like let the pepper grinder run out of peppercorns, he won't notice you bought a new dress today out of the housekeeping budget.
- Friends are important but not essential. Family is essential.

Once I began, it seemed there was no end to the things my mother taught me, and it felt important to get them down in writing. I was a little surprised at how many things she knew. I'd always colluded in my father's superiority to his unintellectual wife. *Our dippy mom.* Even she'd conspired in this. If any of us kids did something impressive, she'd say: 'Oh, you get that from your father.' And by something impressive, sometimes tying our own shoes qualified. Mom had a tendency to gush, probably to make up for the dearth of Dad-praise. But all along, and completely unnoticed by me, she'd been a fount of wisdom.

My brother had warned me she wouldn't know who I was this time, but I found her in the living room, happy as Larry. In between bites of pizza, she was singing 'My Favourite Things'. For the five years Ateca lived with her, she never once remembered her name. Often, she didn't remember her gender and referred to her – very sweetly – as *that man*. But she sang every word to this song, clapping her hands off to one side as if she were singing side-saddle.

'Mom! It's me!'

'What are you doing here?'

'I've come to see you!'

'Really? Really and truly?'

I kissed her cheeks, but she wanted my hand on her mouth for the three kisses. Then she began singing along to the movie again, her face flushed and merry, some pepperoni stuck to her chin.

I told myself that just because she hadn't said my name and just because she greeted everyone, even the mailman, with three kisses, didn't mean she didn't know me. She may not know our relationship any more, but I was certain she knew me. Anyway, how important was a name? And even if she didn't know mine, she still liked my presence – so who cared?

I'd only been away a month and settled easily back into my dead father's office. I'd furnished it with a double mattress I'd rescued from the kerbside down the block. Because it was a San Rafael kerbside, it was cleaner and nicer-smelling than any mattress I'd ever owned. Ateca slept in the room I'd shared with my sister, which was fine by me. I'd no desire to regress that far. I started reading another one of my father's novels – *Cakes and Ale* by Somerset Maugham. It was a first-person narrative about a writer who resembled Somerset Maugham in every respect, and this made him my new best friend.

About a week into my visit, I showed Mom some photographs from her wedding. I'd found them in a Brooks Brothers box deep inside the hall closet. Professionally taken, they were matt black-and-white, 6" × 8".

'Who is that?'

'It's you.'

'I know it's me!'

'I like this one,' I said, holding one of both my parents standing by an MG convertible parked outside the church. My mother's hand was raised, maybe waving goodbye to guests, and my father had a hand on the passenger door handle, probably about to open it for her. Both of their mouths were slightly open, as if they were talking or about to. Little white flecks on their shoulders, probably rice.

'He's a good-looking man.'

'Yeah. He is.'

Then we both stared at the photograph for a while. I fell into it, which is, I suppose, the purpose of photographs. It had been July. The sky would have been deep blue. People's laughter and voices would have filled the air, and if my parents were saying anything to each other, they might have had difficulty hearing what it was. Mom especially seemed to have a question in her face, as if she was saying *What?* Then I thought about how things had panned out for her. A periodically faithless husband, druggy teenage children, getting multiple sclerosis just after her third baby – none of these would have been on her agenda that day. Poor Mom, all those dashed hopes. Then again, maybe she'd faced her life one day, hands on hips, and used her voice that meant business. *So you didn't turn out the way I thought you would – so be it! You are NOT going to drag me down. I repeat, NOT.*

For a quiet person, Mom had a will of iron.

For no obvious reason, I remembered the day I went shopping with her for my only prom dress. Going to JCPenney and Macy's and finally I. Magnin. It was a hot day, and we had lunch in a nice restaurant near Union Square. Being with her on my own was a novelty, and somewhat exhausting. I was not a shopper and she loved shopping. I remembered her smiling a lot, looking happy – and the oppressiveness of pretending I was happy too. That shopping for a prom dress with my mother was a fun and normal thing to do. If she'd dreamed of having a daughter one day, I bet she never imagined an awkward tomboy like me.

When I tried to think of subsequent shopping trips with just me and Mom, nothing occurred to me. Nor could I recall confiding in her about my prom date. This made me sad, and the sadness made me want to write about those days.

Meanwhile, the minutes of wedding photo-gazing kept ticking by soporifically. A car door slammed somewhere, and I could hear birds I didn't know the names of making a racket on the deck. Here we are, I thought. Me and my mother in perfect accord, silently contemplating the day it all began. Maybe she was thinking: *That's a pretty dress. But a dumb colour. Good luck keeping that clean!* Then she made a little snorting sound, like a horse, and I noticed she was asleep. Had probably been asleep for some time.

Cool

Fourteen to eighteen years old
California, 1967–71

I wasn't good at high school. Not academically, not socially. This failure wasn't helped by my parents' regular reminders that high school had been the best days of their lives. *Enjoy yourself!* they were always saying. *I am, I am!* I always lied. They kept assuming I was like them because they'd made me. They wanted to relive their high school triumphs – who wouldn't? They'd done nothing wrong, nothing to deserve a daughter who was useless at being a teenager.

The times didn't help. Everyone was still talking about the summer of love and freedom – it was an exciting time, but it was hard to feel carefree. I read too much and was socially infantile. The pill became available to unmarried women when I was fourteen, ushering us virgins into the dubiously named era of 'free love'. Robert Kennedy and Martin Luther King were assassinated when I was fifteen. Vietnam began to gobble up the brothers of my friends. I attended military funerals and read books like *Johnny Got His Gun* by Dalton Trumbo. Where was the freedom in any of this? Where was the love?

But then I developed a crush on a boy down the road. I thought I was catching a cold, but it was just hormones. When he drove me and my brother to school, he wore mirror sunglasses and used the fast lane the whole time. One day he invited me into his bedroom. I'd come to see my friend, his little sister, but she wasn't home yet.

'Got a new water pipe.'

'Far out,' I said, pretending I was an old hand at getting high. Also pretending *far out* was an expression I was used to using.

After removing all the seeds and stems, he filled the pipe bowl, lit it and sucked the nozzle. Gurgle, gurgle, gurgle.

'The water cools the smoke,' he explained while not exhaling, which made his voice squeaky.

'Oh. Wow,' I said, trying not to think about the bubbles. I had a thing about any drink with bubbles. I couldn't drink milk if it was poured so fast there were bubbles.

'You can take more smoke in,' he continued in his high voice.

His face turned pink and I wondered if he was all right. Then he blew the smoke in my face, presumably because he thought I would enjoy this. I began to think of him as Water Pipe Boy.

'Yeah, yeah. Cool,' I said.

When I stopped coughing, I sucked on the nozzle. I held the smoke in my mouth, then let it out with an exaggerated sigh. I didn't know what inhaling was yet. The whites of his eyes became pink, and then we messed around on his bed for a while. Why did people like kissing? This was my first kiss and it just felt slimy. He lifted my shirt, unhooked my trainer bra, then manfully hid his dismay. I moved his hand away and he seemed relieved. I made the kind of noises I thought girls made, but I began to notice things. His bedroom stank of boy, like my brother's bedroom. Sweaty socks, mainly, and something else. There were dirty clothes on the floor and a half-eaten bowl of Cheerios on the bedside table. Flies had drowned in it. I spotted a *Playboy* on his desk and I felt my crush ebb. I could still feel the space it occupied in my chest, but it was an empty bag now. I straightened my clothes and left. We never did it again, nor did we refer to it.

*

Then there was Nicholas Ross, the sixteen-year-old son of the English couple my parents had befriended because they loved all things British. His family came to dinner one day, a barbecue. He had crinkly blue eyes and tiny freckles, which he hated. Said they'd only appeared since they'd moved to California last year. We spent the evening blushing. Looking away from each other, then looking back at the same moment and blushing. This, obviously, was true love at last. A month later, when I walked into the kitchen, my mother said:

'Those boys! Always killing themselves in cars.' She was talking to my father, who was cutting up a lime for his martini, which meant it was 6pm. 'Sixteen is a crazy age to be driving. It's nuts!'

'She might remember him,' he said, noticing me. I had a pain in my heart which felt uncannily familiar – for wasn't this the story in the 'Teen Angel' lyrics? A sixteen-year-old dies in a car crash and eternal posthumous love is pledged. I'd imagined this scenario many times. Already wept copiously.

'Do you remember him?' asked my mother. 'Nick Ross. That sweet English boy, about your age. Came here with his parents a few months ago.'

'I remember.'

'Very sad, isn't it?'

'Terrible,' said my father, popping a green olive into his drink.

My parents understood nothing important. They were trite.

'It was twenty-eight days ago,' I said. 'And he was Nicholas. Not Nick.'

Then I stormed off to my room to write in my diary. For weeks I cried hot furtive tears, with the tiniest touch of enjoyment for the melodrama of it all.

My love life went downhill for a while after that. I wanted to be a vet, so I volunteered to help at a pet shop on Saturdays. The owner was a quiet man in his forties, given to watching me from the cash register. When there were no customers, there was static in the air between us. One day as I was passing him with two bull terrier puppies, he told me:

'Put the puppies back and come help me with something.'

He pulled me into an embrace and thrust his lardy tongue into my mouth. I froze, disentangled my tongue and walked home. Were kisses just going to get worse?

'I don't think I'll go back next week,' I told my mother.

'Oh dear. Why?'

'Oh, I don't know. The place stinks.' I was sure I'd provoked that tongue. No need to bring shame into our house.

And for a while after that, it was as if I had a sign on my forehead saying *Up For It*. I was still skinny and flat-chested, but that didn't seem to matter. One man in his forties had me sitting on his lap while I licked stamps for his gun control campaign. This was a man my father admired, and it took me several Saturday afternoons to stop sitting on his lap. He used to make funny little noises, almost like a cat purring. At least there were no tongues.

I didn't know why I attracted this kind of attention. Other girls had boyfriends their own age. They went on dates. What was wrong with me? I'd read D.H. Lawrence and Elizabeth Barrett Browning, but so far literary love didn't correspond with any reality I'd observed. I wanted to complain to someone. Someone must be in charge of romantic love. False advertising, I'd claim. And lack of clear warnings.

The summer I turned sixteen, I finally met someone different. His name was Henry Richard Adamson. His birthday was March 16th, he was from Connecticut, and he lived on Quintara Street in the Sunset District of San Francisco. These details are hard-wired to my brain. When my children despair in a few years because I no longer know their names, I'll trot out these facts about Henry, sharp as a tack, and make them wonder if their dad really was their dad. We met in Golden Gate Park while I was getting signatures for a petition against the Vietnam War. He was a twenty-one-year-old Cal Berkeley student with a headband, ponytail and eyes so dark his pupils were indiscernible. My friend was with me, but he didn't flirt with her, oh no. He flirted with *me*. An internal softening occurred. It reminded me of the times I'd almost fainted in church, that same involuntary letting go, half-terrible, half delicious. He wrote down his phone number and said:

'Let's do something sometime. Maybe a flick.'

'Okay,' I whispered, bright pink. Flick? Who ever used that word? I knew I would soon.

Thus commenced my first romantic relationship. We took hikes on Mount Tamalpais, went to flicks, smoked joints, threw frisbees at Point Reyes beach. We held hands and finally kissing was comprehensible, if not completely passionate. I don't remember what we talked about, but he was studying philosophy and English so I imagine our conversations were like runaway trains, going this way and that. I was left behind sometimes, unable to hold on tight enough. How do I know this? He often called me idiot, but affectionately, as if I was a kind of innocent. Once he said *Your bucket has no holes*, and I said *Thank you* as if I understood what he meant. I liked listening to him talk. Under everything, he seemed to be saying *Wow, wow, wow!* He was mercury, quicksilver. He was kaleidoscopic.

The Incredible String Band was often playing on his record player, and The Moody Blues. Sometimes we lay on top of his India print bedspread and listened to 'Nights in White Satin' over and over. When the track ended, he'd leap up and put the needle back to the beginning. I offered to go on the pill, but he kept his clothes on and did not remove mine. There was nothing about Henry I didn't find intoxicating. The patchouli smell of his T-shirts, his frequent girly giggle, his intelligent forehead, the little moustache he sometimes grew. The fact he was older and taller than me, and was going to the same university my beloved father had gone to. Maybe I also liked the way he kept sex out of it. I was writing in my diary every day, sometimes twice. *Dear Diary. I'm going to marry Henry one day. We'll be Mr and Mrs Adamson and grow old and fat, and have nicknames for each other that no one else understands.* I'd drifted by then from Catholicism, otherwise I might have prayed for him to propose.

Even so, Henry was not part of my day-to-day life. Our meetings were intense but erratic, and most of our romantic occasions took place in my imagination. Especially, the worlds of Marin Catholic High School and Henry Richard Adamson had no overlap. As May ended this was more obvious, for June was prom month. I wouldn't go, of course, but it still pressed in on me as another aspect of high school I was a failure at. Maybe I'd babysit that night, or be with Henry. I never knew when that might happen and was in a permanent state of readiness. I told myself that proms weren't cool. I wasn't cool either, but had a keen understanding of what cool was. Henry was cool. I was a cool aspirant.

One day a boy who was not cool either stopped me in the school hall. We'd never spoken. He caught my eye and said:

'Huh. So. Just wondering. Want to go to the prom? With me?'

'Gosh!'

I hadn't said gosh since I was eight. Then I said it again and remembered his name. He had a crew cut. His scalp bristled with short hairs, the bones of his skull revealed in full. It was a nicely shaped head. I'd seen him playing football. He wasn't one of the stars, but I remembered how one time he'd run the length of the field with the ball tucked into his arm, dodging other boys with a kind of bulky grace. There was a nice hawk-ness to his nose and his jaw line was very pronounced. He seemed, improbably, to be a man already – though his awkwardness made me feel older than him.

'Yeah. The prom. Want to go?' By now he was sweating visibly.

'Sure,' I mumbled. I blushed. Then I blushed because I'd blushed.

'Huh!' He smiled broadly, opened his mouth as if about to say something else, something funny. Then he kind of saluted me, turned and walked quickly down the hall.

I didn't feel disloyal to Henry – perhaps because going to the prom wasn't a date in the normal sense. Solo tickets weren't sold, prom dates were sometimes dates of convenience. Nor did I feel it was unfair to say yes to a prom date when my heart was engaged elsewhere. I don't remember feeling responsible for anybody's feelings, and have no defence for this aside from my immaturity.

Arrangements must have been made, about rides and times. No memory of these remains, but the dress does. A yellow full-length frothy dress from I. Magnin. Empire line, with plastic pearls sewn to the seam under the bust. On the night of the prom, my bra (28-inch, AA cup) was lined with the cotton pads my mother used to remove her Noxzema cold cream. My lips were smeared with Frisky Frost, my eyelids with green eyeshadow, and my eyes outlined with black kohl. I did everything possible to bury my true nature. I was not a frothy dress girl. The only thing about myself I'd not hidden was my hair. I let it fall loose down my back, as always. All the girls wore their hair loose and long in those days. The idea was to be able to swing one's head and let hair be a curtain over one's face sometimes, but always act like it was a nuisance and push it back nonchalantly, or twitch one's head.

He knocked on the front door. I opened it with a nervous yank and there he was in his rented blue tuxedo, his broad shoulders stretching the fabric. There was a dab of Clearasil on his forehead, and he smelled of something spicy and chemical. I thanked him for a corsage (yellow gardenia), and we both fumbled with it till it clung sideways to my dress, an inch from my well-buried right nipple. My parents stood in the entrance hall and shook his hand. My mother with genuine warmth, my father with a complex mockery I would not understand for thirty years. We drove in his father's car, a Buick, I think. It was clean but smelt of cigarettes and air spray. A dinner in a local French restaurant followed. With some giggling over the escargot we'd bravely ordered, we admitted we'd never been there before. That generally, our families didn't eat out.

I'd often wondered what happened at a prom, and here it was. The gym was dimly lit and decorated with paper flowers and peace signs. The band – Sons of Champlin – was tuning up. It was magical, but then – perhaps like anything much anticipated, like childhood Christmases, like first kisses, maybe like death would be one day – it became anticlimactic. Unreal. And my own self, with this boy, this stranger – we weren't very real either. Which made it easy to ignore him. The dinner had been almost cosy – but now, self-conscious among peers, I felt myself drift off from him. I answered him politely when addressed, accepting a plastic cup of Coke, shouting monosyllables over the music. Fifteen minutes without looking at him, another fifteen without even thinking about him. I found myself in the bathroom with a group of girls, giggling, smoking, drinking bourbon from Pepsi bottles, backcombing their hair and putting on lipstick. I looked in the wide mirror and for a minute saw myself as one of them. At least I was not obviously one of them, was I? Here we all are, I thought – look at us: Girls at a prom! I knew it was an illusion, that I was an odd duck – but maybe the real illusion was that I thought I was different. I've come to wonder if feeling different is almost a kind of arrogance, a vanity. Maybe every one of those giggling girls had secret insecurities too. Not insecurities identical to mine, and not everyone might have minded as much as I did. But still – maybe we were all looking in the mirror with a kind of hopeful desperation and thinking: *Look at us: Girls at a prom!*

When the band took a break and the DJ put on 'Good Vibrations', I danced with my prom date. I loved that song and it was nice holding onto each other and rocking in place. My arms around his waist, his arms around my back. He felt like I'd thought he would, rock solid, heated. There was a calmness in his arms, while around us seethed a maelstrom of almost frightening adolescence. But when the song sped up and we let go of each other, he became so clumsy I had to look away. Or maybe I just assumed he'd be clumsy because I was not up to fast dancing either. I signalled that I needed to stop, out of breath, and wandered over to some folding chairs. He followed with a lurching gait and my heart sank.

Everything about the evening embarrassed me. The shameful and illogical truth was I felt superior to him. I'd dated a college boy, but I wasn't out of the non-cool woods yet. Like a recent immigrant shunning an even newer immigrant, I didn't want to be dragged back.

Finally, finally, finally, it was over. A forgotten drive home in the spring darkness. He walked me to my door, his tuxedo only slightly in disarray. I hadn't looked at him in the car, and I didn't look now either.

'Look, my corsage is gone,' I said, for something to say. 'Dropped off, I guess.'

'Huh. Oh well.'

Why did he have to begin each sentence with 'Huh'? Henry was so articulate by comparison, I thought prissily. At some point in the evening, the cotton pads in my right bra cup had slipped, so I was a little lopsided. I stooped my shoulders forward, anxious for him to go. I ached to be in bed with my diary. Maybe once I wrote about the prom, it would be real. Maybe I'd had fun after all.

'Goodnight,' he said, and tilted stiffly towards me.

'Goodnight,' I said quickly, leaning back. I went inside, closed the door, waited in the dark hall till I heard him drive off.

'Was it fun?' came my mother's cheery voice from her bedroom down the hall.

'Yeah! Great!'

'I'll make some hot chocolate.'

'No, thanks. Too tired.'

It was cruel to deprive her, to not make up something fun-sounding, but such was my state of confused self-loathing, I didn't care.

When I passed him in school on Monday, I nodded hello, then looked away. He may have acknowledged me, but maybe he didn't. I didn't deserve acknowledgement. Walking to class later, I heard some boys call out *prick tease*, then burst into laughter. I may have misheard, or they may not have meant the words for me – nevertheless, it was so painful, so apt, it lodged straight into me like an arrow, and there it still quivers. It turns out the worst memories are persevered in their pristine original condition, like vacuum-packed mackerel.

And where was Henry, my cool boyfriend? Leading his own life in Berkeley, where he probably didn't consider himself my boyfriend at all. There was the occasional flick or hike, but generally he was absent. I don't recall talking about the prom with him. Our closeness was not based on personal confidences, but a free exchange of abstract ideas. And, I guess, on the dynamic of me looking up to him. That summer I had a job working as a Girl Scout counsellor at Camp We Ch Me near Reno. I wrote Henry most days, using the pre-stamped blank postcards my mother had given me, and he wrote back sometimes. He always signed his name without a capital letter, à la e. e. cummings.

One day he turned up without warning. He'd driven two hundred miles in his little green Renault. Romance on this scale was so exciting I felt nauseous. I got time off my duties and we wandered up a hill, then sat on the brow to look at the view. He gave me a silver ring and the hill trembled. This was it! Holy moly! He silently picked up my hand and slipped the ring on my fingers till he found the one it fitted best. The first finger on my left hand. The ring was a puzzle ring, with two pieces twisted round each other, but they didn't come apart like a normal puzzle ring. They were separate but completely inseparable. Already, I was seeing the ring symbolically. I was looking at it on my old lady finger, remembering this moment on the hill above Camp We Ch Me.

'That's good,' he said. 'I was worried it might not fit.'

'It's beautiful,' I croaked. 'Thank you.'

And that was that. I had to make friendship bracelets with my troop of eight-year-olds, and he drove the two hundred miles back to Berkeley.

When I got home, I went to a family planning clinic and got the pill, prepared myself for full womanhood. His love was real after all, I had the ring to prove it. But by the end of the summer, it was over. He sent me a letter.

Dear Idiot. It has come to my attention that our ways are diverging, and the time has come to think of us as passengers on subways. For a while (a time I will always remember with deep affection) we were riding the same subway. But now it's time for me to get off our subway and catch another one by myself. Subways come and go all day long, and all night long too. There are always subways running. Someone new will get on your subway soon, and maybe one day, you'll see my face in a subway window passing your subway, and we'll both raise our hands and . . .

On and on, with subway metaphors. There were no subways in San Francisco and I struggled with the image. I'd seen *Midnight Cowboy*. The scene where Buck starts hallucinating, runs from Toilet Jesus Man and ends up on the subway – that was pretty nightmarish. Who would want to get on a subway in the first place? I took the letter into my parents' bathroom, which was the only room in the house with a door that locked. I read it over and over and cried so hard my stomach hurt. Years later I read the letter again, but critically, as if it was an academic essay I was marking. I spotted several lines that repeated sentiments, and one that contradicted a previous line. I wondered if he'd really been so cool. Maybe my prom date had been the cool one. Still, no matter how much time passed and how cynical I became: those kisses, those hand holdings. Those mysterious Moody Blues lyrics.

Dear Diary, I'd written the day of the subway letter. *I will never love anyone the way I love Henry. And I will never forget him.* Which would turn out to be true. I took his letters and threw them away, and five minutes later retrieved them. I took off his ring, gave it to my sister, then took it back off her. Hanging in the hall was a large black-and-white photograph, framed by my mother. Henry had taken it one day when we were walking by the bay. I was wearing a daisy in my hair, of course, and one of my white peasant blouses with embroidery on the yoke. Because I was looking at him, I looked like a simpleton.

Sisters

My cousin from San Diego wanted to bring her mother to see my mother one last time. This was my aunt's dying wish, to be reunited with her big sister. They'd not seen each other in over forty years. Mom was never rude about her or to her, that I knew of, but she had a subtle way of letting it be known when someone was not to be bothered with. Now she was senile, things were different.

'Your sister wants to come and see you, Mom,' I said.

'Delightful!'

I knew not everyone liked their siblings. But their long alienation puzzled me because they'd shared an apartment in San Francisco in their twenties, and then again in Seattle along with their brand-new husbands. When I was born, my aunt and uncle had only just moved out of our apartment. In photos from the 1930s and right through the 1940s and early 1950s, my mother appeared friendly with her sister, who was only eighteen months younger. They'd built identical snowmen, gone trick or treating dressed as cowgirls, hunted for Easter eggs together. They'd been each other's bridesmaid. After that, nothing. I didn't know if they fought, or if they did, what about. Maybe they just drifted. Maybe they'd never liked each other, and those photographs recorded times when they'd no choice but to be together. After all, most family occasions could be described as a form of compulsory socialising. Their non-relationship hadn't been a topic of conversation in our house. My aunt and her family lived in San Diego, so we didn't have to worry about running into them in Safeway or downtown.

From early adulthood, I had a correspondence with my aunt. She liked to write, and her letters – and later emails – were always refreshingly blunt and funny. She spoke her mind, and her mind was often full of irreverence. She made no bones about the bitterness she felt towards her absconding father, as well as being convinced her mother had not wanted or loved her. *I'm damaged goods*, she wrote me once, followed by *ha-ha-ha*. She alluded to doing bad things. Bad things to my mother, in fact, but she was vague about the details and just referred to them as in: *Why does your mother shun me? What I did wasn't so bad.* Her revelations always felt slightly scandalous, even titillating. Our mother never confided anything and never complained about her childhood. When I asked her about the father she'd not seen since she was three, she shrugged and said: *It was the depression. Lots of men went off. He wasn't a bad person.* And her mother, who left her and her sister with their grandmother in order to marry again and have another family? My mother smiled her famous smile – like Grace Kelly – and just said: *Oh, Mom! Bless her, she found love again.*

The awareness there were at least two ways to respond to anything seemed important to remember. Did I want to be like my mother – stoical, positive, determined not to be seen as a victim? Or my aunt – funny, indiscreet, determined to see the world as a corrupt place not to be trusted and herself as a survivor of horrendous circumstances? It was a choice between faith and cynicism, between optimism and pessimism. It was interesting, albeit disturbing, that whichever outlook I considered, I thought of it as realism. It occurred to me, briefly, that my mother might be a deeper pessimist than her sister. That perhaps only a fearful and dark outlook could summon her extreme kind of optimism, out of sheer necessity.

My cousin was one year younger than me and like myself, had been a skinny redhead as a kid. I'd gone on a road trip to Seattle with her family when I was thirteen. We spent three weeks stuffing our bras, backcombing our hair, and trying out lipsticks called frosted this and that. We stared at boys continually. Boys of all shapes and sizes, we weren't fussy. We developed new crushes several times a day and fought over crush-focuses, most of whom were oblivious. If a boy noticed us, we froze. Once a boy said hello, and we squealed like pigs and ran away. We wrote down lists of boys we met – and by *met*, we usually meant boys glanced at from our passing car window – with everything we knew about them. Colour of hair and eyes, estimated height, type of T-shirt, whether they wore cut-off jeans or store-bought shorts. We never knew their names, so the list had entries like: blond crewcut, about sixteen, seen getting on downtown bus in Merced, 8.5. The number was their score, with ten being the cutest. We lived in a perpetual state of want, and weren't even sure what we wanted beyond a kiss. Then the summer was over and we didn't see each other again for fifteen years. We wrote, of course, and kept track of each other's lives. Once you fight over boys who don't even notice you, you're connected for life. I never revealed the depth of my mother's indifference to her mother, and now it looked like I'd never need to.

The sister reunion arrived. It was an historic event and Ateca cooked all morning. The house shone, and my mother was all dolled up in a Laura Ashley dress she'd bought for my brother's wedding thirty years ago.

'Mom, look who's here!'

'Who is he?'

'It's a woman. Your sister!'

'My sister? My sister! Wah!'

She kissed her sister's hand loudly three times, and we acted like this was absolutely normal. We took dozens of photographs of the sisters hugging, laughing, and looking for all the world like two old women having a warm conversation. No visual sign of my mother's indifference.

'Barbara, remember that time we jumped from the railway bridge into the river?'

'I think that's just charming. Excuse me, can you please tell me the time?'

We had a nightcap on the deck after our mothers were in bed. We talked about our personal summer of love. I admitted to a second phase of boy-craziness which had occurred when I was about fifty. Unfortunate timing for my first husband.

I whispered, much more cavalierly than I felt:

'But, hey, at least it gave me something to write about.'

In fact, I'd just begun another story about it. Then I held my breath to see if she'd also had a second wave of boy-craziness. If she said no, I could pretend I hadn't either. Not really.

'Yeah, menopause brought some surprises, all right,' she whispered into the half dark, and laughed the throaty chuckle I remembered from 1967.

Then we talked about our mothers. Not only was their alienation a mystery, so were their very different outlooks. Circumstantially, they'd had parallel lives, which led to a discussion about genetic heritage. What else could explain it? An outlook, a philosophical inclination, embedded in DNA.

'But do you really think a person can *will* themselves to be happy, in spite of hardship? That specific events are never an excuse for cynicism and even, well, bitterness? Is it that simple?'

'I don't know. Possibly. But it wouldn't be simple. I think it probably takes great effort,' I said.

I was remembering the times my mother had been so crankily insistent on her cheerful interpretation of events, it resembled unhappiness in every aspect. No matter what awful thing was occurring, she'd react with a cocked eyebrow, then shrug and smile, before trotting out one of her phrases: *Que sera sera. So be it! Don't worry, it's perfectly normal to do/feel/say that*. Was it a good thing to *not* call a spade a spade? To call it, for instance, a rose?

Overall, I gravitated to my mother's style. I sensed it was classier, bigger-hearted, but I didn't always succeed because I loved few things more than ranting and gossiping. Listening to and telling secrets. Even joining in with a session of trashing someone I held only a mild grudge against. I enjoyed having a glass of wine with my cousin, pulling our mothers apart as cold-bloodedly as anthropologists. But I knew it was wrong and I'd feel guilty later, because I was my mother's daughter. It would be nice to say our analysis was imbued with a desire to see our dying mothers in the kindest light possible. That wasn't the case, but if we'd not loved them so much, would we have bothered analysing them at all? We'd have judged them in a minute, a quick hard rant, and changed the subject.

Eventually, our conversation drifted towards an old specu-lation. A fantasy we'd woven. Way back in 1953, before we were born, our parents had all been living in the same one-bedroom apartment in Seattle. My father and her mother had found themselves alone one evening and surrendered to an unwise alcohol-fuelled moment. This was almost certainly untrue but it always tickled us. Not only would it explain our mothers' feud, but also it made us sisters. It was wicked to be gleefully imagining such wickedness, which meant I was probably more my aunt whether I liked it or not.

'Time for bed, sister cousin,' I eventually said.

'Nightie night, sis cuz,' she said, yawning.

*

The next morning, when I popped my head into my mother's bedroom, the toilet down the hall suddenly flushed. She sat up and hissed:

'Who's that?'

'It's just your sister. She slept in Dad's office last night.'

That was a mistake. One eyebrow reared up and I could almost hear her brain registering the many ways in which this sentence was fundamentally wrong. Where was George? He was going to be furious someone was in his office. Anyway, her sister was a no-class person, what on earth was *she* doing here? I braced myself. But after a moment, she just shook her head, smiled and said:

'Well, so be it! I hope he puts the toilet seat down when he's done.'

They Weren't Pretty

Fifty-one years old
Scotland, 2004

After a flurry of internet dating, I ran into a man at our local pub. He was vaguely familiar, and it turned out he lived a few fields from me. He was single and worked offshore. I wasn't sure we had much in common, but I gave him a ride from the airport one day and he touched my knee. It was deeply odd how little shared interests mattered after that knee-touch. Not that I spent much time thinking about it. I missed my marriage. I'd made a huge mistake, and all I wanted was to be safely married again. All the way home from the airport, I kept stopping the car to kiss him. I took the back roads over the Black Isle just for this purpose, and with each kiss, I had fewer and fewer thoughts. In the end, thinking about anything at all just felt like work.

He worked two weeks on, two weeks off on oil rigs in places like the North Sea and the Mediterranean. Sometimes the shifts were four weeks. It fascinated me, how he could live like that. When he was away he worked twelve-hour shifts, seven days a week. Surely that was dangerous? Wouldn't the mindless routine day in, day out, kill something off in a person? And then he was home, with no structure at all, and this seemed equally un-healthy to me.

But it paid well. He bought a plot of land and built a house. It was surrounded by fields and woods, with the closest house about a quarter mile away, just visible. This was going to be our home. I'd watched the process, from breaking ground to furnishing it. It took just over two years, during which he often stayed with me when he was onshore. We spent weekends sanding, painting, varnishing, digging, considering kitchen units, wall colours, floorings. But as it grew closer to being finished, I wondered if it really was our house, not just his house. He'd paid for everything. The design and all the construction decisions had been his alone. I didn't mind taking the back seat most of the time, but one evening he announced the kitchen units were due to arrive the next day. I'd imagined we'd choose them together, so it was a shock.

I was already uneasy because he'd installed very bright lights in each room, and I preferred soft lighting. Getting the lighting right, to my mind, was crucial. When I acted a little peeved about the kitchen units, he made a big deal about letting me choose the cabinet door handles, as if I could be fobbed off. When I chose round wooden knobs, he was unhappy until I said the silver bar-shaped handles were also quite nice. Then he smiled and ordered those. Little things like that worried me.

Finally, we were about to go to bed for the first night in the new house. Some of the rooms were empty still and they echoed. The living room was full of boxes and bags, but our bedroom was already a nest. Candles burned on the windowsill – curtainless because who needed curtains when there were no neighbours? The bed was new, but the quilt was the same one we'd slept under many times. The house smelled of paint, fresh timber and varnish. The bedroom also smelled of his Johnson's baby powder and tea tree oil and my lavender. Because we were used to each other now, no longer insatiable, we lay just resting side by side, head on the pillows. He picked up an old issue of *Field & Stream*. I picked up the newest Anne Tyler novel, which I was reading as slowly as possible so it wouldn't end too quickly. After a while I put it down.

'Just think,' I whispered, looking at the candle flame reflected in the dark window.

'What?'

'No one else in the history of mankind has slept in exactly this space. I'm certain I have never in my entire life slept in a place that had not already been slept in.'

'Huh,' he said.

'It's as if this is the house's wedding night. Tonight it'll lose its virginity.'

'I guess you could be right. Maybe this will be the first time anyone's slept here. Though there's no way to know for certain. Human beings have been around a long time.'

'Well, maybe so. But not exactly here,' I insisted.

'Why? How do you know?' His voice was normal volume.

'Because we are upstairs. In the distant olden days, which are the only days in which people might have lived here, everyone slept near the ground.' Not whispering now either. I was a little annoyed because he always took things so literally, and he hadn't properly appreciated my witty wedding night comment. I turned on my side, away from him. He closed his magazine and sighed.

'What about those ten-storey buildings in Edinburgh? Those are from medieval times. Or older.'

I turned on my back and he picked up his magazine again.

'Well, okay,' I said. 'But that was the city. Edinburgh already existed by then. This is a hillside in the middle of nowhere. The soil's not even good enough for crops.'

'Your point?'

'It is highly unlikely, in fact impossible, that people built tall houses here which have left no trace.' I hated the way I sounded prim. He shuffled himself further up the bed, till he was sitting straight up. Had I ever spoken to him like this before? I noted, but did not remark on, the creaking of the new house. As if it was still getting used to its own existence, and didn't yet understand its limitations or size. As if it was breathing. I was about to say this because it too seemed clever.

'Crap,' he said suddenly. 'Seems a bit arrogant. To claim you know that.'

I pressed my lips together. He'd never used this tone with me before. Almost aggressive. My not-yet-divorced husband had never spoken to me like that. But then he hadn't spoken much at all.

'Everyone knows it,' I said.

'Everyone?'

'Yes, ask anyone. Phone someone right now. Your brother.'

'My brother?'

'Yes. Your brother. He knows everything.'

'Says who?'

'Says you. You think he knows everything.'

'Is this about the oystercatchers again?'

This felt like a hard slap, and my love for him shrivelled up inside my chest. Sizzled and evaporated like a drop of water thrown on a hot frying pan.

'I never blamed anyone for that,' I claimed.

'No, but you wanted to.'

'You couldn't know that. I was sad the mother bird didn't find her nest and her babies died. It was my fault.'

'Yeah, but you moved the nest because I told you the digger was about to move that pile of earth. You blamed me for those baby bird deaths. And I know that for a fact because of that thing you do. With your mouth.'

'What thing?'

'You really don't know?'

'Why would I ask if I knew?'

'I don't know. You have your little tactics to avoid friction. To avoid confrontation, but still make your views known.'

Silence. My heart pounded. These accusations hit at my very nature and were not answerable. If he'd said I never put the rubbish out or I could wear a bit more lipstick – those were the kinds of things that could be fixed, but not this. This was surely the end of our relationship, this had to mean the end. I'd been expecting it since the kitchen unit debacle. He didn't really want to live with me. He'd thought he did, but now he didn't. He was backpedalling as quickly as he could. *Well! Huh!* I could feel my face flushing. How would I explain another break-up to my children? And what about telling my friends, all of whom liked him? I was glad we weren't married so I wouldn't need to change my passport.

Three minutes passed, while the new house yawned and sunk minutely into the foundations. We faced away from each other, and I wriggled my bottom so not even an inch of buttock was touching his. It was tragic, of course, but so inevitable I had to admit to a small measure of relief in my pain. No more waiting and wondering how it would end. It was over right now, and I could take back my rightful role of a soon-to-be-divorced woman with a husband in her extension. The extension of the house I'd lived in for twenty years and – it now appeared – loved more than I'd loved that husband. Then I felt a wave of repulsion, of nausea for the new house. It wasn't mine. It would never be mine. I was cheating on my old house, just sleeping here. Who was I kidding? I scanned the bedroom, pictured packing all the things I considered mine. Bickering over some of the things we'd bought together, like the towels and those blue cups and that wonderful little landscape by a local artist. Lochardil beach.

'Are you crying?' he asked.

'No!' I replied, thinking *Crying in front of someone? Doesn't he know me at all?* 'I'm just tired.'

'That's what you always say when you're mad at me.'

Pause. I didn't know whether to be angry or philosophical. Did it matter any more? Something so liberating about being at the end of things. I could just be myself now, nothing to lose.

'It's not fair.' Indignantly, having chosen anger. 'It's not!' I spat at him.

'You're not making sense. What's not fair?'

'Don't act innocent now. Why should you get to keep Lochardil beach, when it's only me who loves it? You just think it's an investment. You don't . . . you don't love it! You don't love it. You don't . . .'

'Are you talking about that painting we bought at Brown's Gallery?'

I nodded, too overcome now to trust speaking. He moved towards me. Pulled me in, but I wouldn't look at him.

'Oh, for fuck's sake. Is this because I corrected you about no one having slept in this space before?'

'No,' I said, but then I shrugged and nodded a little. After a full minute's silence, he stroked my hair and I couldn't help but enjoy it. The fact it was the last time he would do it gave it poignancy.

'Why do you hate me?' I had to ask. It had to be asked.

'I do not hate you. But you get so intense and you always exaggerate. It can get a little annoying.'

I turned away and sighed heavily, noting he had not said he loved me. I remembered how he flirted with my friends, that he didn't read novels, that he aimed for rabbits in his headlights sometimes. A list of reasons to be glad it was over. Minutes passed, and his hand stroking my head beat down each of my objections. He'd set my son up in business with his own money, taught my other son how to fish, and he cooked the most amazing dumplings I'd ever tasted.

'Jesus, now you're not talking to me? You are . . . exhausting. And I am . . .'

'Shush!' I sat up and touched his mouth. 'Listen, what was that?'

A sudden guttural noise came from outside.

'A dog barking?'

'Except there are no dogs here.'

It came again. If a cow and lion could produce a hybrid, this would be the sound it would made. A low roar, but no aggression – ending in a sad, drawn-out bovine lowing. We crept out of bed and peeked out the window. Once I blew out the candle, the night didn't seem dark at all. In fact, it was a bright night, with a three-quarter moon hanging yellow and lumpish.

'I don't see any dogs.'

The sound came again, closer and from more than one source. It seemed to be right outside the house. He slowly opened the window, and suddenly the shadows in the field resolved themselves into deer. Red deer, tall and rangy. Half a dozen hinds in the patch of field about to become the garden. They were not close to each other, but now they all froze in the same direction, their white bottoms pointed to the house.

'I can smell them. Can you smell them?' I whispered.

'Yeah. They stink.'

After a minute, the deer began feeding again. I could hear them breathing and tugging grass and chewing. The strange low roaring came again, but not from the hinds, who ignored it and carried on eating. It came from three stags, loitering on the hill just above the house. Then came the sound of hooves pounding turf, briefly, and a sudden clattering as antlers crashed into each other.

'Are they killing each other?' I asked, thrilled.

'No. Just figuring out who gets to be the boss. The daddy.'

The hinds still didn't pause in their grazing. We stood there, close enough to touch shoulders, and after a while he closed the window and we went back to bed. We cuddled for warmth. I had lost my angry and frightened feeling, but nothing rushed in to replace it. This was where the deer probably always came this time of year, I thought, and maybe the house being here now made no difference to them. I imagined how this place had been, for years. For centuries. Thousands of centuries. Forested, wild, cold. Wild animals, now long extinct, had grazed right here. Maybe it was true and there had, after all, been another dwelling here before. Maybe an entire village, full of noisy children and yipping dogs and brawling red-faced men. Maybe this new house – which may or may not become my home – would vanish too. First it would become unoccupied, then it would decay, crumble, and eventually the earth would reclaim it. I saw our two pale bodies, suspended horizontally in the air, where the bedroom used to be a million years ago. Maybe this moment of feeling nothing but the new coldness between us, would last a long, long time. No one knew these things.

They weren't pretty, the hinds. Not like Bambi. Their faces were long and moose-like. Their fur was mangy. I kept forgetting deer were wild animals – rough, smelly and slightly unnerving. Not at all how they looked from a distance. Maybe it was the same with love. Prettier from a distance. How could I still be learning such basic things?

He yawned deeply as if none of our conversation had taken place. Was he really so shallow? I had to admire his naturalness, even envy his sense of ease. I was an emotional wreck. Was he or was he not my man? I'd imagined our break-up so vividly, part of me was already looking back on our relationship with my usual mixture of nostalgia and confused regret. His hand strayed to my thigh and stroked it lazily. If our relationship had not ended, it had at least profoundly altered course and I would need to pay closer attention now. I could feel my heart reconfigure itself around this new knowledge, as if atoms of love had been added or taken away. I wasn't sure which. I'd wanted a man to love and here he was. What should I do with him now? I assumed the choice was mine, but within two weeks he texted that we needed to talk. This sounded so classically ominous, I put on my new red summer dress and wore lipstick. I was terrified, but also excited. Something out of my control was about to happen.

'We just want different things,' he said. He said it kindly, with a sweet expression on his face and I liked him all over again.

'Well, maybe,' I said. 'But . . .'

He didn't want to be friends – he said a clean break would be better. Which it was, though for the first few weeks I cried like a baby and couldn't remember anything bad about him. Even those kitchen units seemed beautiful for a spell.

Two Cans of Dogfood

It was a Tuesday night in the middle of December. Or a Wednesday. The days of the week had nothing to distinguish them. My mother was still busy telling Death to get lost because she'd no time – *NONE* – for that kind of baloney. I was getting ready for bed in my father's old office. One wall was all glass and the blinds hadn't worked since 1977. The neighbour's windows looked directly onto our house, so I did what I did every night – undressed with the light out, then switched it back on once I was in bed. I phoned my husband in Scotland to touch base, then read my novel till I felt sleepy enough to sleep. I wasn't sleeping well, which made me cranky. I'd become hyper-aware of the way sleep advanced and receded in waves – which was fatal, because if there's one thing Sleep hates, it's being noticed. Timing was everything, and I lost the knack of slipping under the wave as it receded. At 3am, I heard Sleep laughing in the distance at my beached self, eyes wide open, leg muscles tingling. But I tricked it with the next wave and fell asleep.

I was woken at dawn by birdsong and the sound of Ateca praying loudly in the room next to mine. I took a shower, then walked down San Pedro Road to the levee, cutting through the new development which wasn't politically correct to like – but which I kind of did. Each house was slightly different, but they all had a Cape Cod flavour. Shades of sage green and grey blue

131

on wooden shingles. Dad died before these arrived, but he'd known they were coming and it'd made him furious. More traffic, more pollution, and more damningly – people who couldn't afford golden retrievers. The builders had been required by planning law to include affordable apartments. My parents were new to the middle classes, thanks to the GI Bill. No wonder Dad had been angry. He finally blends in with the lawyers and psychiatrists, when wham! The door opens to his old tribe, the plumbers and truck drivers.

It was an easy walk, flat and not far. The view included the San Rafael Richmond Bridge, the Marin Islands and Mount Tamalpais, a sight that never failed to squeeze my heart. I stopped at Andy's for a coffee and pastry. It was a grocery store, and offering coffee was a recent side-line. Andy was the fifth owner. It had been Rakestraw's, Mayfair, Bruno's, P&X and now it was Andy's.

I sat in a seat by a sunlit window and called my sister. We ranted about people who pissed us both off. Was anything as bonding as a common enemy? We talked almost every day, but not when I was happy. Those were not times to phone my sister because happiness was really a kind of temporary stupidity. It made conversation boring and short, and it irritated her. On the other hand, when I was unhappy, talking with her always made me feel better. Nothing I could say shocked or alienated her. Everything I said was greeted by a version of *I know exactly what you mean*. Maybe bad feelings only felt bad if they had no company. And this didn't just apply to our personal woes. She was a prize-winning reporter at the *San Francisco Chronicle* and according to her, good news was bullshit. Only fools believed it. After our rant about people pissing us off, we ranted about politicians.

Then I went home and wrote. I was working on a story about the time I married an Irish boy in Reno on St Patrick's Day, drunk and wearing a powder blue pantsuit. This was hideous on several levels, but my main concern was my outfit. It was a pantsuit and it was powder blue. If I was capable of wearing something like that, what else would I do for love?

When my mother woke, I told her she was beautiful.

'No! *You're* beautiful,' she replied.

We threw it back at each other a few times, then I said:

'Thanks. I get that from my mother.'

After a pause, she giggled so hard she knocked the electric controls and the hospital bed began swaying from side to side. She never fake-laughed, so I knew she'd got the joke. If had to get dementia, I wanted that kind.

Later I took her to Andy's for an afternoon outing. There were a lot of kerbs to negotiate plus sidewalk cracks, and with each one she gave a cry of dismay. Genuine fear, but also excite-ment as if she was on a roller coaster. When we arrived, I parked her at a table and went to order from the counter. By the time I came back, there were three men sitting with her. She was hold-ing court, and I suddenly noticed she was wearing her trademark red lipstick. Had Ateca applied it? She was waving her hands about in her feminine way, and the men were all leaning in with adoring looks as if she wasn't sitting on a urine-soaked diaper. I stood with my tray for a full minute, contemplating my mother's charisma. For months I'd been feeling sorry for her, patronising her, but here she was – still her magnificent self, and far more beautiful than I'd ever been.

'Are you her daughter?' one finally asked.

'One of them,' I answered. I noted there were no more seats at the table and no one was getting up.

Oh! I was tired suddenly, worn out from shifting my perspec-tive. I wanted to get out of Rakestraw's and take Mom home. I meant P&X. No, I meant Andy's. Damn, who was I kidding? It would always be Rakestraw's to me. Like a second wife seeming an imposter if you knew the first wife. No matter how much happier the new wife made him, she wasn't the real one. I knew

WAH!

Rakestraw's like the back of my hand because when I was eight, nine, ten – it was the only store I was allowed to go to on my own. We'd be out of milk or bread and my mother would give me a few bucks to go to the store. I loved those missions. On arrival I'd act nonchalant, like a grown-up, and begin retrieving the needed items. Then there'd be a loud announcement over the tannoy. All the shoppers would freeze to listen.

'Attention! Attention, please! Cynthia Jones, I've got an important message from your mother. Get dog food. I repeat, dog food. Two cans.'

I'd pretend I wasn't Cynthia Jones and make a wide circuit of the dog food aisle before giving in, blushing so hard even my hands would turn pink. The most surprising thing to me now, five decades later, was that I'd been surprised each time. I never remembered she would forget some item and phone the store. Which means, I suppose, we were more alike than I ever considered.

Powder Blue Pantsuit

Twenty-two years old
California, 1975

One day I met an Irish man. Aside from marrying him, it was a very low-key affair. It all began with blonde Bella from County Galway. I'd sat next to her on a plane a year or two ago. Me and Bella met up sometimes when we were both back in San Francisco, usually at an Irish bar in the Mission. Her figure was very full and she wore tight clothes with low necklines. Everything about her was loud and brassy. She always had a boy in tow and one night she brought a boy for me too.

'Look here,' she shouted at us over the jukebox. 'You two should dance – go on, now. You're a grand couple, so you are.' She put our hands together.

'That's all right,' I shouted to the boy, who hadn't smiled or said anything. Bella embarrassed me. We extricated our hands.

'You sure?' he mouthed. His eyebrows and shoulders seemed to be shrugging an apology.

'Yes! Positive!' I assured him, and found a place to sit alone at the crowded bar. I fumbled in my tobacco pouch to roll a cigarette. It gave me an excuse to avoid eye contact and conversation. I was already wishing I'd not come. I planned to sleep on Bella's sofa later, but all I wanted now was to curl up in my own bed in Santa Cruz.

I met him a few more times after that. He always seemed to be at the bar when we were. I wasn't sure I was going to be a

drinker or smoker forever, but I'd decided to give it my best shot
and the bar was a good place to practise. We fell into being a
couple, the way people do when they're rarely sober and both
a little shy. I woke up one morning in his bed, and with no words
spoken about this transition, we commenced a kind of romance.
He invited me to his brother's house for Sunday dinner. We went
to a barbecue once, and another time to see Blazing Saddles. I
laughed hysterically – he didn't. He didn't seem keen to meet me
where I lived, and I stopped inviting him. I was not sure what
he'd make of my VW van anyway. When we met in Santa Cruz,
it was in a hotel.

He was handsome, with even features and round brown eyes.
He had short hair, no beard and wore ironed polo shirts. In San
Francisco, this was tantamount to being weird. He was like an
extra from a 1950s film. The most attractive thing about him
was his indifference to this fact. He was at ease with himself,
quietly getting on with his life. And of course, there was his
Irish accent. I've always been susceptible to Irish accents.

Once he whispered to me, in his fabulous voice, that he was a
member of the IRA and was wanted by the British Army back in
Ireland.

'What will you do when your visa expires?' I whispered back.

'Go home and be arrested, I suppose,' he said heroically,
shrugging and drinking some beer.

I ravished him right then and there.

He took me shopping, which was a new experience. The
ponytailed boys I knew did not go shopping at all, unless it was
to a flea market, and they rarely spent money on me. In fact,
since Henry Richard Adamson, there'd been a dearth of dating
altogether, perhaps because that would entail the material world
too much. Plus, a traditional relationship would probably
preclude sharing things like crabs or genital herpes. They were
just boys. My Irish man worked on building sites, went to Mass,
drank beer, watched football on television.

'Let's go to the shops. Let me buy you a new frock or something,' he said.

On the surface, it was a great offer – but he kept steering me into stores that sold ugly clothes.

'Actually, I'm not crazy about any of these clothes,' I said politely. I didn't get it. He seemed to want me to look tacky.

But then he smiled his quiet smile and looped my arm through his. I was a sucker for old-fashioned gestures like arm looping, and soon I was trying on all sorts of awful clothes and parading in front of him.

'What do you think?' I said, cringing.

'It's grand. Let's get it.'

'I'm not sure. I want to keep looking.'

'Oh. Okay,' he said, crestfallen. 'Then what about this?'

He held up something even more awful. I burst out laughing.

'Are you kidding?' I gasped.

'Does that mean you like it?'

'Not really. I don't wear pantsuits. And I don't like powder blue.'

'Really? But look at it!' He was incredulous.

'I am looking at it.'

'Sure, but you'd look smashing in it. It would match your stunning eyes. Try it on.'

'Oh, all right.'

I looked at myself in the dressing room mirror. I felt odd and tired. I kept thinking it was just a game, the choice was still mine, that I could talk him out of buying any of these items. But by the powder blue pantsuit time, I was worn out. I witnessed the purchase with a hollow heart, and then agreed the pantsuit needed suitable shoes. Half an hour later, I owned a pair of navy blue Mary Janes and felt completely disoriented. I wondered what Bella would think. Oh, to hell with Bella. This was all her fault anyway. I'd gone from hippie chick to valley girl in a day.

I ended up wearing the powder blue pantsuit simply because he wanted me to, and doing something to please a man was mysteriously sexy. It was interesting to be with a man who hadn't a clue what I was thinking or feeling. Was this how my mother's generation felt, at least initially, with a man? I could see it might be titillating. One evening in Santa Cruz, he got very drunk. We were staying at the same hotel he always booked. I woke up to the sound of him urinating into the metal waste basket in the corner of the room. He stumbled back to bed and fell asleep again. I lay there wondering what to do. What if there were holes in the waste basket and pee was leaking all over the carpet? I quietly lifted myself over him to get out of bed, took the container to the bathroom, poured his pee into the toilet, then rinsed it out. Then I cuddled up to his broad back again and felt proud of my efficiency. Why hadn't I awoken him and told him to clean up his own pee? Because I was being the girl who wore the powder blue pantsuit.

It was not the kind of suit women wore to work in offices. It was more the kind of outfit an un-college-educated girl might wear to church, or to go out for dinner. It was feminine with a fitted jacket and the pants were snug around my bum. In that powder blue pantsuit, I was dangerously close to not being me, which I found refreshing. Sometimes even invigorating. Maybe that's how costumes work for actors. While wearing the powder blue pantsuit, I had conversations with the wives of his friends about the cost of nail varnish and the advantages of certain floor polishers over others. I amazed myself. It was easy to fool people into thinking you were like them. Who else could I be? The possibilities seemed endless. Whenever I put on that powder blue pantsuit, I kept looking in the mirror to make sure I really looked as natural as I uncannily felt. Though not for one minute did I lose awareness of its ugliness. I was fascinated by how ugly it was. It was all a bizarre experiment, I guess.

One night in San Francisco, we were in a Mission Street bar somewhere near 17th Street. It was St Patrick's Eve and I was drinking seven and sevens. I'd discovered I could drink this and feel all right for a long time. Beer made me burp and wine made me sleepy. Me and my Irish man were sitting with Bella and her boyfriend.

'What time is it?' asked Bella.

'Almost midnight,' I said.

'St Patrick's Day!'

'So it is, so it is,' said her boyfriend, grabbing her for a hug. 'I think it would the perfect day to get married, don't you?' he said, winking at me over her head.

'Yes. But not us, dumbie. These two.' She turned around and pointed at us, smiling broadly.

I said nothing. Irish man looked away. I thought he might walk away.

She continued, rubbing her hands together in a business-like way. 'Yes, let's be having you two hitched now. It's the most romantic day in the year to get married.'

No one said a thing, so she just kept talking.

'You don't want him ending up in a British Army prison, do you?' she asked me. 'And anyway, look at the two of you. You make a gorgeous couple.'

I think I shook my head. Maybe I laughed. It seemed ridiculous and I assumed it would never happen. The Irish were mostly talk, especially when they were drinking. But when the bar shut at 2am, the jukebox playing Black Velvet Band, all four of us got into Bella's Ford Mustang and drove to Reno. We arrived just after dawn. I still didn't believe I would get married. We slept for an hour or two in the car, went into a casino bathroom to freshen up and have more drinks (casino-gratis) and eat a fried breakfast (also casino-gratis). I was wearing the powder blue pantsuit but had personalised it with a tie-dyed T-shirt under the jacket. It was holding up well, considering. The Mary Janes were scuffed now, and hence less ugly.

The sky was a different kind of blue than San Francisco. A merciless hard blue with no variations. Downtown Reno didn't have a scrap of beauty. It was ugly, like the pantsuit. I couldn't understand it. Who would choose to come here? Yet the place was throbbing with people ready to throw their money at a casino, even in the morning. We wore sunglasses and smoked continually, walking around and not talking. At last, we found a place. Wedding Bells Chapel was a pink flat-roofed stucco building set back in a weed-filled lot. I remember some ants crawling over red hearts, which were painted over every concrete surface. There were also some pink and purple hearts in velveteen glued to the pulpit. The man who performed the wedding had terrible breath and leered at me. All of this seemed sweet and hilarious. I liked weddings, but only in an ironic way.

By noon, before I'd sobered up, the deed was done. I was Mrs O'Brien and still reverberating from the unexpected thrill of saying those vows. *Do you? Yes, I do.* Those words had power. Even the syllables of those words had power. In some small part of my heart, I had become Mrs O'Brien and I liked it. I sat proudly in the back seat and sneaked my hand into my husband's hand. My *husband's* hand! I decided there was a current running between our hungover hearts via our sweaty hands. Within minutes he had closed his eyes and was snoring, and my empty hand was left palm upwards and ridiculous. I didn't care. All the way back to San Francisco, I kept sneaking glimpses at him. He looked handsome, with his beard stubble and mouth slightly open, some drool drying on his chin. He was incapable of repulsing me. I told myself that in fifty years I'd look back on this day with great nostalgia. *I was so innocent!* my old lady self would reflect. *Both of us so young, but look where it led!* I foresaw forty-three great-grandchildren. Looking at the sparkly ring on my finger, which had recently been on Bella's finger and would soon go back there, I considered un-lapsing my Catholicism for him. That didn't seem such a sacrifice.

*

Most of this time, I was living in my converted VW van parked in front my brother's cottage in Santa Cruz, a mere mile from the hotel. I used his bathroom and kitchen, but he never complained because I kept him in donuts from my shifts at Winchell's, the 24 hour donut outlet. We'd watch Johnny Carson on his little black-and-white television, eat donuts, smoke joints, sleep till noon, then have eggs and hash browns at Sunnyside café for $1.99. That was our main meal of the day. I was saving to go back to Europe, and he was saving to impress a girl. Any girl. It was a fine life, but it felt temporary.

One day we got stoned on the nude beach just north of town. We didn't have clothes on but didn't feel naked. The beach was full of people with no clothes on, so it felt normal. The sea air on my skin felt good, or maybe it was the day itself. Spending time with my brother was like spending time blissfully alone. I could be myself entirely which was always a relief. When we talked, it was never for the sake of talking. We never laughed out of politeness. We were often crude and irreverent. Sometimes we argued and it wasn't unusual for us to travel back from somewhere separately. On this day, we happened to be in harmony. When it was time to go home, we began pulling on our clothes reluctantly. They were sandy and our skin was sticky with salt air.

'Wish we didn't have to,' my brother said, stretching.

'I know.'

'Well, let's not then.'

At what point would we feel naked? We ran across Highway One in full view of cars and people. Didn't feel naked at all. In fact, wearing the powder blue pantsuit felt weirder. We got into my van and began the drive back to town. Aside from my bottom sticking to the plastic seat in an annoying way, the naked-awareness wasn't happening. Then we picked up a hitch-hiker, who at first didn't bat an eyelid. But then:

'Nice mosquito bites,' he mumbled, directing his gaze at my chest.

I saw his eyes in the rear-view mirror and looked down at my defenceless breasts. I felt naked at last. *Thank God!* My more sensible self was always pulling me back from one precipice or another. A little mood shift, and I would suddenly know I had to stop, or leave, or change things. I could go so far and no further. At the same moment I felt naked, I realised the powder blue pantsuit had to go. I was beginning to stray too far from myself. Exactly who I was, was still unclear – but I knew who I was not.

When we got home, I put the powder blue pantsuit in the garbage. I phoned my Irish man and told him I needed a divorce as I was going back to Europe. He agreed quickly. This felt a little insulting, but also a relief.

Then I began to make alterations. Cancelled plans, quit my job, sold my van. Much suddenly seemed unimportant because I was already inhabiting my next location. *London.* Everything wrong with my present life would be rectified there. And then I compressed my emotional ties into a single bundle of farewells. Some would survive the next absence, but it was hard to say which ones. Every goodbye was a cull.

I looked forward to the cultural jolt of London rain and tube rides, doner kebabs and dry British humour. I never loved London more than when I was about to return to it. Though this time I began to wonder if I was happiest somewhere in between cultures. In motion and nowhere in particular. Looking out a plane window at the whiteness of Greenland, or out a train window at the back gardens of South London suburbs, or out an airport bus window at the golden round hills of West Marin. Not talking.

I met Irish man two more times. Once for the immigration interview, which we both passed with flying colours. I was, apparently, a convincing wife of a conventional man even without the powder blue pantsuit. The last time I saw him was at the lawyer's office, to set the divorce in motion. My days of being Mrs O'Brien were officially numbered. A decree nisi would be sent to me in London. He still looked handsome and I ached to touch him. It was as if my libido had no access to the memories stored in my head. We stood in the sun on Market Street outside the lawyer's office.

'Thanks, and good luck with London and all that,' he said shyly.

No hugs or kisses. It was as if we'd never done more than shake hands. He'd never been my husband, after all. Not really. He looked so sweet and timid, so soft. I had a sudden suspicion.

'Hey, tell me the truth. You're not *really* wanted by the British Army, are you?'

'What? Yep, I'm in the IRA. I told you.'

'Huh. Well, not sure I believe that, but good luck anyway. Keep in touch.'

'Of course. Friends, right?'

'Of course.'

And that was that. I boxed my belongings and took them to my parents' basement again.

There was, of course, a family dinner with my father's beef teriyaki and my mother's New York cheesecake. She was wearing red lipstick, and in a blasé way I noticed how pretty she was. She was always pretty. My sister was now nine years old, at the gawky stage, but I could see she'd be cute again as soon as her mouth caught up with her teeth. My brother's hair was driving our dad crazy, but he only made one comment on it that evening.

'You look like a girl, goddammit.'

'Thanks, Dad. You flirting with me?'

We sat on the deck drinking beer while my father barbecued and the current golden retriever chewed up someone's shoe. It felt like just another Oak Drive dinner.

Where was my mother? Probably limping around the kitchen, setting the table, putting flowers in a vase, making a salad. I'd caught her eye earlier, asked if I could help.

'No!' she said. 'You go and enjoy your beer with your father.'

'You sure? You don't need any help?'

'Correct.'

Correct was one of her favourite words even then, and she enunciated it with great relish. Then she smiled her pretty smile and opened her mouth to say something else.

'What? What is it?' I said impatiently.

'Oh, nothing! I'm busy. Go to your father!'

I was relieved when she shooed me away. It colluded with my preferred version of our relationship. Of her as a remote person and me as someone warmer, more socially skilled. For years I'd been telling myself she had no interest in being close, thereby alleviating myself from the task of getting to know her. Even so, standing in the kitchen poised to escape, I suddenly remembered the stories she'd made up when I was a kid. I was always the main character, the hero, and Tinkerbell often had a guest appearance. Where had that mother-daughter intimacy gone? Maybe it faded undramatically and by the time we noticed, we were both too awkward to find our way back. Or more likely, she kept her arms outstretched and about age twelve, I started walking coolly right past them. Exactly as I was doing right now.

'Okay, Mom.'

Then I got another bottle of beer from the refrigerator and went back to my father.

Within a week, I was gazing down on San Francisco Bay, wondering cynically how long it would be before I'd rush back to resuscitate this life, and wasn't it all a bit crazy and tiring and expensive? Bouncing between countries wasn't at all how I'd thought my life would go. It was a constant surprise, but I couldn't see how to break the habit. Bella had pimped me to her friend, but that was all right. He wanted to live in a country not his own for a while, and so – apparently – did I.

Come Home Now!

As Christmas approached, Mom remained on a plateau and nothing much changed from day to day. Mostly, she slept – either in her hospital bed or in her wheelchair in the living room, by the desk, the light filtering through the broken venetian blinds. Her sleep was peaceful. There was no leg twitching or pained expressions on her face. One afternoon I sat near and just let my eyes rest on her sleeping face. More and more, she seemed the most beautiful woman in the world. Then I thought about how mysterious her beauty was. Mysterious and maybe even accidental, because she'd never tried to be beautiful.

Of course, when I was young, I often saw her worried face, which never precluded her being beautiful but which was still awful to behold. I hated making her worry, but not enough to stop doing dangerous things. I just didn't tell her about them – though of course she suspected, otherwise why the worried face? Oh, the ways in which I'd deluded myself! I was working on a story about the summer I turned eighteen and went to Europe on my own. I'd hitched everywhere, lost my virginity to a boy I couldn't remember the name of, was raped by a man I never knew the name of, and discovered Kit Kats (delicious) and beans on toast (vile). The writing of it threw up perspectives I'd not considered before. I'd been raped? How had I buried *that* in a list containing things like beans on toast? I couldn't remember much, but I remembered feeling completely happy. Happy and glad to be out of high school. I also remembered my mother's face when I walked back in the door at the end of the summer. As if I'd come back from the dead. *Is it really you? It's you!*

A decade later, when I'd become a mother and cared about such things, I asked her what that era had been like for her. Not just that summer with me in Europe, but all the times I'd been on the road and out of touch. We were in the kitchen, and she stopped loading the dishwasher to look straight at me. She was in her early fifties, and by then her MS meant she was always holding on to something – a wall, a counter, a chair. There was a smear of her handprints down the hall wall, but her face still didn't have a single wrinkle.

'Well!' she said, as if she'd been waiting years for me to ask a serious question. 'The whole world had gone crazy. Crazy! It was like the earth was spinning *faster* suddenly, and you – all you kids with your long hair and your pot smoking and your hitch-hiking – you just kind of, I don't know – you flew off!'

She fluttered her fingers to demonstrate flying.

'Gravity had stopped working and off you flew. I didn't know if you were alive or dead half the time.'

Yes, my thirty-year-old self had thought. The minute she described my wild days like that, it felt true. Europe had been easy enough to get lost in, very seductive, but finding my way home had been problematic. I had my first English husband by then, a baby on my hip, another in my belly, and I was trying to live in California again. To grab hold of my old life and make it stick this time. And the embarrassing fact was, here I was at my mother's deathbed thirty-five years later and I was experiencing the same old anguish, the same tearing sensation. As if my real self, my child self, was still here in San Rafael waiting for me to inhabit it again. It was probably pretty tired of waiting. I bet it got fed up some days and thought me inconsiderate and friv-olous. Like a child trying on costumes, one after the other, and tossing them rapidly on the floor, not even bothering to fold them up and put them away properly.

My mother was still snoring softly in her wheelchair. I was watching her, and Ateca was watching a Hallmark Christmas Special called *A Very Merry Mix-Up*. I watched her a few more minutes, drank her in till my tank was full, then I got back to snooping around the house as if she was dead already, which made me a cold-blooded vulture. *What?* That's not a good look, so I told myself I was a detective with an honourable mission. The house held vital secrets and clues, especially the deeper recesses of the hall closets and the kitchen cupboards that were rarely opened because they were in awkward positions. I was saving the basement for last, with its cobwebs and low ceilings. Treasure was everywhere. A fondue set from the 1960s instantly took me back to dinner parties where our family felt cutting edge. *Check us out! Melting Swiss cheese over a fire at the dining table!* In the cupboard high above the refrigerator, I pulled out a box containing four gold-rimmed china cups, each with an elegant gold letter J. Probably they'd been wedding presents and remained in the box sixty years because gold paint was *tacky*, but there I was, teetering on a chair and wondering if they were worth anything. Now and then, Ateca glanced over at me but said nothing. I felt watched but not judged, and carried on.

I found hundreds of letters I'd sent in old Rakestraw's bags and manila envelopes all over the house – in hall closets, in the bottom desk drawer along with ancient dog tennis balls, in Mom's side of the closet behind her shoes. I tried reading one, but it made me feel carsick, as if the time travel involved affected my inner ear. Even the sight of my own handwriting, like my own voice when recorded, made me cringe. Maybe I was afraid my letters would contradict the stories I'd been telling myself.

My mother had written me several letters a week for more than forty-five years, which amounted to something like 4,160.

Even the times I was living near her, the letters still arrived. I may have been cavalier reading them, yet I'd needed those letters. Needed my name in her loopy handwriting, her excitable capital letters and exclamation marks. I'd saved most of them, and like my letters here, they slept in folders and carrier bags all over my house in Scotland. I meant to read them again one day, I supposed. Why had she always said I got my writing talent from my father? Dad could write a concise report on the economics of shipping from Novorossiysk, but it was clear *she* was the person who could express her feelings – who needed to express her feelings – in writing. Had she been bumping Dad up all along, because she sensed her own superiority? A mortal crime for a fifties housewife who thought divorce was the devil. Being superior, not the bumping up. She ran the show at home; he paid the bills and made the rules. Anything outside those remits was foreign territory. My father had written me rarely and his notes were blunt and dry. *Dear Daughter. The Bears lost again. C'est la vie. x Dad.* Oddly, the dearth of his letters never put a dent in my belief that I was his favourite.

I came across a stamped unopened envelope addressed to me. The address was a Scottish one from almost forty years ago. In the letter, my mother made a joke about how hard her life was. The fights between Dad and my brother over my brother's ponytail. The sulky moods of my sister, the way she kept rejecting her. Dad getting mad at her on budget night again, over some stupid cheque stub she'd forgotten to fill in. *Heavens to Betsy!* But he was from an Irish family, she said, so he couldn't help being tight with money. Even the dog was not her friend, always running away when she called. *I need you to come home now and help with me with this mess!* She finished the letter with capital letters. *COME HOME NOW.*

Why hadn't she sent it? Maybe she'd lost it under a pile of dirty clothes, written another and posted that one instead. Or maybe she'd already sent too many begging letters and felt humiliated. *Come home now* echoed Ateca's regular commands, but my mother's letter unsettled me for another reason. All those years I'd been telling myself that my mother hadn't tied me to her apron strings. It had suited me to believe that – it let me off the hook – but here was proof of apron strings galore. Damn, damn, damn. It was so annoying to learn I'd been wrong again. I was a fantasist.

Ateca turned off the television and I heard Mom stirring in her wheelchair. A soft whimpering and feminine yawn as she rose from wherever she went when she was asleep. I put the letter away and went to crouch beside her. She opened her eyes and when she saw me, smiled as if she'd not seen me in decades.

'It's you!' she said, reaching for me with both hands.

'It's me,' I replied. Whoever the hell that was.

'Are you all right?'

'Yup.'

Pause. The pause meant she didn't believe me.

'Good,' she said.

I'm home, Mom, I thought. Here I am, at last. As I thought this, it was as if my scattered and ragged selves sighed with relief – it was exhausting, being restless and discontent – and sank into the life I'd left behind, a whole being again. This life was still my shape, a perfect fit. It was tempting to just let gravity have its way and stay. Such a sweet ache of belonging. Why had I hankered after an exile's life? I took her hands in mine and feeling melodramatic, said:

'I'm home now, Mom. Here I am, at last.'

'That makes me happy,' she said immediately, but also casually. As if what I'd said wasn't that big a deal. Then she asked, in her polite way, what she'd already asked a dozen times that day:

'Can you please tell me the time?'

'Time for a little "Do-Re-Mi", Mom?'

'Correct!'

In Orbit

Seventeen years old
Europe, 1971

From the start, nothing about Europe was as I'd imagined. The original plan – as conceived by my parents – had been to be an au pair for three weeks in Dublin, then visit family friends in Belgium, Switzerland and London. It was a loosely knit itinerary, but nevertheless, sitting at our dining table, it made sense to us all. I'd be under the roof of someone they trusted every night.

But things began to go awry as soon as I got on the plane – my first flight! – to Shannon. The stewardess spilled a whole Coke on my mom-sewed India print skirt, creating a stickiness I'd remember for five decades. Even when my skirt dried it was still sticky. My seatmate was a neighbour from home, red-haired Mrs O'Hara, and I was to spend the first night with her family in Limerick. I wasn't tired, so agreed to go out dancing with her nieces. So far, Ireland was darker and dirtier than I'd imagined, and the people were much sharper, cannier. I was besotted. The two nieces, both my age, claimed to be in awe of my fishnet tights and minidress, of the fact I was Californian – *Sure now, what were you thinking, coming to a shite hole like this?* – but they were far above me in every way. As soon as we were out of the house, they began smoking cigarettes, one after the other. They swore fluently and drank straight vodka from cough syrup bottles in their handbags. One of them sported an angry-looking bruise on her neck. They took my naïve jet-lagged self – gawky, pale, taller than anyone there – to a bar and ordered a round of double vodka tonics. When the DJ put on 'Stayin' Alive', they raced to the dance floor squealing, tossed their handbags down and began gyrating. A disco ball rotated on the ceiling, and flecks of light swam over us like pale fish. I danced too, albeit failing to gyrate.

At 10pm, the bar staff called out *Last orders! Last orders!* This meant nothing to me. Orders? Dominican nuns were an order. I'd never been in a bar before. In California, I wouldn't be able to legally enter a bar for three more years. When we stumbled out to the freezing July drizzle, we weren't alone. Three pimply faced boys had attached themselves to us, and the nieces didn't seem bothered about that at all. They were still smoking, drinking, swearing softly and constantly. *Jaysus, will you give me a fag, I'm fecking gasping here.* I'd not slept in almost two days and I wasn't used to vodka, and yet I felt clear-headed, perhaps even sober. Nevertheless, without my noticing, the nieces vanished with their boys and I found myself kissing my boy in a dark wet alley. Maybe I was drunk after all. I didn't feel cold, though part of my brain informed me – quite neutrally – that my skin was numb. We kissed and I was impressed. Look at me, I thought. Not even in Ireland a day, and already in a dark alley being kissed. When I got tired of pretending to enjoy it, I pulled away. I could hear the nieces giggling nearby and hoped it was time to head home.

'Fecking feck. How am I going to walk with these blue balls?'

'What do you mean?' I couldn't see his problem. He wasn't holding flowers of any description.

'Never you fecking mind.'

I could see he was cranky, but I was too happy and sleepy to think about it. As my mother would say – without irony – Ireland was charming, just charming.

When I got off the bus in Dublin the next day, I was met by the couple I was to au pair for. I had much babysitting under my belt by now, and felt prepared. On the car ride home, the husband and wife didn't speak to each other. Nor did they speak to me. It was their Irish reserve, I decided. Their children, a toddler and a baby, were at the childminder's – presumably someone temporary till my arrival – and the house was clean and empty. I was shown my room, which was also clean and very cold. The bathroom was the coldest room I'd ever been in, and this was July. Not only that, but there was no shower and the toilet was bizarre. High above it, clinging to the wall, was a gurgling black box with a chain hanging down to eye level. I looked everywhere for a way to flush the toilet – it needed to be flushed badly – but was afraid of the chain. What if I pulled the gurgling box off the wall and killed myself? Finally, I had to ask. My hostess demonstrated how to flush the toilet, while I stood there blushing, watching my shame swirl away.

'When do I look after the children?' I asked, over a silent meal of fatty lamb chops, chips and peas. I hated peas. And fat. I wished the children were not in bed so early. It had been easy talking to them earlier, even if conversation wasn't possible.

'Oh, yes. Well, I'm not sure,' said the husband, looking nervously at his purse-lipped wife.

'Only if we go out somewhere in the evening,' she said, pouring wine for herself.

'Which is never together,' mumbled her husband.

An awkward pause.

'You don't need to be worrying about the kids, now. You must do what you want here,' she said, smiling, but her voice wasn't friendly. Her eyes flickered over me with impatience.

'Oh. All right,' I said. I didn't want to do anything in particular. I'd only imagined getting to know an Irish family and playing with children.

There was no more talk that evening and I was in my cold bedroom by 9pm, writing in my diary. I was sure that I was in a household about to erupt with rabid unhappiness, and while the dynamics between the husband and wife were quite different from my parents, the atmosphere was unpleasantly familiar. *Dear Diary. I love Ireland, but this house is crummy.* I'd read *On the Road* and also *As I Walked Out One Midsummer Morning.* By morning I had a plan which took something from both books. I took a bus from their suburb into Dublin and bought a backpack from an army navy store. It was brown canvas, with a soft frame and two external pockets. I transferred my favourite items from my new Samsonite suitcase into my backpack, then explained I was going to tour Ireland since they had no apparent need of me. I said it shyly and half hoped I'd be contradicted.

'Super,' said the wife, not looking up from her magazine. The husband was out and the children were in the other room.

'All right if I leave my suitcase here for a while?'

'Of course. On you go!'

And then I was off. Dublin was worth at least one night and day, and I booked into a bed and breakfast for £3.50. A bed and breakfast! The name amused me because it was so literal, so stripped down. Like calling a restaurant a food-and-drink. *I'm hungry, let's find a food-and-drink.* I left my pack, pocketed my key and wandered around the city in a heightened daze. Phoenix Park, O'Connell Street, The Liffey. I'd known there were old buildings in Europe, but they'd been theoretical buildings. I wasn't prepared for their reality and had no defences. California was a bit of fluff. Recent fluff. A hundred and twenty-three years ago, it hadn't even been a state. Here was where real permanence lived. These terraces of grey stone houses, these twelfth-century churches and grand government offices. Could both places – San Rafael and Dublin – exist? Yes, but I wasn't old enough or deep enough to contain both yet, and California slid off my consciousness like the melting popsicle I was eating slid off the stick. Called an ice lolly here. Bought in a paper shop. A shop called a paper shop! It was as funny as bed and breakfast.

Within a few hours I met a boy outside The Buttery at Trinity College. I'd been strolling around the square, enjoying the proximity of books and academia, and noticed him noticing me. I gave him a broad smile. That's how bold Europe made me.

'Fancy a coffee?' he asked. Coffee with an article in front, *a* coffee!

'Sure,' I said, and within a few hours I had lost my virginity.

He offered me beans on toast afterwards, which I found only slightly less disappointing. Why would anyone think soggy toast was a good idea? I found my way back to my bed and breakfast about midnight, not feeling as different as I'd expected but proud to be hymen-less. It was 1971. Virgins were not cool.

The next morning, someone came in my room and sat on my bed. I was so tired. I couldn't open my eyes, but I felt the bed tilt as this person sat and then lay down next to me. Why wasn't I worried? Because it was Nicholas Ross, the English boy who'd died in a car accident last year, and it was nice he was next to me, just lying there. I loved him with all the passion an untried relationship can arouse. I could hear traffic outside, someone in the room next door coughing, the landlady hoovering downstairs. I was in my bed and awake, but I was also not awake because I couldn't open my eyes or move. A delicious paralysis. I was flooded with comfort, and then I fell back asleep.

When I finally woke properly, I remembered losing my virginity and the ghostly visitation but didn't dwell on either. Life was rushing at me with such force, everything faded almost as soon as it happened because I had to be ready for the next new thing. Which right now was an Irish breakfast in the dining room downstairs, with the lace curtains and sideboard topped with bowls of prunes and condiments like Brown Sauce. Another no-nonsense name. Cigarette smoke filled the air.

'You'll be wanting a cooked breakfast,' I was told by an unhealthy-looking person, vaguely female.

'Sure.'

My plate had two fried eggs, crispy at the edges, two strips of bacon called rashers and as thick as slices of ham, a pink square of sausage meat, a slice of fried bread and some fried tomatoes. Soda bread was served on a side dish, with butter. Most of these items were new to me. I ate everything, washing it down with tea. The fried tomatoes – tomatoes with a soft *a* – seemed wrong and tasted terrible. Otherwise, I was happy. So far, travelling was a series of things going wrong, strange food and strange toilets. All this amounted to adventure, which made it fine.

Checking out of the bed and breakfast, I shouldered my pack and embarked on my great adventure, thumbing (occasionally on the wrong side of the road) through Ireland, England and Scotland, followed by Belgium, Switzerland and France. I applied my talent for idealising to Europe itself. My impressions were intense but juvenile. Europe could do no wrong. Every particle of terrible food, every atom of smoke-filled air, each crumbling edifice was wonderful. Nothing said with an accent sounded dumb, no back street was too grubby. I yearned for Europeans to love me too, and then I yearned to *be* European. If only I'd been born here. It didn't matter where, everywhere was equal. Bognor Regis. Sneem. Ballybunion. They were all equal because I was skimming their surfaces, too smitten to properly notice much. Switzerland was clean, and the Swiss ate cheese and cold meat for breakfast. Their chocolate was better than Hershey bars. In France, people washed their bottoms in a separate toilet just for bottoms. In Brussels, I stayed with an American family I'd known all my life, so it just seemed American with a thin layer of foreignness spread over it. Mayonnaise on chips. Waffle stands on street corners. Their son loved Gordon Lightfoot, and forever after I would associate

Brussels with reading a beloved's mind like a paperback novel. I understood that unspoken adoration.

Hitch-hiking was easy. It was a revelation I could go anywhere for free. Nothing bad happened, aside from some shenanigans in France in the back of a van. After hours of driving in silence, with just the occasional attempt to communicate – *Ca va? Très bien, merci! Bon, bon* – he parked in a forest infested with savage man-eating boars, or so he told me. Then he asked for sex using sign language. I said no, in sign language and in words. It became clear he was not asking, but telling me to prepare for the act itself. His tone was so polite, so soft, it was difficult to believe he meant business. Was it possible to sound coarse in French? It was the middle of the night. I had no idea where we were and was more afraid of being eaten by wild boars than dealing with his lust, which was quickly sated. Twice. Despite his refusal to accept my *nons*, it was likely he didn't consider me raped – and in a way, neither did I. Maybe there was a word for sex one agreed to passively, out of politeness and fear of boars. There was so much I didn't know. Later he dropped me off on the outskirts of a small village. The sun was rising, everything was glowing, and the streets were quiet aside from the sound of roosters and the occasional Vesta motorbike. And then there was the aroma of baking bread, wafting out of a bakery window. I stood on the dusty path below and inhaled it. I wasn't hurt. Nothing important had been stolen. *Well, will you look at me*, I told the invisible audience I was convinced cared. *Here I am, an American suburban girl alone in a French village at dawn*. I thought the scene would be great in a movie.

I made lots of friends that summer, mostly drivers and other hitch-hikers. I felt happier than I'd felt since childhood. Even so, one evening in a bleak bed and breakfast near Belfast, loneliness suddenly drenched me like a downpour. Maybe it was the stained floral wallpaper and sour-smelling carpet. No one here knew me, and no one I knew, knew where I was. Who was I, even? There was no obvious answer to this. I had to live through the heaviness, the scariness. I couldn't even write about it in my diary. But by the time I was on the ferry to Scotland the next day, I was returned to my old resilient self. It was as relieving as if I'd just run into an old friend. *Hey, is it really you? It's you!*

Now and then I referred to the itinerary – by now a very grubby piece of paper – and visited each of the family friends, which in my view made me a responsible daughter. No one suggested it wasn't wise to hitch-hike or that I should phone my parents. Maybe I presented such a confident self, they'd not been concerned. Or they privately tutted, but felt it wasn't their place to tell me what to do. A third possibility was that they did remind me of the dangers of the road, of the extent my parents worried, and I simply ignored them. I remember neither guilt nor fear nor homesickness.

Things kept not turning out the way they were supposed to, which was fine because it meant I was having adventures. Six weeks after arriving, I retrieved my suitcase from the house of marital discord in Dublin and took a bus to Shannon airport. I couldn't find the Laker Airways check-in desk. Finally, an airport official explained that Laker Airways had declared bankruptcy a few days ago – hadn't I heard? It had been in all the headlines. Another flight was found which left in five hours. I mulled over my predicament. I'd spent every one of my American Express cheques and only had enough change for a hamburger. I felt sorry for myself – sorry enough to justify slipping a corduroy cap into my pocket. No one said anything as I walked away. Well! I thought. Maybe stealing was like hitch-hiking. Maybe only fools needed money to get by.

When I finally walked into my home, having hitch-hiked from San Francisco airport, it felt like I was re-entering an orbit. My mother dropped the dishcloth she was holding and cried:

'Oh, thank God you're here! I was so worried.' Then she turned and shouted down the hall: 'Come quick! Look who's here!'

My brother appeared from his room, his wiry hair all scrunched up on one side, so I guessed he'd been in bed.

'Hey,' he said, with a grin. 'About time, turd face.'

My sister came scooting from her room, halted and gave me a hard stare. *Are you really my big sister?*

'Hey, Tootsie Pop,' I said and picked her up. She giggled, then wriggled to get down.

'Did you bring me a present?'

'Nope.'

Then my father came down the hall, walked up to me and said:

'Where've you been?' He looked older, I thought. Or sad.

I explained about Laker going bankrupt. And then he said:

'Yeah, yeah, I know about that. Okay, good. Go take a shower. You smell terrible. I'm taking the dog for a walk.' He walked past me, out the door, still looking strange.

'He just means you smell . . . smell like you've been travelling, that's all, honey. You look beautiful. I am so glad to see you.'

'Thanks, Mom.' She'd not hugged me. Neither had my father. We were not a hugging family in those early years. Or maybe it was my smell.

'Your father's glad too,' she whispered. 'It's been hard on him. Not knowing where you were.'

'Didn't you get my postcards?' I'd sent three in six weeks. One said: *I'm at a banquet after starving all my life. Freedom is where it's at. Love and peace, Cynthia.* Wasn't I a considerate daughter?

'Yes, yes. Thank you. Look! I pinned them up.'

'Cool,' I said, noticing my cards on the bulletin board. I had an urge to unpin them, read what I'd written, see if I'd been clever.

'Oh, I could eat you up. Which reminds me, are you hungry? I was just about to put dinner on the table, but now your father's gone out again . . . even though the dog's just had a walk.'

What was going on with my father? Maybe when he heard my voice, the momentum of anxiety had been too strong for him to feel relief. Maybe he'd been pining all summer as if I'd died. Maybe he hadn't been able to walk past my bedroom door without wanting a strong drink. The sight of me now probably confirmed his suspicions because in a way I *had* died. I was no longer someone he even liked the look of. Or maybe he was just having a rotten time anyway, and hadn't been giving me much thought at all. The bills were piling up, he heard about a party he'd not been invited to, his hair was receding.

In the bathroom mirror I considered myself. When I'd left, my hair had been straight and smooth, my cheeks pink and my skin clear. Now I noticed how pale I was, the darkness under my eyes, and the way my hair was wild. Bushy and knotted in places. I was also thinner, I decided. Muscular. I closed my eyes under the hot shower. Europe had been short on showers and it felt good. I thought about the corduroy cap I'd stolen. I hadn't even thought about it, just seen the cap, wanted it, slid it into my bag. Then I remembered the dawn after the boar-infested forest. I'd stood in that tiny French village, alone and sticky-thighed, closed my eyes to the sun for a second and breathed in the smell of bread. When I opened them, a baker was holding out a baguette from his open window. He wasn't young. He had a fat man's face, rosy and round. He didn't want my money and he said something softly in French, which I already knew was the most beautiful language in the world. He blew me a kiss, and I said *merci* and walked away. That bread was best loaf I'd ever tasted. It restored everything.

Get Rid of It

I'd bought a small Christmas tree from Andy's that morning. Hid it in the garage, but now it was in the living room and I was decorating it while my mother was in the bathroom with Ateca. I could hear the shower running, which meant Mom would not be happy. One of the remnants of her personality that defied dementia was her modesty. To be naked in front of anyone was still torture, but boy oh boy, did she need that shower.

It had been a fraught evening. I'd taken us to a friend's house for dinner. They were my parents' oldest friends, and when Dad was alive, having dinner at each other's houses had been a tradition. The men cooked the main course – competitively, always upping the ante – and kept everyone's glass filled, while the women fussed with salads and desserts, serving and clearing plates. Mom, who no one had expected to see at that table again, happily gobbled everything put in front of her. Ateca sat by her side and I sat across from them, feeling as content as a person can feel when their mother keeps not dying and they've just been given the perfect White Russian to drink. But halfway through dinner, the unmistakable aroma of human excrement drifted over the gourmet lasagne and salad with roasted beetroot pierced with rosemary. It was as if someone had slid a freshly soiled diaper over all the dinner plates, and people put their forks down and made small talk. The source was obvious to everyone but Mom, who kept shovelling food in her mouth. I looked at Ateca, and she gave me an eyebrows-raised mouth-downturned *What can I do?* There might have been a small smirk in her look. *Welcome to my life, you spoiled white person who never had to leave your own country to earn enough to feed your kids.*

When she wheeled my freshly showered mother down the hall, I stopped them and told Mom to close her eyes.

'Why?'

'I've got a surprise for you.'

'Delightful!'

She clapped her hands and then pressed them hard on her scrunched-up eyes like a kid. I wheeled her into the living room, turned off the lights and turned on the Christmas tree lights. All the ornaments she'd made over the years were there – the felt angels with pipe cleaner wings, the clowns with sequin eyes glued to thread spools. And all the ornaments she'd bought, each one representing a shopping trip in the past, probably harried and happy in equal measure. My mother loved Christmas. She loved everything about it. She even loved the fruit cake that came in a tin every year from some relative, and which no one else touched. I anticipated squeals of delight and many kisses. Maybe even tears of gratitude.

'Open your eyes, Mom.'

She opened them. Sucked in air through her teeth, then said: 'Oh! Oh! Oh! *What is that?*'

'It's a Christmas tree, Mom.'

'Well, get rid of it!'

'Isn't it pretty?'

'No, it's creepy.'

'But, Mom.'

'She doesn't like new things,' said Ateca, as if I was a dimwit. 'New things scare her.'

'It's not new. She loves Christmas trees.'

'Is it gone yet?' Mom had her hands over her eyes again.

'Take it away,' ordered Ateca in a level tone, so I moved it into my bedroom, trying not to sulk like a fifteen-year-old. The next day, I undecorated the tree and put it in the backyard by the marsh.

I was writing a story about what happened after my father died, referring to a list I'd made at the time. I remembered thinking that if I just wrote facts, they'd amount to something solid and true. At the end of my story, I described a jolly afterlife. My father may have died, but that was okay because now he was at a party down the hall, and I'd catch up with him later. I liked that idea very much and it made a good ending. But when I pictured catching sight of Dad's blond head bobbing in a party crowd, my throat hurt and my eyes watered. I wanted to believe in that party room so badly.

I went back to Scotland a week before Christmas. My husband was getting a new knee and I wanted to be there with him. Luckily for my conscience, though less so for my ego, Mom had a fantastic Christmas without me. Ateca's son, wife and four children came to stay for a few weeks. My sister visited on Christmas Day and reported they cooked a pig in the backyard, and guess what, someone had dumped a perfectly good Christmas tree there.

'A whole pig?'

'I kid you not. I saw the ears, the little piggy tail.'

'What, on a spit?'

'No, the Fijian way. Underground.'

They'd dug up Dad's overgrown zucchini beds, lit a fire, laid the pig on top, then buried the whole shebang for hours.

'How was Mom?'

'The truth?'

'Yes.' I braced myself to hear she'd locked herself in the bathroom.

'Happier than I've ever seen her.'

'No.'

'Yes.'

Ateca later told me the youngest grandchildren had called my mother *Favourite Momma* in Fijian and covered her in kisses all day long. My children had never taken to their grand-mother with spontaneous physical affection. What was wrong with us all?

A Year is a Circle

Sixty years old
Scotland and California, 2013

It was Valentine's Day, the day of hearts beating fast, but my father's heart beat too fast and then it stopped. I cried a bit and waited to feel depressed, but instead noticed that death was suddenly everywhere. Within a week, Uncle Lew died. Then Judith from over the road. Nelson Mandela began to die. Being alive or being dead started to feel like the only difference between people that really mattered. There they were and here we were, a pitiful handful by comparison. I couldn't stop thinking about the huge gang my dad had joined, and imagined them not acting dead. Like Road Runner who kept running in mid-air because no one had told him the cliff ran out.

My father had loved his life as if it was a thing outside himself, an expensive car or a beautiful woman. If he was still aware somehow, I bet he wished he still had that life. Or would he? Maybe there was a better party down the hall behind a locked door, the one that the ride-share driver had told me about decades ago on my way to Mexico with Cowboy. Just because you can't hear anything doesn't mean it's silent in that room, or that it doesn't exist. I pictured the dead with their favourite tipple looking for their also-dead siblings, friends, parents, grandparents. Just like you do at a party when you arrive alone – cruise around with a silly half-smile till you spot a familiar face. I imagined Dad's mother spotting him across the room.

Grandma, without her liver spots and paunch. Her face lighting up, then his face lighting up too. *Hey, Mom, is that really you? It is you! Oh my God!*

February kept chugging along very slowly. I went to California for the funeral, an event I'd imagined so often it felt like a memory. In addition to the death cluster in Dad's wake, there was a miraculous pregnancy, a dispute between neighbours who'd been friends for decades, and my roses bloomed early. I began thinking this was a peculiar month and it was because Dad had died. Then I figured this heightened awareness might only be applied to new loss – like new love.

In March, one of my daughters announced her third pregnancy. My other daughter was accepted onto a university programme in New Orleans, and I tried not to think of guns. Time continued to be sluggish, as if it was constantly yawning. I began to read newspapers with more attention. A family of four died in the Lake District when their living room dropped into a sinkhole. Someone working in an office in Virginia pulled out a gun and shot three people from his window. I took note of these deaths and shivered at the randomness. At least Dad got to get old.

In April, I met some Italian cousins I hadn't known the existence of, and we – me and my second husband – spent a week at their house in Domodossola, Italy. It turned out I was related to an entire village, and a dozen relatives followed us everywhere and gave us gifts. Every dinner began after 9pm and lasted hours, and grief hadn't killed my appetite. Or maybe I was not grief-stricken. Maybe I was delaying grief by imagining he was in some secret party down the hall. We stayed in Italy long enough for me to imagine moving there, learning Italian, making a new home. Then I imagined getting homesick for Scotland, as well as for California. Layers and layers of homesickness. Maybe I would feel homesick even if I'd never left home. Thatcher died.

I hadn't liked her, but I was repelled by people's glee over this. Death is death. Dead people have no defences, damn it. Then the country-and-western singer George Jones died. My dad's name was also George Jones. *Not a good year for the George Jones's*, I could hear him say.

In May, I heard my first two novels would be reincarnated as e-books. Having novels out of print was humiliating. They sat on Amazon, brazenly announcing my failure, costing one penny. *How much are they paying you?* That's how Dad greeted every announcement of an accepted story. Not much. Sometimes nothing. My firstborn moved near us, for work reasons. My youngest made plans to move away from us, to Glasgow, for university. He'd be home for another three months, but he acted as if he was already gone. I missed their child-selves, because I'd felt closer to them then. I lived in a perpetual state of nostalgia for their freckles and the sight of them crunching their way through my cinnamon toast.

I went home to California again. Mom was incredibly calm and happy – I was very sad. Dad's *New Yorkers* were still on the coffee table. He'd been sitting in his chair next to them when the now legendary conversation took place. *So, Dad*, said my brother, *would you like to keep spending time in the hospital? Or would you prefer to stay home from now on, stop all medication and let nature run its course? Hospice or hospital, what do you want?* Dad had sighed hard and said: *Jesus Christ. I want to go to a decent Italian restaurant. And then I want to get drunk.*

Me and my sister drove to Santa Barbara to meet an old friend of our father's. I brought a sandwich baggie full of his ashes in case he felt left out. My husband came too. I'd always struggled with merging my two worlds socially, but he was a force for good on that road trip.

*

In June, I tried to finish my novel inspired by my parents. How had they stayed married for sixty years without killing each other? Their house was often tense with angry words or silence, but I remembered them smiling at each other – real smiles – and sometimes laughing hysterically. One morning when they were in their seventies, I opened their bedroom door to find them asleep, their arms around each other. It was hard to capture the complexity of a long marriage. I wanted to tell the truth, or a truth, about the thing that replaced romance and felt like hatred some days.

I phoned my mother every week. She always sounded the same. *I'm fine! How are you! I love you!* One day I pushed her a little. *What are you doing right now?* And she said: *I'm looking at the blinds. And they're cryingly sad.* Only a four-year-old or an eighty-four- year-old would think of using words this way. Those blinds hadn't been raised in two decades. Dad kept meaning to get them fixed. Iain Banks died of cancer. Dad, keep an eye out for this guy, I thought. *Proper writer. Made tons of money.*

In July, I was awarded a grant by the Society of Authors to finish my novel. This made me feel like a proper writer for at least ten minutes. My husband and I went to Portugal for a week. In the afternoons, after I swam, we drank beer and played cards on our balcony. I won three times, he won 254 times. He got a funny expression and pretended he didn't care when I won. Then we fell out over where to eat. He wanted to eat chicken madras at the same Indian restaurant every night. *We're in a Portuguese fishing town!* I said, sounding like my dad. *Eat the goddamn fish!* All my children (aside from the pregnant daughter) ran in a marathon called Tough Mudder. At the end they were covered in mud, blue-lipped and could not speak. *Well done!* I said and hoped they never repeated this.

Dad's good ear had been his right one, so when we walked he'd always been on my left. Now, when I took a walk alone, I turned to my left and imagined him there with his terrible dog,

Beau. Dad wore shorts and his knees were scabbed from all the falling down he'd done lately. He was wearing the desert boots he'd been so delighted to find back in the stores. Then I looked straight ahead and there were his younger, thinner selves in his lumberjack shirts and old Levi's, and I was trying to catch up to him because it was going to be fun where he was going. Some days his older self with the scabbed knees suggested we walk to Andy's for coffee, extend our time together. Now I always answered *Of course!* I often put him off when he was alive, saying I was in a hurry. No time for Andy's coffee. Elmore Leonard died. My sister's favourite author. *Dad – look who's here! Ask him if his first book really was true.*

It was now five months since my father died. I thought about him more, not less. I visualised him in empty seats, like the back seat as we were driving to town. He hated the back seat, so he always gave me his *what-the-hell* expression. He seemed close, and appeared to accept being dead with equanimity. That old head-tilting and self-mocking shrug. *Hey, what can I do? It's your mother's fault.* His silly expressions always made me smile, but they made me cry now too. I was experiencing missing him in very slow motion. I slowly realised I'd always been slow. By the time I got used to being pregnant, I had a toddler.

In August my sister took some of Dad's ashes to Trinity, where they stayed every summer in a cabin. Lots of people toasted him by the swimming hole and poured their drinks into the river. She told me this on the phone. For the millionth time I wondered why I was living six thousand miles away. I was offered a job at Edinburgh University. This meant I was a proper writer – *I am! I am!* I chanted to myself. It almost worked. At the end of August, Seamus Heaney died. So did John Bellany. Had famous people always died so frequently? Since Dad died, all I heard on the news was the deaths of other amazing people.

*

In September, two of my children visited their dad in Thailand, where he had a series of young girlfriends who spoke little English. This could sound sleazy if you said it a certain way, but I imagined him having proper relationships with these girls. Feel real affection and respect – maybe even love. It was easy to be judgemental, but in a way it was every man's dream. Firm flesh, no challenging discussions, the possibility of romance. I tried to believe he was truly okay, otherwise I'd ruined his life. He hadn't been easy to live with – he never put the clean cups and bowls back on the right shelves, and he had a way of sneering when I got upset. He'd been annoying, but I was beginning to realise everyone was annoying if you spent much time with them. No doubt, I'd been an annoying wife. And now I was married to a high school teacher and my children's father lived in Thailand with a girl whose name I couldn't remember. My dad used to make fun of that first husband. Now I detected some respect, at least for his choice of girlfriend. *Aha! A tiny tame Thai*, he said, then chuckled. *Wise choice.*

A man was killed on the Black Isle overtaking a tractor. Flowers covered the spot, as if the place where people last breathe retains a remnant of them. Souls? I wondered if we secretly miss the mystery of religion. Pretend to be atheists in the same way people used to pretend to be religious – mostly because everyone else is.

October, and time was regaining normal speed. A week before Dad died, he'd said on the phone: *My life is awry! I'm leaking time!* My children kept moving and I felt stable by comparison. For years I'd craved stability, and now it just happened without me even trying. My daughter's baby was in breach, with a month to go. A storm in the Philippines killed over ten thousand people. Life seemed so cheap, when you saw the photos of bodies, all piled up, but I couldn't bear the thought of her losing this baby. A helicopter crashed into the North Sea, just after another helicopter crashed into a Glasgow pub. *Not a good year for helicopters*, said Dad.

My husband lost two stone. We went for a bike ride, but gave up after the first hill. I couldn't remember hills being such a problem before. We celebrated our fifth wedding anniversary. This was my second marriage and his fourth. I was Wife Number Four! This meant I could never take myself seriously. Our house was littered with wedding presents from his previous marriages. Our mantelpiece alone had three of these reminders. One of them was the model sailboat I'd given him for his third marriage. It made me laugh, in a self-mocking way. A fourth wife could never be smug. A second or possibly a third wife could believe she'd be different, but not a fourth wife. I wasn't just his wife, I was his *current* wife. I fully expected his fickle heart to tire of me one day. I had maybe five more years, tops. I intended to enjoy them. He played guitar every night while I read, and we both liked Dylan and Joni. He told awful jokes and laughed at them, but no one's perfect. He mended clothes and sewed the buttons back on, and for that alone I was willing to risk heartbreak. He thought Dad had liked him. My father despised every man I introduced him to. He was polite but made fun of them the instant they were out of earshot. *How's Pedro*, he'd ask on the phone. *His name's Peter, Dad. Yeah, whatever*, he'd answer.

My dad's old fishing buddy died. *Dad – look for Deke! Trout season, right?* My husband was thinner and thinner. I wondered if he'd spotted Wife Number Five already. A man who used to give me lifts died. I read it in the paper, and it just said *died suddenly*. Did he die in the middle of a sentence? *Pass the salt and . . . ?* Doris Lessing died. I thought she was already dead, but still.

November arrived, and it snowed for four days. I stayed home from work because the road was icy. Scotland's winters had never failed to feel like a novelty to Dad. I pictured him with his favourite dog in the snow, because I'd no doubt that wherever Dad was, Beau was there too, licking his bare legs. Then I pictured him with every dog he'd owned, a long row of them. I tried to remember names but could only think of four. Then I pictured him with his dead friends and parents. I pretended he was not entirely gone, that no one was. If this was true, I hoped he was okay with it. I tried to finish my novel about my parents' marriage, but lost faith in it. What made me think my novel added so much to the world?

I remembered Dad saying, with a snort of laughter (when I nagged him to be more protective of her): *Oh, your mother! She's going to outlive me, damn it!* He'd probably fantasised about widowerhood. A parallel life, where he got to marry a soulmate. Then I remembered how he came home early from his book club last year, went straight to sit next to Mom and tried to hold her hand. Had he worried about how she'd manage without him? Or had he been frightened of dying, and already missing the deep familiarity of his own life with her? Was it an *I'm sorry* gesture? *I'm sorry I left you at home tonight, and for all the other nights.* She'd not been enthusiastic about taking his hand. He had to coax her, and then I took a photo because it felt important.

I fought with my sister by text, while shopping in Tesco. It was upsetting. My cousin wrote to say her mother was going into hospice care. My aunt was hot on her husband's heels. I gave a reading in my local library to three middle-aged women and some old guy who snored. This should have been demoralising, but I loved it. Me and my sister made up. I'd never forget our terrible words to each other, but *C'est la vie!* as Mom would say.

December. Another grandchild was born. She weighed almost 6 lb and had – to her mum's horror – bright red hair. Nelson Mandela finished dying. A snowstorm hit and we had power cuts. Thousands of trees fell. A truck driver died on the A9. He was delivering produce for Marks & Spencer. I made Christmas cards on the kitchen table. The photo this year was one my husband had taken of our snowy track. I glued the photo on some card and sprinkled glitter on it. Glitter was everywhere. Floor, chairs, kettle, my glass of port. Paul Torday died of cancer. A fine and modest writer. Wrote *Salmon Fishing in the Yemen* when he retired. This fact encouraged me.

Christmas came and no one fought. I had a rotten cold and went through the holiday in a Lemsip fug. I had great kids and friends and a husband who might or might not stay forever. I was one of the luckiest women on earth. I didn't have to remind myself not to send Dad a gift, and this didn't make me cry. I wore his L.L.Bean watch and often forgot to let it remind me of the brevity of life, or of Dad. I just liked the watch. My daughter decided red hair was beautiful after all.

January. It was almost a year since Dad died. I didn't want it to be more than a year. A year felt like a circle, and as long as I could say Dad was alive this time last year, he was still here.

A friend's father died of Parkinson's. And then someone's mother died. And then another friend's mother died. Parents were dropping like flies. We walked around stunned at their desertion, but as far as I could tell, no one was incapacitated. I suddenly wanted a dog. It had been four years since I had a dog, long enough in anyone's life to be dog-less, and I set about persuading my husband it was a good idea. He said no on the grounds he'd never had a dog, and was therefore not a dog person. Within a week of the dog idea being rejected, I was only speaking to him when necessary. Then one night he said:

'Okay, I have five words for you.'

'What are the first letters?' We liked to play word games.

'G. A. F. D.'

I thought of God and fine dinners.

'I give up.'

'Get a fucking dog.'

I didn't tell him that was actually four words, because in this second marriage I was learning to stop while I was winning. Ever since I'd lowered my expectations of marriage in general, I'd been much happier. Sometimes I looked back on my first marriage and cringed. I'd been naïve, looking for everything in one person. I reserved a golden Lab puppy online, though both ironically and typically, I started having second thoughts. Dogs were a tie. And barking could be irritating. Was it a mistake? It had been the most beautiful year, weather-wise. I didn't think Scotland had ever been so consistently beautiful.

In February, on Valentine's Day, we got our puppy. *Check her out, Dad. Nice dog*, he said. *Shame about the man.*

I was always on the look-out for signs that Dad might still be around. Thinking of him made my throat ache, but it was a pleasant ache – perhaps because I was at an age when feeling *anything* was good. Some days I chose to think we had a conscious existence after death, and Dad *gathered round* me. He sat in chairs, on benches, in my car, at my desk. He was all his ages, and sometimes he was with his sister or his buddies. One night I was alone, listening to Dad's Glenn Miller CD, setting the table. I lit the candles, set out the wine glasses, and pictured Dad sitting in the living room by the fire. Heard him shout through to me: *Not here, silly. I want to sit in the kitchen with the wine.* So I turned my head to the table and the CD jammed. The song was 'In the Mood', and the line it jammed on was about the loving daddy with the beautiful eyes. I was wearing Dad's green L.L.Bean sweater, and it still smelt of wood-smoke from the fires he lit every night last winter.

Maybe there were graduations of death, as in: freshly dead, meandering, long time gone. Like jet lag, where for a few days

173

part of you is still in the place you left. Maybe being dead was like waking up, only you didn't need to pee first thing. Or, as is commonly accepted, a sudden un-dramatic nothingness. Noise and light and sensation snuffed, like a light switch flicked to *off*. Then the slow alterations which end with us becoming the dirt vegetables grow in, leading to the nourishment of some other life form. Thus, we joined the world in a new way. It was a fact that every person who ever lived was still here – in some form or other – but still, no one could tell me how life began. And nobody knew what happened to consciousness or to memories when we died. As long as those question were unanswered, I was hoping for something a little more engaging than nothing-ness after the heart stopped. I was fine with becoming food for a cete of badgers or even some sorority sisters, but I saw no reason for that to preclude the party room.

Hey, I'm over here! Dad would call to me over the heads of strangers, waving his hands like mad. *Have a martini. You won't believe what lime tastes like here.*

God is God

'Come home! God is calling your mother right now,' Ateca told me on the phone at the end of March.

'How do you know?'

'What?'

'How do you know God is calling her?'

'I hear Him, Sister. Sometimes in the afternoon, but mostly at night.'

Now I was really intrigued. She was so specific.

'Really? You hear his voice out loud? Is he saying her name?' Then I had to add, because I needed to know: 'Was it a man's voice?'

'No, Sister,' she said in a patronising way, as if even a five-year-old knew what I didn't. 'God is not man. Not woman. God is God!'

This time the church sent a deacon for the Last Rites, not a priest. Maybe they were demoting her for crying wolf. *This'll teach you to say you're dying, and then not!* I looked forward to it because deep down I kept hoping to be swept back into Catholicism. As a child, I'd loved it, especially Midnight Mass. The nativity had everything. Maiden in distress followed by royal rescue, and babies were cute. Fantastic stories, lots of candles, stained-glass windows, incense, holy cards that promised wish fulfilment – and no matter how bad you were, the confessional wiped the slate clean every week. Catholics had all the fun.

The deacon was in his fifties with a beer belly, wearing jeans that were too tight, a Gap T-shirt and a Giants baseball cap. Something about his face reminded me of a pig I knew once, and I made a mental note to write the story of Priscilla later. I still had one of her teeth, and every time I saw it I remembered the best kisses of my life. Meanwhile, the deacon was laying out a white lace-edged cloth on the dining table. He lit a single candle and asked us to join him in saying the Lord's Prayer. I would have preferred it if he'd been wearing a dog collar or at least a black suit, but I complied. My mother and I knew all the words, but he didn't seem impressed.

He anointed her from his little bottle of holy water and said:

'In the name of the Father, the Son and the Holy Spirit. Amen.'

'Wah!' my mother said. Her voice was young today, as if it didn't know her age.

He made the sign of the cross on her forehead and then he drew the sign of the cross in the air, mumbled some Latin and slipped a host onto her waiting tongue. I enjoyed the candle, the prayer, the holy water being used in such solemn sequence – a magic spell cast over Mom, promising everlasting life in heaven. I stuck out my tongue for a host and held my breath, ready for my re-entry into the fold. My soul was bouncing around in my chest – *Yippee, let's go! Here we are at last!* But then, with no warning, he began talking about his wife's psoriasis. And then his dog's ticks, which might lead to Lyme disease. And then his son's expensive lifestyle at Stanford. It was like coming out of a matinee to find it still broad daylight and the world its ordinary self. We didn't respond to his chatter. My mother had her hostess face on, polite interest not quite disguising blatant indifference. I nodded once or twice, shook my head in sympathy. I didn't care about his wife or son or dog. His self-importance irritated me. I wanted spiritual sustenance, I wanted wisdom and heart-soaring inspiration. My mother probably just wanted him to shut up so she could have her bear claw, which was already sitting on a plate in the kitchen. He kept talking about his life, cackling at his puns.

'Okay, thanks, Father,' I had to say finally, standing up and extending my hand to shake his.

'I'm not really a Father,' he said. 'Call me Don.'

He shook my hand after a second's frown, turned to my mother, slapped his broad hands together and boomed:

'That's you done, Barbara. You're good to go now!'

'I love you, goodbye!' said my mother. This was code for *Go away!*

'I love you too,' said the deacon, beaming.

I walked him to his car, and on the way back to the house I ran into Isiah, who may have been there a while. He had a way of stepping into the shrubbery and standing very still. Isiah was one of the Fijian men who wanted to marry Ateca. I didn't blame him. Her cooking was exceptional and she had an air of such certainty, no one could fail to feel safe in her presence.

'Isiah!' I said, startling him. 'Go on in. Ateca's in the kitchen.'

'No, no, better not.' He was tall and sad-faced.

That meant she'd told him she didn't want to see him for a while.

'Okay. See you later,' I said, and went back inside.

'He still there?' Ateca asked me. She was shelling prawns from Andy's – not full price, because no matter where Ateca shopped, she acted like she was in Fiji. She would have talked the fish guy down five dollars at least.

'Isiah? Yeah. How did you know?'

'Ha! I know,' she answered, laughing and shaking her head. 'Don't ask me how, but I always know.'

She knew because she's psychic. How do I know? Because while I was writing about her, she sent me a text message. *The Bible says we have to bless each other so we can live in love. I bless you. I bless your heart. Your life. Your health and home. Your family. Your finances. Today is a day of blessing! Please pass this blessing on.*

I sent it back to her, and she responded immediately with a throbbing red heart.

The jury was still out on God, but I believed entirely in Ateca.

Priscilla the Pig

Twenty-three years old
Scotland, 1976

I was in Scotland, living in the countryside, and I was in love with Priscilla. She was a large white pig. That was what she looked like, and also the name of her breed. To my mind, this was as quaint as Brown Sauce and paper shop. Puzzling too – why waste an opportunity to make up a name? It seemed so British, that pared-down modesty that shouted gargantuan confidence. It saved time too, because you immediately knew what to expect, when told you were about to see a large white pig. You saw Priscilla. Except she wasn't really white, she was flesh-coloured. Like a redhead's skin tone, with mud caked to her stumpy legs and the underside of her belly. Her eyes were tiny, brown and human. She looked at me when I talked. Mostly.

Back-to-the-Landers the papers called us. We considered ourselves country people, but that was an illusion. For one thing, I loved Priscilla and only city dwellers and suburbanites fell in love with farm animals. For another, we got lots of things wrong. Priscilla's field turned into a mud bath within days of her arrival because it was too small. The challenge of extending her field was so daunting, dozens of sheets of paper were covered in solutions – none of which came to fruition.

We paid a pig farm man to bring a stud pig to mate with Priscilla and we pretended to ignore her unhappy squeals. It was natural! John Seymour said so in his self-sufficiency guide. Then the pig farm man took his pig away and I proceeded to fatten up pregnant Priscilla. I kept her shed full of clean straw and her trough full of clean water. Fed her kitchen scraps and pig food. Stroked her, scratched her back, cooed and sang to her, and lo – she grew rotund. So rotund, she could hardly walk. We read up on piglet births and complications of pig labour. We chose piglet names. Charlotte, Toby, Cat after Cat Stevens who I loved. I wanted to be like Cat Stevens' 'Hard Headed Woman', despite all evidence indicating my brain was comprised of oatmeal. I imagined men falling in love with my toughness and confidence. I was Pig Girl.

Two months earlier, I'd hitched from London to Scotland with the lyrics of 'Woodstock' playing in my head – about being stardust and needing to get ourselves back to the garden. It was the peak year of my hippiedom. I was as far from my upbringing as I would ever be again, and I thought I was very hunky-dory. I knew about the cottage in Scotland because a few friends from London had already moved there. We didn't call it a commune, that word had too many middle-class connotations. In fact, we didn't call it a farm either. It was too small for that. We were just a bunch of friends living together in an old cottage in the far north. The owner of the house, an acquaintance, was currently in prison for selling stolen goods. We hippies didn't give a fig about crime as long as it wasn't violent. He'd instructed us to modernise the cottage in lieu of rent. Once I arrived and settled in, the deal seemed reasonable. No time stipulations, which was lucky because progress was slow due to lack of funds and lack of skills.

There were about half a dozen of us, but people came and went. There was the Irish boy who teased everyone all the time. And a boy from Sheffield who had the trusting look of a boy adored by his mother. Quite the opposite was a short squat ex-army man who scared me slightly because he had a rifle. He shot rabbits and the occasional pheasant or goose, which we ate.

There were also the twins from Yorkshire, very pretty girls and very practical in the kitchen. And of course, there was the man who ran the show, the one who used to sell us dope in London. I thought of him as Mr Cool. He was the oldest by far and a dominant person by nature, though he was cowed by his much younger girlfriend with blonde hair past her waist. Mr and Mrs Cool had the best bedroom at the gable end of the cottage, whereas I had the box room with the teeny window. I had a crush on them both, but then I had a crush on everyone – except scary Gun Man. Each person seemed unfathomably glamorous. I could only compare this to the kind of love A-list celebrities inspire in fans – not from me, needless to say, because my friends far outshone them.

We planted peas and potatoes and lettuces and carrots, and consulted the John Seymour book for everything. How far apart to plant the lettuces, how to make rabbit stew, yoghurt from goat's milk and rose hip syrup from rose hips. Summer arrived and it was the hottest on record. None of us had the right clothes, and sometimes we girls just wore our bras and shorts made from old jeans. We continually congratulated ourselves on leaving London behind. The grass in Hyde Park was yellow now and water was rationed. Look at us! Barefoot, drinking home-made Ribena, lazing in the shade. Our garden chairs were ripped-out plastic car seats with stuffing pouring out, and I thought them beautiful.

The cottage had previously been a farmworker dwelling attached to a byre for livestock. It sat, a long one-storey building with a corrugated iron roof, in the middle of cow fields about seven miles south of Fraserburgh. We'd knocked out the dividing wall and put in electricity, but we'd no running water aside from a single tap in the kitchen. There was a free-standing boiler in the porch which we filled up with buckets from the kitchen tap. The porch was where rabbits were skinned and gutted and pheasants were plucked. It was also where we had showers by scooping jugs of water from the boiler over our heads. It was almost entirely glassed-in, so I could look out over fields. Sometimes Priscilla stood at her fence, which was ten yards away, and we communed a while. Or that's what I told myself as I serenaded her, naked and shivering. Our toilet was a bucket with an old wooden toilet seat precariously stuck on top. When the bucket became disgusting, we dumped it in a hole we'd dug. It filled quicker than John Seymour led us to believe it would. It was a two-cesspit summer.

For a while, I was utterly happy. Me and Priscilla were in love. It was a love that overrode the pettiness of species or indeed, gender. She made a special noise when I fed her, and I was pretty sure she didn't make that particular snuffling snort to anyone else. Sometimes I went out to see her before I went to bed. It would still be light at midnight, being so far north, and she always trotted over to me. Or, increasingly, waddled. I told her my current thoughts on life, my woes and hopes, and she stood still to let me talk – as long as I kept scratching her head. No pigs are pretty, and Priscilla wasn't an exception. She was ugly, but ugly to such a glorious extent it strayed into beauty. I'd no evidence anyone else thought her beautiful, but I never tired of looking at her. The sight of her *pleased* me. Her skin was rough with individual bristles poking out here and there, sharp as pins, but it was also warm and curiously pleasant to touch. She exfoliated my fingers.

One July night, I was telling her that I finally knew what I wanted from life. I wanted – *all* I wanted – was to own an old stone cottage with fields around it, like this one. I loved everything about country life. I even loved the smell of silage. I'd have a huge field for a pig just like her, with a cosy pigsty in the corner out of the wind. It would be close to my cottage, so I could sit on the doorstep and easily see my pig. Of course I also wanted a man to love, but that was nothing new. A husband inside my dream cottage, maybe mending some farm tool or feeding the fire. Did I want to be a housewife? Was I *allowed* to want to be a housewife with the new women's lib movement insisting that housewives were exploited slaves? It was tricky knowing what to think. Last year I'd given my mother *The Women's Room* and after she read it, she turned on me. *How dare you consider me exploited! I chose to be a housewife. I chose to stay home and raise you darn kids. Now scoot out of here.* She hardly ever lost her temper, so I'd scooted. Now I felt uneasy about the lowly status libbers assigned to housewifery. Like my mother, that life would suit me. I liked cooking and I wanted babies. Maybe six. I was so excited to know what I wanted, the next day I wrote my family and told them all, in separate letters. I even suggested if they cared to support my dream of buying a cottage, cheques were acceptable.

The postman called our house Kinky Cottage. I felt he didn't fully appreciate our serious intent. He had the habit of bringing our post inside the house. Just opened the door without knocking and shouted out *Post!* I thought this meant he wanted to be friends with us, that he was – in effect – visiting us, and I'd offer him a cup of tea. He always refused because he was the postman, just delivering letters to people who weren't organised enough to have a letterbox or slot in their door. He brought me weekly, sometimes daily, letters from my mother, periodic letters from my siblings, and none from my father. Once I sent my mother a photograph of my friends sitting outside the cottage on the old car seats, and my mother wrote back and said they looked like losers. But normally her letters were full of domestic news with lots of exclamation marks, always finishing with variations of *I miss you. When are you coming home? We all miss you.* Sometimes she even asked after Priscilla. *How's that pig of yours?* My brother's letters were often crude, referring to his boners, the breast sizes of girls he wanted to know better, and how frustrating his life was. Even writing letters to me was frustrating. He compared it to *dry humping an old mountain goat.*

Once he sent a postcard that just said: *When you coming home, jerk?*

I didn't miss my family and I didn't write often. When I did, I wrote two versions of my life – a wholesome account with humorous anecdotes to my parents, and tales of exaggerated debauchery and woe to my siblings. Once this backfired because my mother read the letter intended for my brother, in which I claimed to be strung out, miserable and starving. My mother didn't catch the bragging undertone and I received a letter from her, in her loopy longhand, informing me a ticket was waiting for me at Heathrow and she would meet my flight in San Francisco in two weeks. I wrote back immediately, assuring her I was not starving or suicidal, and encouraged her to get a refund. Letters took five days or so, and all our arguments and misunderstandings took place in painful slow motion. I could have called from a phone box in Fraserburgh and reversed the charges, if it had occurred to me.

Near the end of Priscilla's gestation, just after my twenty-third birthday, I met someone. It was a Wednesday night and I was working in a local hotel bar, reading a novel and shovelling peanuts into my mouth as was my wont. I looked up and there he was. Tall, with a confidence in his loose stride as he came in the door. As an aesthetic experience, it was classically visceral. He walked through my innards as he approached, casually thrumming down to my knees. Wearing faded jeans, he had a white T-shirt that looked new, and his shoes were soft golden leather. It was almost 6pm and every other man in the place was wearing grubby work gear. On their feet were hobnailed boots, and each of their heads sported a cap. Or bunnet, as they called it. I swallowed my peanuts, cleared my throat and said:

'Can I help you?'

He didn't answer right away. Just stood at the bar, emanating light and silently staring at the bottles behind me. His lips, I noticed, were adorably chapped.

'Oh! Well, yes. Something cold and wet would be quite good. Do you have any real ales?'

A clear intelligent voice with an odd inflection. Foreign and privately educated, was my guess. I noticed the other men had become quiet. They weren't staring, but they were listening because this man was odd. Oh, he would not be popular in this bar, I thought. This was not a place for outsiders. Especially, I suspected, male foreigners, possibly royal, with expensive shoes.

'Sorry, just draught Tetley's or McEwan's. Also, bottled cider and stout.'

'Oh, I see. I'll have a Manhattan then, please.' Every syllable enunciated crisply, with an intriguing upturn at the end, as if he was asking a question.

'I'm sorry, we don't have the ingredients for that.'

'Any Prosecco?'

'No.'

'Red wine?'

'No wine of any kind.' I detected sniggers from the drinkers behind him. One of them mumbled *Try a Snowball, ya puffter*, but my foreigner didn't notice.

'You might like a Black Velvet,' I said. 'Half stout, half cider. It's kind of nice with peanuts.' That was true.

He laughed almost silently, more of an audible smile – even his laugh was serene and aristocratic – and agreed to try it.

'Where are you from? Not here, by the sound of it.'

'Near San Francisco,' I said, focusing on pouring. I took pride in making Black Velvets. The creamy top not mixing with the dark liquid below. I hoped he'd ask for nuts so he'd get the full experience.

'Are you? Flower child.' Then he sang the opening lines to 'San Francisco (Be Sure to Wear Some Flowers in Your Hair)'.

'Well, Haight-Ashbury is full of heroin addicts now, and since Altamont the whole peace and love thing has kind of gone downhill.'

'Well, it had to happen, I suppose,' he offered cheerfully. 'Still, a beautiful city last time I saw it.'

Meeting someone who'd been there brought the city right into the bar. It did exist, after all – silly me, I kept forgetting. He was from Cape Town, it transpired. Over ten thousand miles from California, but it felt like we were from the same place anyway. We were both foreigners, outsiders in a place full of people born within five miles. Had I been lonely all along? An expat, suffering a self-imposed exile and pretending to have fun? It was hard otherwise to account for the feeling of kinship.

He sat by himself, reading *Heat and Dust* by Ruth Prawer Jhabvala, sipping his dark sweet drink. I'd read that book, maybe we could talk about it. Discuss whether he preferred the Olivia or the Anne strand. I hoped it was Olivia, but I was prepared to champion Anne if he preferred Anne. His chair was by the window, and the setting sun gave him a halo. I noted I was no longer in the least hungry. In fact, I felt a little sick. Snippets of Doric filled the air. *Oh tuaavin awa. Ya ken fit like. A heard yer bidie-in's in a richt sotter. Aye. Weel. Nae need tae fash yersel aboot it.* If I didn't concentrate, it sounded like a foreign language, a cross between German and Swedish.

I was an old hand at flirting, but this was the first time I felt my femininity as a telekinetic ability. Something invisible and potent was streaking out of me and heading straight for Cape Town man. He kept looking up from his book and watching me. This was embarrassing but mostly exciting. And perhaps also a little worrying, because it had a mind of its own, my new power. It wasn't asking for my permission – it was just intent on reeling in a man. I tried to ignore the Fourth of July in my head. Kept pouring pints, half-joining the bar banter, even picked up my novel when things were quiet. But in between times, I loitered near him and chatted. When I asked if he wanted another drink, he asked for lemonade and explained he didn't drink alcohol, being a Buddhist. The pint of Black Velvet had been an aberration, he didn't know what had made him order that. He was in a funny mood.

'Yeah, well, drink's a bit overrated,' I mumbled, thinking *he likes me, he likes me, he likes me!*

We chatted more. I told him about our cottage. About Priscilla. Her freckles, the noise she made when eating, her pregnancy. He asked the right questions. How long to go? Did she need special food? He was a BP man, had been working on a rig in the North Sea Forties Field. His bed was in the bunkhouse at St Fergus, which he called St Fungus, and he'd been so enchanted with the early evening sun earlier, he'd taken a long wander. His job was scaffolding. Dangerous but good money. He was headed to a rig off Angola soon. At 10pm closing time, I took a tray to his table to load up the empty glasses.

'You can come back with me, if you like. Sleep on the sofa.'

'Yeah?'

'Sure.'

'Why not. Better than St Fungus.'

He liked my old car, so I let him drive. He was a fast driver, which didn't seem very Buddhist-like, but I didn't say anything. I was just wondering if it was too straight, too conventional, to care that I didn't know his name, when he said:

'Hey, so what's your name?'

The windows were open and the summer night was rushing around our heads.

I told him, and he took one hand off the steering wheel, offered it to me solemnly. 'Nice to meet you, Cynthia. My name's Christopher.'

'Nice to meet you too,' I said.

I liked that it was Christopher, not Chris. It meant he took himself seriously, which was refreshing. Only Priscilla understood that I took myself seriously too. I took his hand and a jolt went through mine, which travelled up my arm like a snake.

'Did you feel that?'

'Yeah,' I said hoarsely.

'Static electricity. Our clothes, I guess.'

'I guess,' I said casually, thinking I'd need to learn to control my new power.

Everyone was drinking Newcastle Brown and Carlsberg Special that summer, and normally I did too, but when we got back I made us both a cup of tea. Then I waited till everyone had gone to bed so we could kiss. A kiss delayed by a mere four hours, and yet it had been excruciating. I put on Graham Nash's *Songs for Beginners*, and when I stood up from the turntable, he pulled me into a slow waltz. It was strange. I couldn't remember the last time I properly danced with a man. Maybe high school, with the prom date who'd waited for my goodnight kiss in vain. I loved this album. It wasn't especially good for dancing, even slow dancing – Nash was always jumping around, rhythmwise – but we danced anyway. Sometime during 'Simple Man' I realised we were kissing. I'd never been caught unaware like that – so lost in a moment that I'd stopped thinking.

'We're not going to have sex, you know.' He said this kindly but without hesitation, as if he didn't care how I responded. A declaration, not up for discussion.

'All right,' I said, then dived back into the kiss. We were sitting on the sofa now, me half on his lap. Dory Previn was being happily suicidal on the record player.

'All right,' he echoed.

Two or three minutes passed. Maybe forty-five. I had never been kissed, or kissed, so passionately. He was the prince with the spell-breaking kiss.

'Why not?' I asked, pulling away.

'Why not what?' he asked, getting up to turn the record over.

'Why can't we, you know.'

'Have sex? Because I'm a Buddhist. Remember?'

'Oh yeah. But we can do more of this? Kissing and stuff?'

'Sure,' he said. 'That doesn't really count.'

'Because I think I love you. I mean kissing. I mean, I love kissing you.'

He came back and sat down, said:

'Besides, I have to leave soon. It wouldn't be right to start something.'

'Soon? How soon are you leaving?'

'I'm just waiting to find out what day the Angola job starts. I don't know when I'll be back. Or if.'

We could not, would not, have sex. He would leave and I would never see him again. Kissing a soldier leaving for the front might have felt this way. I kissed him so hard my bones melted. I fell inside those kisses, feeling gravity's tug. Maybe falling in love was literally about *falling*. I'd never experienced love as vertigo.

In the morning, I drove him to St Fergus to collect his things. Three days passed and I don't remember much from them, aside from the blond hairs on the back of his neck, his shoes on the floor by my bed, the smell of his skin (like sea salt and cucumber) and his eyes. They were green and small, often crinkled up as if laughing, though he rarely laughed and never loudly. My lips were swollen. I'd developed a kissing technique where I traversed his mouth minutely with my lips, giving each centimetre its share of attention. A gentle tug here, a lighter touch there. Tongue kissing followed, but lip kissing was hard to beat. Maybe lips had nerve endings that released a narcotic into the bloodstream. And of course, there were our fully clothed bodies pressing into each other in a delicious torture. He slept with me in my single bed in my tiny box room with the tiny window wide open, through which cows occasionally looked, sometimes licking the glass. We snuggled and giggled and kissed, often (I fancied) falling asleep at the same time, turning in unison till dawn. When we weren't kissing, we were talking. We talked about religion, meditation, books, our countries, our childhoods. I'd been missing the kind of talk where no subject was too silly or taboo.

189

'Do you ever get homesick?' he asked me once in the middle of the afternoon. We were sitting on the front steps, and I could see Priscilla sleeping in the shade of her only tree.

'Nope,' I said, stroking his feet. 'Do you?'

'I think so.'

'You don't know?'

'No. When I go home, sometimes the homesick feeling still comes.'

He had long toes with little tufts of blond hair. When I stroked the space between the little bones of his ankles, he sighed and whispered, *Yes, there*. Now and then I wondered just where Buddhists drew the line, sexually. Kissing and stroking ankle bones seemed a little hypocritical, but I didn't say anything in case he stopped kissing me.

'Maybe you just feel sad sometimes.'

'Maybe. But I worry it's a grass-is-always-greener thing. In which case, I'm fucked.'

Another time I told him about my mother saying my friends looked like losers.

'Of course she would,' he said.

'But they're not!'

'She doesn't really think they're losers, silly. She's jealous of them. They get to spend time with you.'

I softened towards my parents during those long hot days with Christopher Parker. Judged them less harshly. Maybe my father's dearth of letters didn't indicate anger, they were more like a sulk.

Aside from Gun Man, who was suspicious of vegetarianism, my housemates accepted Christopher Parker with the casual friendliness they extended to everyone who liked them. A houseful of golden retrievers, tails wagging. All forms of Christianity were out of fashion, but Buddhism was in. They were interested in how he emptied his mind. I had no desire to empty my mind because I needed all my brain cells ticking over just to keep afloat. While he meditated, I answered letters, weeded the carrots, made bread. I liked to set his few belongings in a neat pile by my bed. His battered copy of *Siddhartha*, his ChapStick, his loose change and comb.

The heat continued to be enervating. Flies circled over the kitchen table constantly, and no one was fast enough to swat them dead. We didn't have a refrigerator and the goat milk kept turning. Everyone complained about the heat, but not me. It was a time of lurching from one kiss to another like a drunk, my skin so sensitised it hummed.

On Christopher Parker's last night, we got dressed up in our finery – mostly our cleanest hip-hugging floor-sweeping jeans – and went to a dance at Lonmay church hall. This was a rectangular stone building, plain as could be, next to a small church and cemetery. Beech trees shadowed the church and hall, with the evening sun flickering down through dark clusters of nests. Big black birds were making a racket up there.

I took Christopher's arm as we walked towards the door, gave it a little squeeze and he squeezed me back.

'Crows,' I said.

'Rooks. A rookery,' he correctly gently, looking up, thereby forever imbuing rookeries with romance. Nothing remained ordinary in our wake.

People may have stared as we walked into the hall, but I didn't notice. No one said anything unwelcoming. There was a long table with cups of juice and a tea urn. The women were all on one side of the hall, some sitting on long benches, and the men were on the opposite side. We stood at the back of the hall by the long tables, and tried to look casual. We were under-dressed despite our efforts. The men wore their black trousers belted high, and if they wore jeans, they weren't Levi's and the hem was above their shoes. The band struck up, playing cover songs like 'Knock Three Times' and 'Crying in the Chapel'. We danced, sometimes together, sometimes by ourselves. That uncanny current was still running between us, and I was always aware when Christopher was near. When he left the hall to find the toilet, the room briefly died. As I was watching the band, I sensed he was back. Turned around and there he was. One of the Yorkshire twins did a belly dance that caused a short fuss, then everyone ignored her and returned to their own dancing. We were not asked to dance by the locals, nor did we ask them.

'What do you think they make of us?' We'd gone outside to smoke, and were alone.

'That we're show-offs, I think,' said Christopher. 'City folk, come to mock them.'

'No! I think they like us. They might even be a bit jealous.'

'Well, I don't think they're jealous,' he said softly. 'Why would they be? They like their lives.'

'But I want them to like us,' I whined, slipping an arm around his waist. Buddhists could be slightly annoying, I thought with the tiny part of my brain that was immune to kiss-sedation. They could make a person feel bad about having an ego.

'No, you don't. Not really.' He smoothed the hair around my face. 'All this is just an interlude for you.'

Then it was time.

'Write me, all right? I'll write you,' I whispered at dawn, limp with teetering on a knife-edge of desire.

'Of course I'll write. Dear Miss Kiss, I'll say.'

And then I drove him to Aberdeen airport and he left. Was I upset? No. I was glad he was gone so I could love him without the distraction of his presence.

I told Priscilla all about Christopher that night. In fact, I couldn't wait to. I'd never admit to my friends that mere kissing had sent me to the moon. Even I knew that sounded dumb. I went out to her field about ten, and there she was, looking gorgeous in the moonlight. *Not long to go now, Momma*, I crooned, running a hand across her belly full of piglets. I thought I could feel the babies wriggling. It felt far longer than three days since I'd visited her like this, alone at night. Pre-Christopher Parker time was in another realm, and it was like trying to remember what it felt like before I'd ever had a joint. Then after a few minutes, she was back to being my dear Priscilla. I found her favourite spot, just between her ears, and scratched vigorously while she made the pig-equivalent of purring. A steady asthmatic rumble. *Well, I met a lovely man*, I began. *And now I get it about kissing.* I noticed she'd gained more weight, which was as it should be. I'd lost weight, which also, I supposed, was as it should be. The kisses had made food hard to swallow. Yet as I told Priscilla about the experience, I remembered that not much had happened. Nothing that would normally change a person. I couldn't even call him a boyfriend. He was just a boy I'd known for three days and enjoyed kissing.

The days began to pass at normal speed again. I pulled weeds, cleaned out Priscilla's shed and worked in the bar. I painted my tiny room grey and no one liked it but me. I began to paint a mural on the living room wall, from floor to ceiling. The wall was plaster and lath, yellowed with age, and no one cared what I did to it. I copied the back cover of *Tea for the Tillerman* and painted it in watercolour with a tiny brush – but all the time, I was daydreaming about *him*. I played Nick Drake albums constantly, and every lyric was personally relevant. It was over. Or was it? His physical absence, his farewell with no word of return – these were just the obstacles all protagonists faced before the happy ending. He'd be back. I imagined converting him to an un-celibate version of Buddhism. I'd become that kind of Buddhist too, to keep him company, and we'd have a heap of Buddhist babies. I'd let him give them all South African names, or Buddhist names, whatever he liked. And I'd learn how to knit so we could all be cosy when it got cold and he wouldn't miss Cape Town. We'd be in the old stone cottage surrounded by fields, of course. The dream grew and grew. There were roses climbing up the walls and a clothes line stretched between fruit trees. It was refreshing to feel such clarity about my future. I missed him, but I was content missing him. In fact, it was exquisite, it was *enough* – just knowing my perfect man existed out there somewhere.

I wrote him long letters and he wrote long letters back, via other men going ashore and posting them. Some days I got three letters from him, and the postman presented them to me with a flourish. He wrote about the Angolan sun looking bigger than the Scottish sun, about fish that looked like the fish in Dr Seuss books, about his co-workers, one of whom practised a violin every night on the deck. About books and meditating in the toilet, which was the only private place if his bunkmate was there. One letter was ten pages long. He worked twelve-hour shifts but didn't complain. *I don't know where the time goes but I assure you, its passage is painless.* I figured he was lonely out on that rig in the middle of the ocean, lonelier than me. Imagine being a Buddhist vegetarian celibate among a hundred or so porn-addicted booze-deprived drinkers, mostly with wives at home they cheated on whenever they had a chance and *See you, you got a problem with that*? He was a freak, and wrote me letters so he could be himself to someone. He referred to our kisses sometimes, but never to the possibility of resuming them. Either he was content with a virtual relationship, or he was more restrained than me. I could never resist finishing my letters without a verbose wish for the return of his lips.

Finally, the day came for the piglet births, and we took it in shifts to check Priscilla every half hour. On and off, all day and all night for two weeks. I made up a pig labour song and sang it constantly, to get her in the mood. *Keep breathing, keep humming, your darling babies are coming!* Eventually, after much consultation of the John Seymour Self-Sufficiency Guide and the pig farm man, we conceded that Priscilla was not pregnant. She was just fat from over-feeding. I was surprised and disappointed, but not overly. My love for Priscilla was unconditional, but the men of the house were not happy – all that money wasted! They were farmers, not pet-pig keepers. They'd been misled and plotted to kill Priscilla, inspired by the chapter called 'Slaughtering Your Pig'. I was shocked but didn't say anything, except a weak *Do we have to?*

We were in the age of Women's Liberation, as I said, but traditional roles were nevertheless adhered to on pig-killing day. We girls were in the house drinking tea and the boys – *men* now, as I briefly thought of them – were at the business of killing. I'd said goodbye to Priscilla earlier, pretending to her it was just another day and tears weren't running down my face. This was how I imagined a mother talked to her child with terminal cancer, cleverly keeping fear at bay. *You're the best pig ever, I love you very much and everything is going to be all right.* I climbed over the fence to put my arms around her solid grunting body. *Priscilla, I'm so sorry!* I must have hugged too hard, because suddenly she jerked away and toddled off to her shed. Normally she didn't mind how hard I hugged, so maybe she knew something was up. I went back to the cottage, feeling like Judas.

When the deed was done, the boys – back to being *boys* now – drifted back into the cottage, pale and laughing nervously. Except for Gun Man, who was quietly aglow. I didn't go to the shed to look at Priscilla's body, now referred to as bacon. Over the next few days, she was butchered, following the chapter called 'Butchering Your Pig'. Mr Cool knew how fond I'd been of her and saved one of her teeth for me. It was a tusk, yellow and curved, and he glued a silver ring into it so I could wear it on a necklace.

'Thank you,' I said, though I never wore necklaces.

The meat was stored in a barrel full of brine, according to the directions. We would have free organic meat for a year at least. All was well. But then, it was not. We were terrible amateurs and some small step of the process had been omitted or misunderstood. There was a smell. It became obvious the meat had turned and was inedible. Priscilla had gone to waste. And then the hottest summer on record was over. I was still grieving for Priscilla and could hardly look at her field. It was no longer just mud, but already turning green as if she'd never existed. I could have prevented her demise and tortured myself imagining rescue scenarios. In one of them, I led her on a rope away from the cottage in the middle of the night, a bag of pig food slung over my shoulder.

Meanwhile, I kept writing long letters to Christopher and he kept writing back. I kept his letters in my sock drawer, nestled with my other letters and my passport. Then his letters stopped. I wrote a few more, then one day I decided he'd met someone else. Some old girlfriend he ran into while in Cape Town for his two weeks off. I hated him. He'd not been who I thought. Maybe he wasn't even Buddhist. He was engaged. Married, even. Or maybe he had syphilis and that was the real reason for his gallant abstinence. Or he was impotent! Everything I remembered from our time was tainted. Nothing, as I imagined, and this sense of unreality spread to the world around me. Was *anything* as I perceived it?

At the end of November someone told me he'd died. He'd fallen off a rig scaffolding forty miles offshore from Angola and died instantly. I asked someone else, and they'd heard the same rumour. It took a few minutes, very large minutes, to adjust my perspective. All the implications filed in slowly, a solemn slow march, and my perceptions did a backflip to their original position. He'd not been a bastard, he'd been my one true love. I kept imagining deep blue African skies, against which his body was falling. His arms and legs thrashing the air, his perfect mouth open in a scream. Maybe he was thinking: *This was not the plan for today*. Assuming my face flashed before him, I travelled backwards in time and over the seas till I was right there with him, falling through the air, calming him, telling him – like I told Priscilla – everything was going to be all right because I loved him. *Hold tight.* I couldn't imagine past the falling, not the actual impact. Was it the sea or the rig? I hoped it was quick. I didn't know his family so couldn't send condolences, as my mother had raised me to do. In fact, I didn't know anyone who'd known him much at all.

Time recommenced, and on the surface nothing was different in my days even though Christopher Parker had unpeeled from the land of the living and was now nowhere. Or elsewhere, because as every good lapsed Catholic knows, the jury is out on immortality. Then I remembered him telling me about the six rebirth realms of Bhavacakra. How you could come back as anything, and how the way you lived your life determined your next life form. This made me feel slightly better, because if true, I'd almost certainly see him again. In fact, I bet he was heading my way right now, maybe as a seagull. Given the location of his demise, that would be most logical non-human life form. Oh God, what if he was a fish? That would take too long, and since I never opened my eyes underwater, our chances of resuming our platonic affair were nil. Of course, he could also be setting up home in a new human embryo right now, someone who might sweep my as-yet-unconceived daughter off her feet one day. Not as comforting as a tame seagull perching on my shoulder next week, but beggars can't be choosers. At least I'd get to see him again.

I retrieved and polished up every memory I could summon, for they'd quadrupled in value. His quiet laugh, those expensive shoes, the taste and feel of his skin. His lower lip, the way it felt between my own lips, and how that feeling would then shoot straight down my body to my toes. We probably never would have had those six children, but I missed them just the same. I began to write a poem. *Christopher Parker stood as a marker at crossroad number forty-three.* I'd turned in one direction because of him, and now I was at a dead end. Freedom used to be fun. Now it just made me tired and a tiny bit panicky.

Meanwhile, my mother's letters kept arriving, several a week, and each one contained *I love you, I love you, I love you.* My brother still wrote variations of *When the hell are you going to get your skinny butt home?* My father wrote one letter. It contained a cheque for $25 and two sentences: *If you put this money towards buying a cottage, don't bother coming home again. Which reminds me, when are you coming home?*

Everything was changing. My car died and we pushed it behind the cottage where three other cars already rusted. One by one, my friends began to leave. I waved them each away, feeling irrationally abandoned. Time began to pass sluggishly. I minded the sad lonely sound of the wind now, and nothing about my body hummed any more. I painted pictures of flowers and suns and moons for Christmas presents, tried to read and write, but mostly I sat in my tiny grey-painted room and felt nothing. People's voices came from a long way off. It, whatever it was, was over.

I packed my belongings into my backpack – Priscilla's tooth tucked inside a sock – and flew home just before Christmas. What would happen next? Something would. Experience had taught me I would most likely be all right. Maybe I'd try college again. When you didn't know what to do, learning seemed a good plan. All that flight, I thought about death. Not Christopher's, but my own. I was a third of the way through my life already, and at the rate time was going, I'd be dead before I'd figured anything out. If I died old, I'd probably have a few months first of waking up every day and asking myself if this was my last morning. On the day of my death, I'd think: *Nah, I don't believe I'll die today*, and then I'd close my eyes and die. And all the things I'd done and felt and learned, all the people I'd known and all the people I'd loved – all of Christopher Parker's kisses – they'd disappear with me. These thoughts didn't make me sad. They felt true and therefore interesting, almost romantic. Was there anything intimations of mortality couldn't cure? *Death, come get me!*

But then our plane began bucking and creaking. Lights flashed and the pilot told us to put on our seat-belts. A minute later, in a less calm voice, he ordered the crew to strap themselves in too. The plane dropped hard, like it had dropped straight onto something solid, concrete – *whoomph!* – and I lifted off my seat. With sickening clarity, I understood none of the safety equipment we'd been shown earlier – the oxygen masks, the life jackets, the whistles – would be used. Somewhere close, a child was screaming and a man was whimpering. I tried to remember the words of the Lord's Prayer, but like everyone around me, I found myself swearing instead. *Shit, shit, shit. Fuck.* Late bloomers should never die young, that much was obvious.

Then, as suddenly it started, the turbulence stopped. I was not dead, none of us were, and trivial preoccupations recommenced. Queues for the toilet formed, books were opened, drinks were poured. Children were told to stop whining, and spouses told spouses to stop arguing. It was soporific, and somewhere over Canada I fell asleep. I dreamed of finding a new room in a familiar house. When I woke, it occurred to me those kisses had been like that. As if I'd stumbled upon a secret door to *real* kissing, as opposed to the tongue wrangling I'd engaged in up to then. What if I'd never met Christopher Parker? Well, you don't miss what you've never had. Probably lots of people go through their lives thinking they know kisses.

Hospice Doghouse

I'd been home three weeks, during which time my mother continued to not die. She wasn't even ebbing. She had colour in her cheeks and took an interest in everything. *The Sound of Music* was still a daily necessity, and after that came food, especially bear claws. Sometimes I put on one of Dad's jazz albums, Ella Fitzgerald or Glenn Miller. I'd stand in front of her wheelchair, take her hands and we'd more or less dance while singing a song about someone making us love them, even though we didn't want to do it, we didn't want to do it. Having fun with my mother was easy now. I suppose it had been easy when I was five years old too, dancing silly around the living room with her. I'd no memories of this, but no doubt those times occurred. Now I was filled with gratitude because she'd stayed alive till I learned to really appreciate her. So considerate, not to die beforehand. I sang and swayed and wriggled, all the time holding onto her hand unless I was doing a twirl and had to let one of her hands go briefly. She'd leave her hand mid-air till I caught it up again, and then she'd giggle so hard tears came.

Maybe my presence was perverting the natural course of events and she'd be dead by now – only I kept turning up, forcing her maternal instincts to rev back into action. And they were fierce, those instincts. They pretty much overrode everything, even dementia. Or maybe she was just terrible at dying. Maybe dying was one of those things some people were naturally good at – born die-ers, like born musicians – and others were just amateurs. Meanwhile, my list was growing.

Things I Learned from My Mother:

- If you are not a success in high school, then be assured you are a freak – but still lovable to your mother.
- If you go to college, then you are a genius. Not as smart as your father of course, but awe-inspiring just the same.
- If you have any good or clever qualities, be certain you got those from your father.
- If you have any bad or weak tendencies, be certain you got those from your father too.
- If you are beautiful, loyal and honest, be certain this is no protection against a pretty crap life.
- If you have endured sixty years of marriage with a sexy funny man who cheats on you even though you're a good wife and physically frail, you will happily outlive him by many years in the company of someone of uncertain gender from a third world country.
- If you are speechless for any reason, simply raise open hands to the sky, smile and say: *Wah!*

One day, on the phone, the doctor explained the hospice's rules to me. You got kicked out if you didn't croak in six months. Ideally, in under three months. This was her seventh month. My mother was in Hospice Doghouse and he just wanted me to know.

'Thanks, Doctor. Let's hope she gets a move on.'

He didn't laugh.

I was proud she was being awkward. Not only did it mean she was a rebel, but it also meant I got more of her. I kept think-ing of all the years I'd ignored her, avoided her. Even on a vacation cruise with her when I was fourteen, I'd acted as if she wasn't there. I'd been a terrible daughter, wasted all those chances of closeness – but now I embraced my guilt because it seemed to have a function. It informed and sharpened every recollection of that SS *Lurline* bound for Hawaii with us on board. I didn't want forgetfulness or forgiveness, I wanted to be haunted by regret because it was a way of feeling close to her. What else did we have now, but my past crimes and omissions?

About a week into my visit, I decided to take my mother to see a movie. Ateca came too, as I was inexpert at moving my mother from her wheelchair into the car and out again. Several times I'd almost dropped her in a parking lot.

'Move your bottom now!' Ateca barked. 'That's right, honey. Park your butt right here.' She guided my mother's rear end by holding onto the belt loop at the back of her jeans.

When was the last time my mother had been to see a movie? I'd no idea, but she used to love going to movies. We were a movie family. Northgate Mall was essentially the same as I remembered from adolescence. Florescent lights buzzing in wide corridors, populated by shoals of pimply teens and overweight women in their forties. About a quarter of them were pushing strollers with whiny runny-nosed toddlers, and telling the kids to shut the hell up. Otherwise the shoppers, even the teens, were silent. Their faces seemed both dazed and sedated. Was this outing a terrible idea after all? I pushed my mother's chair quickly, not wanting her to notice, much less absorb the atmosphere. What if this was her last sighting of the outside world?

'Close your eyes, Mom.'

'What?'

'Nothing.'

'Look!' she squealed. 'A See's candy store!'

So we stopped in See's, an oasis of white, and inhaled the smell of chocolate. I bought the standard box. We were a See's family, and I knew exactly which chocolates were nestled inside. The coffee cream was mine, and so was the dark chocolate almond cluster, but I'd have to act fast. They were my mother's favourites too.

The movie choices were not good, but it didn't really matter because my mother was asleep before the previews finished. The place was packed and I enjoyed myself. I was, after all, a child of this suburb, and it was peaceful sitting in the dark eating chocolate. Mom was snoring softly and Ateca sat on my other side, laughing her head off. At one point the hero was winning. It was quiet, not even music was playing. Then there was a very loud bang as the baddie came out of nowhere and fired a gun. My mother shot forward and into the silence shouted:

'Turn that down!'

It was her old self that shouted, the Mom from my teenage years who got angry when I played my records too loud and woke my sister. Her voice which said: *I mean business, darn it!*

'Turn that down, I said!'

Oh God, I loved her cranky voice.

SS Lurline

Fourteen years old
California and the Pacific Ocean, 1967

The ages of eleven, twelve and thirteen seemed to go on forever. They didn't leave many clear memories, though I viscerally recall watching the classroom clock, which slowed down after lunch until one minute took two hours to pass. And the way summers seemed to bisect my life entirely, so when school began again, I had to reacquaint myself with everything. The location of the toilets, the numbers on the classroom doors, the teachers' names. Of course I remembered everything, but in a semi-fictional way. The rooms were never the exact same size and were never in exactly the same place. The nuns never had the same voices or faces they'd had at the beginning of summer. As if without my daily witnessing of these things and people, they had no reality, no solidity. Those years I was still growing, a process I couldn't believe would end because I'd never not been getting taller. But the day came when my favourite shoes lasted till the soles flapped off, and time itself sped up. Everything turned into a blur, a helter-skelter too fast for proper thinking.

The Cold War was at its height by my fourteenth birthday, but all I cared about was my new two-piece bathing suit. It wasn't just the Cold War – there was Vietnam and the atomic bomb too. There wasn't a good reason – an un-embarrassing reason – for my indifference. I was hanging onto childhood by the skin of my adolescent teeth. I had a new bathing suit because we were going to Hawaii on a cruise ship called SS *Lurline*. Even now, it seems unlikely. We were not a vacation family, nor were we a swimming family. I lacked buoyancy and failed beginners' class twice, flailing and sputtering my way across the short pool length. These failures had been greeted with good humour and even pride by my parents. In fact, many failures were greeted with head-shaking cancelled out by an affectionate smile. It was the house of proud under-achievers, the implication being only winners were losers because only they cared about winning. It was flawless logic. The only challenge was success, should it ever arrive.

My new bathing suit was green with white polka dots – a two-piece but not a bikini. The top half looped down under my bust in a little apron to cover my middle modestly. The bra cups were rigidly empty, and I had to make sure I didn't bump into anything, otherwise I'd look like my chest had caved in. I was my full adult height and weighed 95 lb. I had no curves. Not one. I loved my new bathing suit, but I was worried I'd drown in it. Hawaiian beaches had surfers, which meant waves and undertows. I also worried in case I got my period and couldn't go swimming, or worse – it began while I was wearing my new suit. I wasn't used to periods yet. I'd only had three. The first had been momentous but also cliché, occurring in the family bathroom.

Yikes! How did I cut myself there?

Oh, okay, now I remember.

Where did Mom put those diaper-things?

Oh Jesus, what now?

I'm supposed to tuck each end of the towel into these little metal loops attached to an elastic band around my waist?

I'm a butterfingers. I still spill my milk every night.

This is nuts.

Are you telling me every girl has to do this? Every month?

Whether I wanted to be a woman or not, womanhood had its hooks in me. Hormones drenched me in optimism, followed by deluges of pessimism and irritability.

'I am not listening,' my mother would say placidly, when I'd snap something nasty in her direction. 'You're just tired, honey. Or hungry. Eat something.'

Being rude to my mother was not as satisfying as being rude to my father. He would react with equal crankiness, and then off we'd go, both saying horrible things we meant.

Growing up seemed a process intent on eroding my child self, that person I'd so solidly, so comfortably, been up to now. Who was I? I'd always known that, for heaven's sake. More worryingly, I couldn't remember what it felt like to be five, or six, or even seven. That freckled girl with scabs on her knees and a crush on her father? She was like a person I'd met briefly and remembered with some embarrassment.

My reading habits moved from *Nancy Drew* and *The Hardy Boys* to Steinbeck, Hemingway and Somerset Maugham. I cried for an hour when I finished *Of Mice and Men*, and spent days feeling superior to anyone acting happy. I was shocked by how sad a story could make me feel, and perhaps also a little shocked at how much pleasure melancholy gave me. When I finished *The Sun Also Rises*, I was filled with a delicious weariness. Ha! There was nothing about the man-woman relationship I didn't know now. The bottom line was black, just as I suspected. What a relief. No more fretting, because if all was hopeless then what else was there to do but enjoy life? No one close to me had died yet. I had five grandparents, including a great-grandmother who had come west in a covered wagon. Even our golden retriever was still alive, though he'd ceased talking to me. Inhabiting fictional tragedies offered me a depth of experience which my life so far – lucky me – had not. But I still never read the newspaper.

*

My sister arrived a year ago via a planned caesarean. *BABY!* had been scribbled on the calendar for months, along with a dentist appointment for my brother the same day. I headed to the school bus that morning, just as my parents were getting in the car to go to the hospital. My mother was always beautiful, even now. It was easy to forget she was pregnant. Her dark hair was pushed back from her forehead by a black band, and she wore red lipstick. My father was wearing his trademark gold corduroy jacket and thick-framed glasses.

'See you later,' he said. Then he smirked and added: 'Have a nice day.' I knew he meant it, and also understood he couldn't say the phrase *Have a nice day* without an ironic tone because it was a corny thing to say. Failure may be applauded, but corniness, never. Bad taste in clothes was also frowned on. Polyester was the devil.

'Have a nice baby,' I told them both, and off I went.

I hadn't given any thought to my mother's upcoming ordeal. Being sliced open, for instance. Or having a newborn to take care of, as well as two adolescents in an era of well-publicised drug danger. She hadn't seemed worried, so neither was I.

In the afternoon, Sister Agnes came into my eighth-grade classroom and with a serious face, asked me to come to the office. I assumed I was in trouble again. Just a week ago, I'd decided morning prayer time was a good time to clean out my desk. I still didn't understand the problem. Life was puzzling and unfair.

'You've got a new sister,' Sister Agnes said softly but also happily.

I smiled. I knew I was getting a sibling, but a sister? Even better.

'Your father called from the hospital,' she continued, obviously waiting for some verbal response from me.

'Can I go home early?'

'No.'

My sister was born in an historic year. When she was two months, the *San Francisco Chronicle* told us to brace ourselves for the upcoming 'Summer of Love'. There was something suspicious about this phrase – how could they predict something so abstract? Summer, yes. But love? Could love be forecast like the weather? As soon as school was out, thousands of young people from all over the country would be coming to San Francisco to wear flowers in their hair, have sex with strangers, get high and listen to the Grateful Dead in Golden Gate Park.

I was proud of our city – and glad not to be living in Sacramento any more – but it was all happening so quickly. I could remember when I had to wear a hat and gloves to go shopping at I. Magnin. Now people sometimes didn't even bother with shoes. One Sunday that summer, our family drove around Haight-Ashbury as if we were tourists. My sister was on my mother's lap in the front, and me and my brother sat in the back. The car was a nifty little Hillman Minx because we were superior to families who drove around in ostentatious fat American station wagons. No one ever said this out loud because that would have been snobby, and snobby-ness was the devil.

'Stop staring at those girls,' my mother ordered my father.

'I'm not staring. I'm looking.'

'Mom, Mom!'

'What?'

'What's wrong with her boobies? They're wobbling like Jell-O,' said my eleven-year-old brother, his face hanging out the window.

'Do not call them that. They are breasts.' She enunciated each syllable, which meant she was cranky. 'Turn the car around,' she told my father.

Ponytailed boys with beards, girls with long hair swinging, and on all their faces a look of sleepy joy. These were hippies? I was excited. Would I be a hippie too? Anything at all could happen. I might even grow breasts, now the whole puberty thing had kicked in. But even with that optimism, I never imagined our family would cross the ocean in a luxury liner to Hawaii next summer.

Our family outings up until then had been visits to our grandparents in Redding at Easter and Thanksgiving, and camping in our local campground. When I was very young, we'd gone to a cabin in Viola. Going to Hawaii was like going to the moon. How had it come about? My father worked for Matson ship lines, so maybe it was a free passage due to a last-minute cancellation. My father was not coming on SS *Lurline* due to work – he'd fly to Hawaii and meet us there. Then it turned out my sister, now eighteen months, wouldn't be coming either. I wasn't sure why. Perhaps my mother foresaw her slipping between the railings and being left behind, bobbing in the ship's wake. More likely she needed time off from taking care of a toddler. She'd not been well since the birth. Not our dancing-around-the-kitchen mom at all. We weren't told why, but we'd noticed she'd begun to walk with a limp and often took naps on the sofa.

When the day of departure came, it was our Italian grandmother who drove us to Los Angeles. We called her Nina, which was her name and short for Caterina. Thirty-nine when I was born, maybe she hadn't felt old enough to be called Grandma. But she was fifty-four years old that summer and I noticed her skin had become looser, as if she was shrinking inside herself. I was still proud of her, as I was of my mother. Some of my friends had dowdy fat moms and old ladies for grandmas. I had a mom and grandma men whistled at. I waited in mute anticipation to wake up beautiful too.

We left before dawn and when we weren't dozing off, we sang. Mostly songs Nina taught us. 'I've Been Working on the Railroad', '99 Bottles of Beer', 'Mairzy Doats'. We ate bologna sandwiches and drank cans of warm Shasta soda. Los Angeles was not as pretty as San Francisco – it was flat, for one thing, and full of freeways – but it scored points for not being familiar. It was early afternoon, but how could that be? Waking up in my bed at home and having a late lunch in Los Angeles was as close as I'd come to time travel. If travelling expanded time, then logically travellers had longer lives than stay-at-homes. Could be useful information, I thought.

My mother passed my sister to my grandmother at the gangplank.

'Thanks, Mom,' she said tearfully. 'Don't forget she needs a hat in the sun.'

'Don't worry,' said Nina. 'She'll be just fine.'

'She'll take it off and throw it away. I've lost three hats this year. You've got to watch her.'

'Sure, I'll watch her. She'll be fine.'

My mother kissed them both, hard and quick, then marched us up the gangplank.

Maybe she felt an umbilical cord connecting her to her baby stretching out, like silly putty. We found our deck and stood at the rail. I could see Nina holding my sister, streamers fluttering from the ship to shore. She was wriggling to get down, but Nina had a good hold of her and kept kissing the top of her head. Was I a little jealous? I was the first grandchild and considered myself her favourite. I had a fantasy in which my parents died – painlessly of course, with a direct flight to heaven – and I lived with her. Nina's house had white bread and Frosted Flakes, two items banned from ours. Plus, she was always happy.

Everyone onboard and onshore was laughing and calling *Bon Voyage! See you later, alligator! Send me a postcard!* The air was full of blown kisses. Then the ship's horn blew – spine-tingling, like a train whistle, only lower, louder, hollow somehow. The engines thrumming, black smoke pouring from the funnels, we drew away into the west where we could see nothing but sea and sky. The seagulls were frenzied, as if making the most of our last minutes near land, wheeling and crying. People started to drift away, but I stood a while and got used to the vibrations and noise of the engines. I watched the California coast become a lump of dark land. It took a surprisingly short time. We were slipping across the surface of the globe and I felt the top of my skull lift off.

We must have shared a stateroom with our mother, but I don't remember her there. I clearly remember getting the top bunk because I was the older, and my brother whining:

'But I'll drown in your vomit and die. Then you'll be sorry.'

He had a point. I'd been carsick all my life, why would I be immune to sea-motion? But I was adept at vomiting – it might have been my main skill. I had the same strategies every carsick person learns – to not close your eyes and avoid the back seat. I would *not* throw up on my brother. Even so, I was astounded by the sheer frequency of seasickness. I didn't lose my appetite, but I kept nothing down. By the end of the second day, my mother was worried enough to ask the ship's doctor. He prescribed suppositories since I couldn't keep pills down, but I was too squeamish to use them. I flushed them away, one by one, and began to conceal my puking. Another skill. The invisible inaudible vomit.

In between throwing up, I had a great time. Nothing I'd done in my life so far was as thrilling as what I was doing right now. Being on SS *Lurline*, headed across the Pacific to Hawaii with my new green two-piece bathing suit tucked away in my suitcase – incredible. Like a city, SS *Lurline* had theatres, swimming pools, stores, beauty salons, tennis courts, bars and restaurants. It even had a daily newspaper called *The Polynesian*. This didn't just list things like baseball scores and the weather in New York; it also had the day's programme of events – dance classes, exercise clubs, the staff show, hula lessons, golf driving, Mardi Gras

Night. On 21 August 1968 it listed twenty-four activities. It also had the news:

In Saigon, six hundred Viet Cong using home-made grenades overran an Allied outpost near Da Nang killing all thirty-four defendants: nine American Marines, a Navy Seabee and twenty-four Vietnamese popular force. Allied troops killed nearly three hundred Communist soldiers in scattered battles.

I knew these terrible things were happening in the world, but they were peripheral, like mosquitos buzzing around my bed in the dark. Not distracting enough to prevent me falling asleep. In six months, a friend's big brother would be delivered home from Vietnam in a casket and make the war real. A year from now, my mother would sometimes look at me as if I frightened her.

Our mother made us dress up when it was our turn to sit at the captain's table. It was a windy evening and the ship was rolling from side to side. I was all right on deck where I could keep an eye on the horizon, but the minute we walked down the grand stairs into the dining room I was in trouble. I wanted to warn my mother, but she was making small talk with the captain in the charming voice she reserved for such occasions. Wearing a simple pink linen shift she'd made from a McColl's pattern and her hair in a neat flip, she looked like her icon – Jackie Kennedy. Though Jackie had recently fallen from grace with her engagement to Onassis, who my mother considered trash on the grounds that he was rich and old and looked like a bull frog. 'Jackie's become a common little gold-digger,' I heard her say – not bitterly, but with dismay as if it was a personal betrayal. I ate the first course and excused myself to find the closest bathroom. All the cubicles were locked. In the end, I threw up in the potpourri basket by the sink. I watched my vomit seep out from the bottom. 'Humph,' I said aloud, in case anyone was looking and wondered if it was my vomit. Obviously not, if I was humph-ing at it.

*

Me and my brother were feral. When we discovered we could order anything just by quoting our stateroom number, we became reckless spenders. We spent hours at the bar drinking Shirley Temples, which led to a revelation from the bartender:

'She was here once, you know.'

'Who?'

'Shirley Temple, of course,' he said, as he slid our pink drinks over the shiny bar. 'Right here, where you are sitting right now.'

We were too stunned to respond. Just sucked on our straws and ate our cherries. I loved Shirley Temple.

'Sure, they've all had a drink here. Elvis. Carole Lombard. Myrna Loy. Charleston Heston. I could go on and on.'

Was he telling the truth? We weren't sure, but even so I felt myself levitate into the upper realms and floated there a minute, breathing the same air Shirley Temple had breathed. Only it couldn't be the same air and the bartender was probably fibbing anyway. We scampered off to buy Butterfingers and *Archie* comics at the ship's store.

The crew were nice to us, but it couldn't have been because we looked cute. We didn't. We looked like nerdy juvenile delinquents. My brother was my height by then, about five foot six. We were skinny, freckled, sunburned, red-headed – and as far as I can remember, we wore the same shorts and T-shirts every day. Maybe the crew smiled out of kindness, because they thought we were neglected. Or maybe they were taking tip money each time we made a purchase. It didn't matter. It only mattered that we felt unsupervised and safe, which might be the definition of happiness for all children.

What else did we do with our freedom? Played game after game of ping-pong on the deck. Spied on the old ladies in their exercise classes. Sneaked onto the first-class decks, knocked on doors and ran away giggling. We stole small things, like hats left

213

on the deck chairs. We finished off alcoholic drinks abandoned by fellow passengers. We didn't like the taste. We did it because not liking the taste and drinking it anyway was hilarious. Oh, why was being bad so much fun? We had a history of being bad. Silly misdemeanours I could hardly recall, aside from the fact our mother would tell our father to spank us when he returned home from work. Was throwing missals during Mass really such a crime? Riding the conveyor belt in the backroom of the supermarket? Maybe good behaviour comes easier to only children. Badness was plainly more fun in the company of a sibling. I know this for a fact, because after I left home and my crimes really began to mount up, I didn't have much fun at all.

The Russians are Coming, The Russians are Coming played twice a day, and we watched it four times. It was a satire on the Cold War, but we didn't know that. We both loved it from start to end because it was irreverent and had a great love story. The parents fought constantly and realistically, which was cheering, but the real love story was between the Russian sailor and the babysitter. Alexi was so tall, so sweet. When he said *I love you, Alison Palmer* in his funny accent, I felt something in my chest open up, felt air ripple through my innermost tissues and organs. I decided to buy a shirt like Alison Palmer's – ribbed cotton, tight, scooped low in front. In our stateroom mirror, I emulated her smile, half-shy, half-sensual. My brother didn't notice because he was busy being in love with Alison Palmer, practising his nonchalant yet sincere Alexi smile. We were besotted, and how did we express this? We raced up and down corridors and decks, and in a ridiculous Russian accent, repeated one of the film's lines. *Emergency, emergency, everybody to get from street*. It was our anthem for the trip. We couldn't say it without laughing like hyenas and we didn't even know why. I don't relate this with pride or even comprehension. We were strange and, as mentioned earlier, not cute.

*

On the third day out, *The Polynesian* reported: *U.S. Air Force jets dropped 350,000 lb of blockbusters into the jungles around Saigon as part of the Allied drive to crush Communism. The U.S. Command reported the loss of the 300th American plane over North Vietnam. Under heavy guard, Hubert Humphrey led 100,000 marchers in the Labour Day parade in New York. There was heckling between anti-war demonstrators and Nixon backers.* The bad old world was coming closer, but I just got sillier and sillier. Maybe it was the proximity of impending adulthood that gave the last days of childhood that extra sweetness. And all along, forgotten entirely, was our mother. How did she spend her *Lurline* days? One possible scenario:

In the minutes after we skip out of the stateroom, she sighs. Slumps. Shakes herself and tells herself to stop feeling sorry for herself, then she slumps again. Oh, it is hard, hard, hard to be happy, even here on the world's most luxurious ocean liner. And she's lonely, because no one knows her fears. It's the middle of the afternoon. Her left leg, all the way from her toes to her thigh, is numb. It doesn't throb or hurt. Aside from the slight tingling, it is entirely without sensation. She strokes her bare leg, as she tends to whenever she feels unseen. Her fingers feel her flesh, but her flesh does not feel her fingers. It's like she's feeling someone else's leg. When she walks, she has to consciously lift her left foot off the ground and try not to drag it. She worries about tripping, about falling, but above all, she worries about people seeing her and thinking: *There goes that poor cripple.*

Now she makes her way to the tiny bathroom. Leans against the wall for support and looks into the mirror. Not long ago, she used to examine the skin around her eyes for wrinkles. Pucker her lips and pinch her cheeks to make them pink. Now she yearns for that recent vanity, that preoccupation with something normal. What is happening now is not normal. Maybe after a while it will seem normal, but not yet. She looks in the mirror, frowns, puts on her lipstick and tells herself: *You have multiple sclerosis. Oh yes, you do. You have multiple sclerosis and that's all there is to it.* She often talks to herself like this, as if she and herself are old acquaintances who barely tolerate each other. Sometimes she scolds herself, sometimes she complains about her husband. Lately, she spends a lot of time just making sure she remembers the state of things. The truth. No one knows what causes MS and there is no cure. She prays sometimes, not because she's a devout believer, but to hedge her bets. In her suitcase are some items from the ship. Like her children, the *Lurline* experience has brought out the kleptomaniac in her. She thinks of them as souvenirs, and in squirrelling them away has already enjoyed looking back on this trip across the Pacific. The miniature fan that was part of the table decorations one night. Two spoons and a fork, with the letter M engraved – M for Matson, the ship line that owned SS *Lurline*. Now she eyes the soap dish under the mirror. Could she take it right now? Perhaps better to leave it till the last morning. Then her thoughts race back to her illness, her permanent companion. Oh, it is so unfair. She's been good. She's tried to be a good person every day. Ahead lay walking sticks. A wheelchair. Incontinence. Impairment of speech, possibly. Impairment of sight, almost certainly. Memory loss. But the hardest loss is mobility. Even thinking this makes her pine for dancing, for running, for skipping. For just walking quickly anywhere, without thinking about it. It amazes her she ever took walking for granted.

She thinks of her children briefly, about once every ten minutes. They're on a constant loop and bring her back from fretting. She thinks of her baby and calculates what she'll be doing right this minute. Napping, eating, getting a bath. Then she thinks of the older two. *Where are those darn kids?* She comforts herself: *What can they get up to on a ship?* Cruise liners are what rich people use, and rich people are safe people. Then she thinks of her husband, back in San Francisco. Her handsome blond husband who still makes her heart turn over when he walks in the door after work, darn him. The sight of him, just that. Well, he's probably flirting with that new secretary or the divorcee down the block. But she smiles wryly thinking this, because he's not been unfaithful and she imagines he never will be. He's been sweet about her MS. Protective, consoling. No one else knows, it's their secret. Then she looks out her porthole at the vast Pacific – those rolling swells of navy-black water – and thinks: *Well! Here I am, on a luxury liner on my way to Hawaii. Got myself a successful husband, three healthy children, and I still have my figure.* She pictures her home town in the valley, and thinks: *Boy oh boy, if they could see me now.* Then I think she cries a little. She sounds like a little girl. I've rarely seen her cry, but I think that's because she's private and proud, not because she's never sad. Even in her crying, she's still pretty.

Of course, I could be wrong. Another possibility:

The minute her children leave the stateroom, she's delighted, smiles her secret smile. She can be herself! She can finish the magazine she's reading, and she doesn't have to share the See's candy. She doesn't give her children or her husband a second thought. She believes a cure for MS is just around the corner, because good gravy! Things always turn out all right in the end, don't they?

Our beautiful white ship was coming closer and closer to Honolulu. The endless days were coming to an end. On the last morning, the decks were lined with passengers claiming to see porpoises, whales, even an albatross. I tried to see us as a bird might. A floating white city – a wedding cake of a city – teeming with a thousand humans mostly unaware of each other, my small family pocketed among them. My brother was nearby, staring at a girl wearing a bikini. I assumed it was with a kind of sweet ache, because that is how I felt about Alexi. Maybe we'd both become familiar with that ache, and the sweetness of it.

And when we became old and stopped feeling much, maybe we'd greet this memory like an old friend because it would make us feel something. My mother was still in the stateroom, probably rehearsing her upcoming reunion with her husband. She wouldn't tell him about the bar bill we'd run up – not till later, when they were relaxing somewhere. She'd tell it like a funny story and deflect his anger. My father would struggle to keep his smile, but he'd manage.

'Your children did what?' he'd say.

I stood by the deck, watching the approaching land without joy. It was like watching the end of *The Russians are Coming, The Russians are Coming*. A sadness simply because it was over. The way the end of a novel made me sad. The ending of anything seemed worth mourning, because it was a miniature death. I sighed and thought of my green two-piece bathing suit, in which I would almost certainly drown soon. Why had I thought it lovely? I willed the ship to drop anchor now, to halt its relentless forward movement into the future. And then the next minute I headed back to our stateroom to pack. I was so unhappy. I was ecstatic with unhappiness.

Love Letters

I was snooping through my mother's house as she lay dying. Again. On the bookshelves in their bedroom, I found Dad's master's thesis titled 'Longshore Unionism on Puget Sound 1957', typed by my mother when I was four. At the back of my mother's sock drawer, I found some small cellophane envelopes containing snippets of our childish hair. But the biggest treasure was in an old I. Magnin box in the hall closet. It was stuffed with letters they'd written to each other during the months leading up to their wedding. My father had already begun his new job in Washington, while she was still a secretary in the San Francisco office where they'd met. I knew this story. I'd written a whole novel inspired by their marriage – but here was original source material.

My mother's letters were full of practicalities and confidence. *One of your friends, Kenzie, I think, wants to bring two guests to the wedding, is that all right? It's okay dokey with me. The mechanic phoned to say your car is ready to pick up, should I pay him? Your mother wants the recipe for my cheesecake.* She'd typed these letters, not a single typo, yet they were conversational, effortless, as if they'd been typed without a care in the world. In one of the letters, she opened by saying: *I am KAPUT. Last night my sister came in about 2am, drunk as a skunk, and we stayed up to dawn talking about YOU KNOW WHO.*

My father's letters, on the other hand, handwritten on office stationery, seemed sweetly insecure and romantic. He talked about finding the apartment they'd live in, choosing their bed and how he couldn't wait to see her in it. He kept thinking about her in a certain strappy dress she'd worn a lot last time he was home, and could she remember to pack that for the honeymoon? Sometimes he crossed out words so completely, it was impossible to guess what he'd decided to delete. In one letter he included a sketch of the shelves he planned to build for his growing collection of Penguins. He often finished by saying he was going to walk to the mailbox *right now to mail this letter*, even though it was almost midnight, because the first mail collection was 5am and he'd never manage that. He signed off with the name he was known by then, plus French endearments. *Je t'aime, ma femme chérie. Mickey.*

This, I reflected, was a stark contrast to the tone of letters he'd written to Claire, a woman he'd known before Mom. Technically she'd never been a lover or girlfriend – yet those letters attested to a non-platonic frisson. We read them, me and my sister, when we finally met Claire the year he died. Those letters had no cross-outs. They were more intimate – less careful, less romantic than his letters to our mother – as if he was drunk and she was the only person he could pour his heart out to. They certainly weren't like the letters he wrote me and my sister – rare, brief and usually containing some reprimand embedded in humour. The Claire letters made me think of a Chekhov story, *The Lady with the Dog.* The way the man had two lives, public and private, and his secret life was the more real.

While I guiltlessly read letters not addressed to me, the television blared from the living room. Not *The Sound of Music*, which was therapeutic and high culture, but normal television with commercials about haemorrhoids every ten seconds. There'd been a time when this would have felt sinful. A venial sin, but sinful nevertheless. Shows like *Peyton Place* were the devil. The first time I came home to find Ateca with my mother in front of the television in broad daylight, I'd been stunned.

'Mom hates daytime TV,' I told her quietly, trying to keep a judgemental tone from creeping in.

'What? Your mother loves *General Hospital*,' she said loudly, and then laughed hard. 'Hoo boy, she loves that Dr Drake too much!'

'Are you sure? She can hardly walk away.' This was mean, but I couldn't help myself. 'How do you know she likes it?'

'Because she never falls asleep. Anything else, she closes her eyes. Like this.' She closed her eyes in case I needed a visual aid.

'Huh.'

'And she loves *Divorce Court* too.'

I'd grown up believing we were not a daytime television family, but now I had to consider another possibility. Maybe Mom *was* a daytime television person, deep down. Dementia, I'd noticed, had a way of stripping away artifice. Maybe watching *General Hospital* was the equivalent of eating a whole box of See's candy by herself every day.

I left Mom just after Easter, with Ateca crying as usual, making me feel like an emotionally frozen person. I felt guilty, driving away from that house. I *was* guilty. My place was there, by my mother's deathbed to the end, and nothing should have been getting in the way of that. Why, why, why did I keep leaving her? I had a job I loved and I'd already taken too much time off, but the most flattering *not necessarily true* reason was because I was a mother, as well as a grandmother and wife. Altogether, I had thirteen family members in Scotland, and the momentum of those relationships was more powerful than my daughterly duties.

I got on the airporter feeling the pull of my Scottish people as if they were gravity itself, but still – none of them could put a dent in my guilt at leaving my mother's deathbed. It was a deeply familiar and upsetting feeling. Above all, it was frightening, because while I was in its grip, I couldn't imagine it ending. What saved me? The same thing that always saved me. After fifteen minutes, as the bus rolled into the Waldo Tunnel and I noticed the rainbow looked like it needed repainting, I began to make up stories. To think about the past and fill in the gaps with imagination.

I'd squirrelled half a dozen of the love letters into my bag and I pulled one out now. I'd already read it but was convinced further readings would reveal more. I was used to viewing my father as a cocky serial adulterer, but those crossed-out words niggled me and I had to consider a more flattering possibility. Maybe he'd been lonely in his marriage. Out-and-out lonely, the kind that has a bad smell and breeds naughty impulses. In which case, those affairs had not been about sex, but genuine quests for love. Maybe some of those other women had even broken his heart. Mom was many good things – attractive, honest, loyal – but her letters reminded me how self-sufficient she'd been, how content in her own skin. Maybe a frustrating partner for an insecure man who craved emotional intimacy and free-flowing confidences.

All the way home on the plane, even while watching movies on my minuscule screen, I kept thinking about my father going out to mail those letters in the middle of the night. It would have been cold, but he'd left his warm hotel room because he wasn't tired yet and needed to do something. I understood that restlessness. And I recognised that sense of urgency. The need to reach someone so badly, a walk to the mailbox at midnight wasn't a chore at all. It was a joy.

There he goes: a skinny man looking about fifteen, striding through the shadowy streets of downtown Seattle. He's clutching a stamped letter addressed to Miss Bobbie Jean Swarts, which was her name then. He grew up in a small town, he's still not at ease in the city. He walks quickly and keeps darting glances around. He gets to the mailbox, looks around, then kisses the envelope and slips it in. On the way back to his hotel, he goes a little slower and whistles 'Goodnight, Irene'. He imagines his letter being delivered to her apartment, maybe the day after tomorrow. He knows just how she'll look when she sees it. The way her lips will part, and her eyes crinkle up a little. She's so goddamn pretty when she looks like that, like a movie star, and he always has to touch her somewhere. Her knee, shoulder, hand. Mouth. He tries to keep her face at the front of his thoughts as long as he can, because everything else in his life right now scares the hell out of him.

Our Lady of Solitude

Sixty years old
California, 2013

My sister was a reporter for the *San Francisco Chronicle*. She'd been a columnist, a prize-winning feature writer, a copy editor, and now she was a crime reporter. Which made her a hero. Unlike myself and everyone else I knew, she lived at the rock face every day. She was familiar with parts of the city I was too afraid to enter, and she interviewed victims of terrible injustices and tragic accidents. If they were unwilling or unconscious or dead, she interviewed their loved ones or random witnesses. Listened to the details of shootings, knifings, drownings, rapes, violence of all kinds. Then she wrote about it, so us wimps could experience the world from the safe distance of our nice kitchens, sipping fresh coffee and making tut-tut noises. Once she told me the paper liked their crime reporters to be women because victims and witnesses were more likely to open up to women. The areas she ventured into were often dangerous, so they sent her with a male photographer. This never reassured me. Were male photographers known for physical courage, skilled in defensive arts? I imagined them screaming like little girls and hiding behind my sister, while she wielded her pencil like a sabre. Which meant that, like my brother, she was a good person to have adventures with.

It had been six months since Dad died, and we were hatching a plan to meet Claire, his secret lover. Or was she? There was no proof but plenty of indicators, and together we'd fabricated a whole romance. We missed our father dreadfully, and we told ourselves visiting Claire would essentially be a tribute to him. It would also be a trip on his behalf, of course. He'd known Claire longer than he'd known our mother, and they'd been writing letters since college days. We knew about her because he'd always confided in us. Our mother hadn't known about his post office box in town, nor had our brother. It was reserved for Claire letters. Whenever he said her name, he had a particular stupefied look, as if he was saying *love* in slow motion.

So there we were, newly fatherless, two daddy's girls about to head out to visit one of his favourite people and feeling not one whit of disloyalty to our mother, who was no doubt sitting in her wheelchair by the desk right now, munching pastries and watching *The Sound of Music*. *I'm so proud of you*, we could imagine Dad saying, shaking his head and chuckling that chuckle he had when something tickled him and he knew it shouldn't. We were in my sister's old Corolla hatchback with the dog-hair-covered seats and seat belts that didn't work. It wasn't that she didn't believe in seat belts as death-preventers – it was a lack of funds to fix them. As for cleaning cars, her disbelief in that was like atheism. It had no grey areas. There was no point, ever, in removing garbage from the car or vacuuming dog hair. Her thick hair was tied back in a ponytail and she was wearing dark glasses, non-trendy jeans, a faded Bear's T-shirt and her charity store sneakers. She looked like she didn't give a damn, and also gorgeous. Her dog Scout was on the back seat. After our Dad's terrible dog Beau, Scout was the worst dog in the world. Also, after Beau, the most loved. He was huge with long black hair, like a bear, and when he jumped on people he knocked them over. He had a running sore on his neck, which in my sister's view was one of his more endearing attributes. He normally sat on the passenger front seat, so when I sat there instead, he lurched forward to try and sit on my lap.

'No!' I said firmly. 'No! Get back, Scout!'

But his front paws were already on the dashboard, and with his rear legs planted on my lap, he commenced to whip my face with his tail. *Thwack, thwack!* I tried to push him off, but one of my hands landed on his running sore and I said *goddammit*, sounding uncannily like our father. This made my sister laugh and say in a funny voice:

'Oh, silly Scout, you just wanna be next to your momma, don't you?'

I started giggling, which surprised me. The whole scenario was intensely irritating. Maybe it was the idea of how we looked. My squeamishness, my sister's glee, Scout being oblivious to everything but his entitlement to the front seat. There was something timeless and classically absurd about the moment.

I'd loved my sister since she was born, in a blurry semi-maternal way. She was only four or five when I left home, but the age gap had shrunk to nothing ten years ago when we both became single. Without telling each other and six thousand miles apart, we each flew from the safety of our nests, much to the dismay of many. Were we frightened, lonely, anxious about the future? We were aware those responses were appropriate, but mostly we were not. Not in the beginning. We giggled like insane people everywhere we went. In cars, with our children in the backseat wearing exasperated expressions. In bars and restaurants and parks. In our parents' house at the dinner table, all of us still under the impression our parents were immortal. In Starbucks on 4th Street in San Rafael, my ten-year-old son took a photograph showing us with eyes closed and our mouths wide open – presumably cackling. My head was thrown back as if I couldn't get enough oxygen otherwise.

I was lucky. I'd been close to my brother till the time we both married, putting the brakes on our hitch-hiking and train-hopping adventures. And now, just when I needed another cohort, here was a sister for me to play with. My only experience of sibling rivalry was the fear my brother and sister would gang up on me one day. That they'd have fun without me, talk about me and laugh. It was a secret fear, and ridiculous because *of course* they'd do those things – I did them already, with one or the other of them. Betrayal was integral to being one of three, albeit a non-vicious betrayal. More like gossip, really.

Me and my brother had mainly done dangerous things. Me and my sister mainly talked. We talked for hundreds of hours, maybe a year's worth of hours per decade. It was such a relief to speak to someone who instantly and consistently replied: *I know! Me too!* We talked about people who annoyed us, about politics and dogs, about our exes and our dates, about our children. Compared to adventures with my brother, it was a physically sedate time. Love was uppermost on our mind, and romance and passion, but we mostly behaved. How could it be otherwise? Our children were constantly there wanting things like food, Pokémon cards, the television to be fixed. Now and then, clean sheets.

That era ended about five years ago when I remarried and my sister found the perfect boyfriend. Not being single had led to less giggling, and some days that seemed a high price. Hence my relief when giddiness resurfaced now in her old Corolla, *thank you, Scout*. It was a September morning, about nine, and already baking hot. Scout was in the back seat again, emitting a low whine of self-pity and the occasional fart. The engine whined too – *pleeeeeeze don't try to start me* – and we had to jump-start it. Finally, with a sound like gunshot and a roar followed by black exhaust, we were off. Rufus

Wainwright's 'Hallelujah' blasted out of the speakers. It was our anthem from our single days, and I briefly wondered why we didn't talk much about them any more. Maybe they hadn't happened as I remembered – how would I know, if we didn't compare notes? Then I was caught up in the moment. The commute traffic cramming us into a lane we needed out of, the sky as blue as it never was in Scotland, my sister shouting at other drivers – *Come on, ya dumbass, give me some space!* She drove with one hand so she could make gestures and beep her horn every few minutes. She was a fabulous person to go on a road trip with, and we hollered out those 'Hallelujah' lyrics as if we'd written them, as if we were pulling them from our guts. Damn right, love was just a cold and broken hallelujah.

We were not alone. My second husband sat quietly on the back seat next to Scout, instinctively understanding his temporary effacement was necessary. That because I hardly saw her these days, I'd want to talk to her, not him. That this was a *sister* trip. I was grateful, in a spoiled brat kind of way, and mentally gave him a thousand brownie points while me and my sister commenced talking about our dead father and Claire. Had they been lovers over the years? Or even at the beginning? Dad had implied they had, but that might have been male pride. We couldn't decide. Since Christopher Parker's kisses forty-odd years ago, I knew all about the enduring quality of nonconsummation. What was romance, if not an absence, a postponement, a regret? Or – and this was not my favourite visual – maybe Dad and Claire had been meeting in a Hotel Five once a month for sixty-three years. Maybe he'd had a proper double life with her. In which case, he'd not told his daughters everything after all.

'Remember her letters?'

'Of course,' my sister said. 'I read them all the time.'

'Me too.'

It wasn't true. We were both exaggerators.

'Sometimes I wonder why he saved them. You couldn't call them romantic. Or even indiscreet,' she said.

'Maybe they were in code. In case Mom found them.'

'God, that was a great day.'

'The desk day?'

'Yeah. Wasn't it? I think about it all the time.'

Another exaggeration. But those letters had been pivotal. They were how we found out where she lived. It had been easy to sort out our father's desk, and a good post-funeral distraction. He'd not been a hoarder, and the contents of each drawer were minimal and logical. A combination of practical and sentimental. The top right drawer contained items like scissors, tape, pencils and a pencil sharpener. The drawer under it had three old not-ticking watches (I recognised one as my grandfather's) and four pairs of glasses, presumably the ones that had been replaced by stronger prescriptions. In the top left drawer we found new chequebooks and unopened bank statements. One envelope had a new credit card inside, which made me sad.

In the drawer below that, we found a manila folder with a dozen letters from Claire, written over the previous ten years. We'd watched our father mail letters to her over the decades, mostly postcards, but we'd never seen her letters to him. They turned out to be warm and newsy and funny, with little moans about how banal young people were these days, even the ones in their fifties, and as for getting to grips with the internet, well! *The world is obviously going to the dogs.* We tried to read between the typewritten lines. There was nothing alluding to an affair, but couldn't that omission tell a story too? Otherwise, why the post office box?

On top of the desk, alongside his magnetic paper clip box and his business card carousel, was a round wooden box full of keys. Each one was tied with a string to a label in his neat bold handwriting. *Boat. Garage. Basement.* Then, to our delight, *P.O. Box.* The key attached had a number engraved on it. We hopped in the car and raced to the post office, but after many tries during which we talked to the key and sang open-up songs, nothing happened. When his last P.O. bill had gone unpaid, presumably the box had been emptied and a new lock installed. It felt so anticlimactic, that key not turning in the lock. That was not supposed to happen, damn it. We were supposed to spend the afternoon reading letters addressed to a man who no longer had secrets, because what's the narrative point of finding a key that doesn't work?

'Pity he never wrote down his life story,' my sister said, as we drank coffee on the deck later, recovering from our disappointment.

'Yeah,' I agreed. 'He was a good writer, but aside from work reports, he'd no interest in writing.'

His desk was as close to an autobiography as we'd get.

The windows were down. There was air con in the Corolla, but of course it was broken and the hot air rushed around the car, sending dog hair and other less identifiable particles spinning. It was full of valley smells. Rotten fruit, hot tarmac, now and then a whiff of diesel exhaust. Scout licked the back of my neck from time to time, which I stopped minding after a while. I passed bottles of water to my sister, and behind me, to my husband. He was huddled up to Scout.

'Cute,' I said. 'You look like a couple.'

'Thanks,' he said, with a fake smile.

'Albeit an inter-species couple. Still cute.'

He smiled again, this time less fake, and gave me the finger. I blew him a kiss and put Etta James on because no one sang about lonely days ending like her.

We were on 101, which was not as scenic as Highway One following the coast – but in a way it made that other route seem touristy. We were on the real road, the road people used to get somewhere, like work or home. We stopped for a break at Soledad. I'd heard of Soledad State Prison – it was famous, but now I learned its real name was Correctional Training Facility, which seemed strangely generic and in need of an article like *the*. Soledad meant solitude in Spanish – apt for solitary confinement – but that was just a coincidence because the place was named after a mission built by the Franciscan fathers in 1791. We followed the signs down a dusty road to an empty parking lot by a small pink stucco church, very simple and traditional. It looked like all twenty-one of the rebuilt missions. The sign in front said *Nuestra Señora de la Soledad* – Our Lady of Solitude.

'According to Wikipedia,' said my husband, reading from his phone, 'it was a name applied to Mary by the Marians, whatever they are. The first Lady of Solitude dates back to 1506, when the Castilian Queen Juana immersed herself in mourning after the early death of her beloved husband.'

'Kind of romantic. And sad,' I said, reaching back to touch his arm. 'To feel life unbearable without someone you love.'

'Huh,' said my sister. 'Or maybe she just wanted an excuse to be alone.'

'Oh, come on,' protested my husband.

'Hey, it happens! Women like to be alone sometimes!'

My sister had announced the end of her marriage to our parents via a short but eloquent speech. Very brave. Something dry and factual, along the lines of: *It's not good between us any more. I've left him.* I, on the other hand, told our parents in a letter. It was verbose, as if I was trying to bury the lead. Midway through the third paragraph, I mentioned some problems in the marital department that might require a major adjustment, then I went on to describe how my sixteen-year-old wanted to leave school and train to become a chef. Weeks went by and I had no reply to my postal announcement, so I phoned home. My mother answered and immediately said:

'Hold on, I'll get your father.'

This was not a sign of anything in particular, it was a friendly rote reply. Maybe she'd long ago given up competing to be the favoured parent and wanted to save time. I listened to her shout *George! George! Come quick!* and heard a door open and footsteps. It was easy to picture home. The sailboat photograph on the wall where it'd always hung, the dog asleep on the hall rug, the shadowy living room with the broken blinds half down. My father's cranky face as he approached. *What is it, Barbara? I told you, I'm busy!* I felt a little sick. *It's Cynthia on the phone*, she said. *Oh*, he said.

'So, did you get my letter?' I asked him, after our hellos.

'Sure,' he said.

'About us splitting up?'

A pause filled with his sigh.

'*Yes.*'

'What do you think?'

'I think it's a pretty dumb idea.'

Then he went on to tell me a story about a friend of theirs who'd divorced her husband on the grounds of infidelity.

'Now he's remarried to a twenty-five-year-old girl and his business is booming.' He chuckled.

'And his ex-wife? Your friend?'

'Haven't seen her around much, no one invites divorced women to parties. Heard she was living somewhere in the Canal,' he said sombrely. The Canal was short for the Canal District, and code for abject poverty.

'Oh dear.'

'Yeah, and lonely as hell, I gather. Drinks a lot.'

The upshot being I was now a social pariah and also bound for hard times. Divorce was obviously a man's game.

When my parents came to Scotland a few months after the split, they saw my not-divorced-yet husband walking past the kitchen window to his own door in the extension. My father went out to the garden and greeted him like they were old friends, shaking hands, laughing – which was ironic because he'd given me clear messages since my wedding day, I'd married a geek. But when my husband came into the kitchen to get something for his makeshift kitchen, my mother lifted her hands and blocked him from her view.

'Hi, Barbara,' he said. 'How are you?'

She then wiggled her fingers in front of her face and made *lalala* noises as if saying *I'm not listening*. She knew I was at fault but here she was, snubbing the poor sinned-against husband. It looked like no matter what stupid thing I did, she was going to stick with me.

Mission Soledad was evidently not a popular tourist site. There were no other people in sight. The air was dry and dusty, smelling vaguely of garlic and onions. Nothing was pretty. Potato chip bags, Coke cans and other trash had drifted up against the chain-link fence at the back of the church museum, as if the place had been closed for years. The land was flat and dotted with scrubby bushes and the ragged bits left after crops were harvested. There was the distant drone of traffic and a closer drone of yellow jackets. On the ground – when I stopped to look closely – ants were marching in columns, steadily intent on their own war of domination and survival. High above, turkey vultures circled lazily. The only things approaching beauty were an iron bell hanging from a curved post capped with dry guano, and four palm trees standing asymmetrically around the building.

'It's so atmospheric,' my sister said. 'Don't you think?'

I agreed, and we exchanged a complicit smile, but my husband began walking away towards the flat empty fields beyond the churchyard.

'You okay?' I called.

He lifted one hand with a thumbs up but didn't turn around. Were his shoulders sagging a bit? I had neglected him, I told myself. He hated being here. He didn't think it was atmospheric, he thought it was weird to think that. Soledad was as different from Scotland as it was possible to be. I stared at his retreating figure, and the further away he got, the more alone he looked.

'Jesus, I'm such a bad wife.'

'Nah,' my sister said.

'But look. I've driven him away.'

'Don't be silly. He's probably just looking for a place to pee.'

Ten years earlier and newly single, me and my sister had begun flying to each other regularly. We often had a glass of wine or beer, but were never as drunk as our giggling sounded because our intoxication came from rapport – the deep kind that dissolved inhibitions. We bought matching padded bras in Victoria's Secret, looked at dating sites and flirted shamelessly in bars, in parks, in grocery stores. Sisters who looked nothing like sisters, united in giddiness. I suppose we were loathsome in our happiness. Simultaneously, we were miserable. Our father disapproved of us and we were destined for lonely poverty-stricken futures. When we eventually died no one would notice for days. Maybe weeks. When we sang along to Rufus Wainwright's 'Hallelujah', we were aware how corny we sounded, how melodramatic, how off-key. And that made us laugh harder, even though we were extremely miserable. Love couldn't be a hallelujah victory march for us, nothing could. For one thing, we shared the worry gene. We got it from our mother, the very person we'd intended to never become. The woman who used to lie awake, convinced we were dying in a wrecked car, or homeless and lost in a foreign country. Who called the highway patrol so often, they knew her name. *No, Mrs Jones, no road fatalities tonight.* How had this happened? We'd made choices like our father, but responded to them as if we were our mother. It was hell, having a contradictory nature, and it was probably confusing for the people around us.

Once when I was visiting her in Oakland, we stayed up late talking about our children. They enjoyed unprecedented freedom now we were single, but did they also suffer? Not obviously, we assured each other – or was it just convenient to view it that way? Surely there'd been upset, sadness, even trauma.

'But the kids know we love them. That's the main thing, right?' I eventually offered.

'Yeah, maybe.'

'And you know what else?' I could feel an epiphany swelling up. Not sure what words would convey it, because I'd no idea what it was yet. Like spotting something approaching in the distance in the vague shape of something good. With my sister, I could always trust the vague shape to evolve into something or other.

'What?'

'Well . . . we were loved too.' Aha! Was it as simple as that? *Yes!*

'Oh, Jesus.'

'Okay, sorry. But it's obvious, right?'

'Well, sure, I guess. You mean when we were kids?'

'It doesn't matter when. Once you're loved by your parents, you're loved. It's done. Like a polio vaccine.'

'Huh.'

Then I couldn't stop myself.

'We were loved! Mom and Dad loved us. They still do. Can't you feel it in here?'

I ran my hand down the middle of my front, ending with a pat on my belly. Which due to four pregnancies was a little pouch so soft I could sink my fingers into it, and frequently did when I needed a fidget object. She continued to look at me sceptically.

'Of course, I know. Jesus Christ. You're tired. You always get like this when you're tired. All sentimental and idealistic.'

'*I am not,*' I replied as petulantly as any tired three-year-old, and from there the evening began to dissolve – because of course, we weren't always giggling. That would be bizarre.

'Ah, come on, you're always playing the love card.' She said *love card* in a silly way, as if the words described something infantile. A kiddie television show or a pink feather boa.

'I am not! Jesus Christ almighty.' I felt like crying suddenly. 'You're the one who's tired! You always get cynical when you're tired.'

On and on – she called me a prissy Pollyanna, I called her a pathetic Eeyore – and then, suddenly flat, we stood up and started clearing the table.

'Yikes, what's that thing?' I asked as we faced each other, about to head to our bedrooms.

I put my finger on her chest and she fell for it. Looked down, and I quickly tickled her under her chin. Then I managed a quick plunge to one of her armpits before she pushed me away, making muffled squawking noises because she didn't want to wake the kids.

'Fuck you,' she mouthed. She mouthed it beautifully, stretching her mouth expressively.

'Fuck you too,' I whispered, and tried to kiss her but she dodged me.

During this time, she was living in a small rented basement apartment which she told her children was just as nice as the three-bedroomed house with a view they used to live in. And life was still hunky-dory. Everything was as it should be and there was nothing whatsoever to worry about. She so thoroughly convinced her children their situation was entirely normal, her six-year-old described a new kid in class as being weird because her parents were un-divorced. My sister had to explain this was not necessarily a freaky thing to be. That, strange as it seemed, some mommies wanted to stay married to the daddies. Really? Yes, really.

She was the only person I knew whose cutlery drawer was without divisions for forks, knives and spoons. She had no wine glasses and drank Pinot Noir from plastic kiddie cups. When her refrigerator was empty, she'd pile her kids into the car and take them to a burger place for dinner. She didn't believe in pyjamas for herself or her children. Everyone in her house, from infancy onwards, slept in the clothes they were wearing when they got tired. And everyone slept in the same enormous bed. Whenever milk spilled or pizza fell on the floor, she'd call the dog to clean it up. She was chronically exhausted and anxious about money, but I never heard her shout at her children. She never made them wash their hair if they didn't want to or clean their rooms. She never said no when they asked for another pet, and always laughed when they farted or burped. She was, in short, a glorious mother and her children adored her.

'Wonder why they called it *Our Lady of Solitude*?' my husband asked suddenly. We were swatting the flies who had finally found us. 'I mean, why name a church after loneliness? All the other missions are named after saints.'

'Solitude is not the same as loneliness,' I said, wincing as I heard how pedantic I sounded.

'Still,' he replied. 'And who got to choose it?'

'Oh, some homesick padre, probably,' my sister offered, half smiling. 'Someone with no friends, who decided to make a thing of it. Like it was a good thing, being an outcast.'

Then she said *shit*, because Scout was pooping on someone's grave. She scooped it up with some twigs, tossed it over the fence, and then we went back to the car and drove off. Two hours later we stopped for a late lunch in Paso Robles. We had unremarkable sandwiches and weak coffee served by a somnolent waitress in her late teens. We chewed silently and cooled down. When we finished my husband paid with the quiet graciousness I'd grown used to and depended on, in a confused feminist way. Then we walked around and saw nicer places to eat, with avocado and langoustines and crispy kale on the menu.

'Oh well,' my sister said. 'Typical.'

'Yeah. Oh well,' I said.

'But I really liked the place we had lunch,' protested my husband, maybe because when you're from Wakefield in Yorkshire, things like langoustines and avocadoes are just scary.

It was about 3pm now. Not a breath of wind. Walking slowly around downtown Paso Robles, we were speechless and shiny with sweat. After letting Scout out to pee and drink some water, we got back in the car and kept driving. There was hardly any traffic, and none that was speeding or overtaking – as if all the drivers had agreed to obey a choreography law. We passed wineries and vineyards, lettuce fields and rows of apricot trees, dusty wooden houses set in yards full of dead grass. The highway was perfectly straight. Sometimes there was a shimmer above it, a heat mirage. I let my thoughts wander, while the valley air pumped itself around me. I'd ceased noticing the dog smell. I'd ceased caring I wasn't strapped in. The car went over heat cracks on the highway, setting up a soporific rhythm. At last, we saw the Santa Ynez mountains in the distance.

Look, Dad, look!

Goddamn! he replied appreciatively.

Like most towns, the entrance to Santa Barbara was a little disappointing. Just another set of freeway turn-offs and retail outlets. The Pacific Ocean was visible, a thin grey line on the horizon – not pretty yet. We found Claire's apartment building and then suddenly there she was. I'd seen photos of her eighteen-year-old self, and the sight of her now gave me a visceral jolt, as if she was someone I'd known all my life. Or as if Dad was secreted inside me somehow, and it was his recognition, his joyful leaping. *It's you, it's you!*

'Was your trip hell?' she asked in a low voice. 'Come on in, I'll fix you a martini.'

She was old and sweet, but not at all a sweet old lady. She was pretty – proper pretty, not just pretty for her age. I understood – me and my sister both did – what our father had seen in her. Within the first three minutes, we knew she was fun. *Fun.* A much-misused word. Fun was not going to a circus or a party or telling jokes. Fun was seeing the humour in things that weren't meant to be funny with someone else who also saw it that way. It was indulging in small naughty acts with someone. Our father had been fun. Our mother liked having fun, she was even funny sometimes, but she was not fun. She made us laugh, but we mostly laughed at her, which was more cruel-sounding than it was.

Later I excused myself, went into her bathroom and emptied some of Dad's ashes into the back of her highest cupboard. Behind a gift basket of soap, a small heap of the man who'd always carried a torch for her. Then we checked into our hotel, where I swam in my underpants and T-shirt because I had no swimsuit. I had the good tired feeling that comes from being too hot all day and from laughing hard. My sister, who did not like swimming, sat at the side and we talked in between my languid laps. Scout was under her lounger, panting.

'So, what do you think now?' I asked.

'Oh, they definitely bonked. But it never would have lasted if they'd married.'

'True,' I said, after a minute. 'She wouldn't have put up with him.'

'Which means, I guess, he married the right one.'

'Yeah,' I said. 'It was a good move.'

The truth was, we admired dysfunctional marriages. Happy couples with perfect smiles – holding hands or worse, wearing identical clothes – were to be despised. Maybe this preference was the main legacy of our parents' marriage.

'Anyway, maybe not having each other was the whole thing,' she added.

'Yeah?'

'Yeah. No one gets to adore someone for sixty years *and* live with them. It's physically and emotionally not possible. I'm not even sure it's legal.'

Then my husband appeared by the pool, reminding me of his existence, and I was flooded with appreciation and even a kind of shock. My God, by a pure fluke I'd married a kind and attractive man! Nevertheless, I couldn't help noticing he looked like most British tourists in California – a bit pink and dazed. And were those socks with his sandals? At least we wouldn't have to put our marriage to the sixty-year test, I thought. We'd be lucky to get to twenty.

We took Claire out to dinner, a place on the pier where we ordered oysters and dry martinis in Dad's honour. Beyond the windows was the familiar Pacific, my favourite ocean, presently in an iridescent mood. The sun sank slowly into the sea like a glowing marshmallow. I half expected to hear a loud hiss, and then it was gone. At our request, Claire was talking about seeing Dad for the first time. It was in her English 101 class, and even though he looked young, he seemed like a man because he'd been a soldier. As she talked, she started looking younger. Pink and happy. She insisted he'd been a good friend, maybe her best friend, but never a boyfriend. Heavens, she'd been engaged to a medical student all that time! The medical student was often busy studying, so our dad had escorted her to parties and dances. They used to meet in the eucalyptus grove on campus and just talk, talk, talk. Sometimes he brought some beers, or a lemonade bottle full of liquor – she couldn't remember what kind, it was just liquor. They'd drink and smoke for hours. Then when she was studying in Paris on her year abroad – *such an exciting place to be when you're young*, she told us – she broke her engagement because our father's letters were so much funnier than the ones her fiancé wrote.

'Aha!' I couldn't help saying.

'But I'm not saying I broke up with him to be with your father,' she said. 'We were entirely platonic. It was just that I realised how boring my life would be, married to a man who took himself so seriously.'

'I get that,' my sister said. 'Serious self-regard is the kiss of death.'

Claire laughed and added: 'My God, his letters were unreadable. I threw them away, half-read. But I've still got all your dad's letters.'

What?

But we were too slow to react, and she began to talk about going on to London from Paris for a while. I understood that. Lots of Americans need to slum it in Europe at least once in their life.

'And by the time I was back in California, your parents had met.'

'Oh no!' we cried.

'No, no, it's okay. I had someone else by then too. An older man, I was crazy about him! Even later when I found out he had an ex-wife and kids, I still adored him. We got married lickety-split, and then we both went to your parents' wedding.'

This was news to us. Our mother had met her? I'd seen wedding photos, but here was a real live witness.

'What was their wedding like?'

'Oh, it was fun. *My God, real fun,*' she told us in a confidential tone, hinting at hedonism. 'Maybe a hundred people at the reception. Very noisy, everybody laughing and talking loud. No one sitting out dances. Lots of champagne.'

'Wow,' said my sister. 'So, did you and Dad, uh, dance together?'

'Well, sure we did!'

'Was it a slow dance?' I had to ask.

'Oh, I don't remember. Maybe.'

Wine-drinking pause.

'Okay, but just so you know,' my sister said disarmingly, 'we wouldn't mind if you'd been more than friends.'

Another pause, and my husband said:

'So, if you don't mind my asking, were you?' It was his first contribution to the conversation, and I could have crawled onto his lap and French kissed him.

Claire smiled, then sidestepped his question entirely by spilling her wine, leaving me to imagine versions of that evening in Sausalito at the Alta Mira hotel. They'd danced slowly together one last time. *If only you'd stayed here, not gone to Europe*, he might have whispered, his lips grazing her ear. Or something funnier, blacker, because that was their relationship. *Close call, baby. Could have been us.* Then she probably waved our parents goodbye, along with everyone else. Along with her husband. Watched Mom and Dad in their going-away outfits – Mom in a classic grey dress, her waist impossibly tiny; Dad in a corduroy jacket and khaki pants – walking down the steps to their waiting MG convertible, laughing and brushing rice off their clothes. They would have been half drunk, and that wouldn't be worrying a single person, not even their mothers. Twenty-year-old Claire probably stayed on to watch their car till it disappeared down the twisty hill to the bay, maybe shaking her head slightly, smiling and blowing them a last kiss. Then she'd turn to her brand-new husband and kiss him too.

'Want a cigarette?' he'd ask, intuiting she'd just had a moment.

'Damn tootin'.'

And he'd light two at the same time in his mouth, then slip one between her lips before blowing a perfect smoke ring. All of which were actions intended to persuade her she'd married the right one.

After dinner, we had coffee and then brandy.

'So, can I just return to Dad again for a minute?' my sister asked, in tenacious reporter style.

'Of course,' said Claire. 'What else do you want to know?'

'Did you see each other after the wedding?'

'Oh, I don't think so. Hard to remember. Maybe a few times. At least once, anyway.'

'What happened when you met?' my sister asked.

'We had dinner, I think.'

'And then?'

'And then we just carried on writing letters,' she said, smiling enigmatically. Or maybe not enigmatically. The truth must be allowed to be anticlimactic, after all. Then she signalled to the waiter for the bill.

As we wound our way back up the valley the next day, we were tired and not talking much. My husband sat in the front – I'd had my fill of sisterly conversation, and felt generous now. I watched the neat rows of fruit and vegetables slide by, each one a different shade of green. Now and then I spotted people working in the fields, and I liked that – people improved scenery sometimes, and so did houses if there weren't too many. Scout's head flopped out the other window, ears flapping, eyes closed.

He looked dead, but whenever a bug whipped his face he flinched. My husband and sister talked a bit. I only caught occasional words and mainly noticed the pattern of their voices. His was enquiring, hers was lower and delivered in the sweet even voice she used when interviewing strangers. Sometimes I heard them laugh spontaneously, and that made me happy. I wanted them to like each other.

As we approached the Bay Area, passing signs for San Jose, Sunnyvale and then San Francisco, it occurred to me we'd been having adventures all along, me and my sister. Just because we hadn't hopped freight trains or hitch-hiked, didn't mean we hadn't taken risks. Anything at all might have happened, even on this trip. A bus might have pushed us off the road into a concrete barrier at seventy miles an hour. A black widow spider might have crawled up our legs and bitten us while we were wandering around Soledad. What if a bee had stung us, and we'd become allergic to bee stings? Or if an earthquake – the big one – had cracked the state from Baja right the way up to Oregon? It was a miracle, our mother would say, that we were both still alive. That our children were alive and well. *Thank God you're safe!*

'Hey,' I said to my husband and sister. I had to lean forward and shout because of the wind. 'Let's go out for dinner tonight. My treat. Pizza at that place on Jack London Square?'

You could sit at that bar having a gin and tonic, and suddenly everyone would stop talking because a train was coming through, the wheels going clickety-clack and the whistle filling the air like an elongated sad-in-a-good-way balloon. They agreed it was a good idea and I sat back. We'd be there in fifteen minutes, if the traffic wasn't bad. But thinking about time passing quickly reminded me we were flying back to Scotland in three days and I had a little preview of how much I was going to miss my sister. Tiny pains in my throat, in my chest. Pinpricks of love, I told myself, then smiled because I imagined what she would say if I told her about my pinpricks of love. I tried to catch her eyes in the rear-view mirror and when she finally glanced at my reflection, she made a goofy face. Then she raised both eyebrows and smiled just like our mother did when she was saying *Wah!*

Last night, after we took Claire back to her apartment, we'd accepted a nightcap on her balcony. Port, along with thin slices of sourdough and Manchego cheese. It was a harvest moon, deep orange. She didn't turn the lights on, just lit a candle. We could clearly hear the surf now, and it reminded me of listening to my asthmatic brother breathing at night when we shared a room. The same gravely whooshing in and the higher-pitched sucking back out. She showed us some letters our father had written to her. The earliest predated his meeting our mother – 4th May 1951 – and began *Dearest Shadow: It is a crappy spring night. I just got off work (ugh) five hours ago, and am now five dollars poorer but ten martinis richer.* A later letter contained this: *I am going to be the brightest star to hit the American literary world since P.G. Wodehouse. I'm going to crack it wide open.* Another, dated less than a year before his marriage to our mother, finished with this: *Let me know, Shad, when you're coming back to the States. Give me a few hours to sever any impediments I've picked up in the last year.* The most recent was dated ten years ago, and included these lines: *Exciting news here. My darling daughters, without collusion, have each dumped their nerdy husbands. I'm so proud of them!*

When it was time to go, she hugged my husband and told him he was a saint to put up with us all. Then she turned to me and my sister and kissed us too. Two kisses each, one on each cheek, European style. She half whispered – was she crying? – that meeting us felt like Dad's parting gift to her.

'I'm so glad – *so glad* – I didn't marry Mickey, because . . . well, look at you girls!'

I didn't know what to say, but I was glad I'd left some of Dad in her bathroom.

Had they had an affair? Possibly, but who cared. There were deeper and bigger things between people than affairs. Not every relationship has a name.

Scoot In

'Sister, you better get here quick!' This was whispered, because Ateca had taken the phone to my mother's deathbed, where my mother was too close to death to say hello but conscious enough to require tact. 'God is ready for your mother.'

'Okay, okay. I'm on my way.'

But it was hard to summon a sense of urgency. At the end of May the hospice had given my mother another extension, but they'd made it clear that if she was still alive in September, she was on her own. It was now early June. I booked my flight and then set about cancelling things. I got a little cranky. *This better damn well be worth it.* My sister met my flight, and we spent most of the ride home laughing about stupid stuff. Death could find no entry with us, no siree! It held no weight, because our mother thought dying was in bad taste, it was what losers did. I arrived home to find Ateca putting Mom to bed.

'Look, Barbarajones! Look who's come all the way from Scotland to see you.'

Mom was lying on her back, looking young because gravity was pulling her wrinkles out. Her pyjamas were pink with purple daisies on them. Nylon, not cotton. Nothing about those pyjamas said *Mom*. Where were her soft checked L.L.Bean pyjamas? Her Lanz nightgown? I kissed her cheeks and smelled toothpaste.

'Is it really you, all the way from Scotland?'

'Yeah, it's me.'

'Come here, you.' She pulled me in for three kisses, this time on the mouth. 'Are you all right?'

'Yeah, I'm just tired,' I said.

'Why don't you climb in with me?' She lifted her blanket up. 'Come on, scoot in.'

'That's kind, Mom, but no, thanks.'

I went to bed in my dead father's office down the hall. I hadn't been to bed in two days and it was good to stretch out and sink into sleep. But I woke in a few hours because someone was unlocking the front door. I listened to the key in the door, the door opening and then footsteps. It was dark, and I couldn't see my watch because I was unable to move. Ateca had left earlier and said she'd be back the next day. Presumably, she'd changed her mind. I went back to sleep but was awoken again by footsteps outside my door, going up the hall to my mother's bedroom, then down again past my door. Ateca must be having a restless night, I thought. I heard the refrigerator door open and close, then more footsteps. In the morning, her bedroom door remained shut and I heard no praying, which was unusual – but I was too groggy to think much about it. I made coffee with the coffee I'd bought a month ago, when suddenly she walked through the front door.

'Morning, Sister.'

'I thought you were in bed,' I said. I told her about the noises in the night, the footsteps. She laughed her barking laugh. *Ha! Ha! Ha!*

'Oh, yes, that is your father. George Jones is still here. Up and down the hall all night sometimes!' Then she sighed as if it was a little tedious, but certainly not weird.

And thus commenced my final deathbed visit, though I didn't know that at the time. I settled back into my San Rafael routine. Phoned my friends, arranged to meet for dinner, for coffee, for walks, hung up my clothes in the closet.

Then I set up my laptop on my dad's old desk and began working on a story about the first time I lived in London. So much surprised me. What kind of kid – I'd been nineteen – embraced urban squalor and loneliness over Marin County and family? Yet I'd jumped that ship of familial love and material ease without a second thought. Maybe it was just the times. None of my friends had valued middle-class comfort either. We used to brag about how little we spent on everything. Laugh at people who had ambitions, or for whom nice cars were important. And the more I wrote, the more I remembered the intoxication of anonymity. How familial love – *how being known* – could feel oppressive.

On and off, I kept thinking about the footsteps. Dead or not, I was definitely up for a visit from Dad. I *missed* him. Even seeing his old *New Yorkers* made me cry. One day I googled nocturnal visitations, and one of the links that came up was narcolepsy. I clicked on it and read about sleep paralysis with audio and visual hallucinations. They often occur in that blurry place that's neither sleep nor consciousness. Jet lag is sometimes a factor, and the sounds are often of footsteps and doors opening and closing. This was not reassuring news. I wanted to believe the thing that made me happy, so I went back to the search bar and typed in *Loved ones returning as ghosts*.

The next day, I hid Mom's pink pyjamas with purple daisies in the hall closet, and put her L.L.Bean pyjamas at the top of her pyjama pile. I brushed her hair, held her hands and tried to believe these were my last days with her. Tried to be fully present, not always daydreaming or reading or writing or walking. But it would be a full year before I began to regret not scooting into her bed that first night. Hospital bed or not, *I should have done it*. I was such a prude.

*

Hi Ho Silver Lining

Nineteen years old
London, 1972

I used one of the addresses I'd garnered hitching through Europe the previous summer and stayed with some Vietnamese brothers in west London. Much shorter than me, they were very skinny, very sweet, and almost constantly absent as they worked long shifts at the airport. They gave me strong tea and fat joints, and the occasional bowl of noodles or rice. My first full day in London, I bought *The Daily Mail* and scoured the ads while sitting in a café. I took a pocket of ten-pence pieces, shillings and tuppences to the payphone on the corner, and by evening I had set up job interviews and viewings for rooms in flats. On the way to the first job interview, I went into a shop to buy a navy blue, just-above-the-knee skirt, and I also bought a pair of flesh-coloured tights in a plastic egg – neither of which I would wear again. I stuffed my bell-bottoms into my bag, combed my hair and got a job. And then I got a room too.

I said goodbye to the Vietnamese brothers and moved to Hither Green, to share a flat with a tiny (everyone was tiny) woman who worked as a solicitor. At twenty-five, she already seemed older than my mother. My bedsheets were orange nylon. Slippery when cold and sweaty when warm. Like the non-absorbent toilet paper in her bathroom, the sheets seemed intentionally awful. The solicitor woman told me to keep my food on a single shelf, which I loaded with my frugal shopping.

Eggs, oats, bread, apples. Old money had just become new money, and everything had two prices. Eggs cost six new pence (or one and tuppence ha'penny old money) for half a dozen. I earned £20 a week. I spent £5 on rent, £8 on groceries and tube fares, and the remaining I put in a savings account at Woolwich Building Society, where they entered my weekly deposit by pen. I remember these things because I took my solvency seriously. I even kept track of my income and outgoings in a little book.

I wrote my friends, my parents, my siblings. My Italian grandmother. They all got their own letter, because I wanted to get as many letters as possible. It was a lonely period, but I didn't consider going home. If only I'd been an un-lapsed Catholic, then I could've prayed for bilocation. Be in both places at once. Sometimes I wrote to my old boyfriend, Foam Man, but he hardly ever wrote back. I was nineteen and had no friends. London was not how I imagined it would be, not how I remembered it. That was summer and this was fall, but even so – I was bewildered. As if I'd been tricked somehow. Travelling through a place was not remotely the same as living there. But it was silly to expect the thrill I'd felt that summer and it was time to grow up. Look around! Nobody in London was thrilled to be there. No one smiled, no one looked healthy. I would be happily unhappy too.

Perversely, because I was in one of the world's most famous cities, I avoided tourist attractions. I concentrated on becoming invisible, a chameleon, so I would know what it felt like to be British. I truly imagined that was possible. At the end of the year, I would still not know where Buckingham Palace was, or London Tower or the British Museum, but I would know the spiral staircase at Holborn underground station like the back of my hand. Weekend nights were spent shivering or sweating in my orange nylon-sheeted bed and listening to people laugh outside on the street, coming home from the pub. Everyone was having fun but me.

I worked for a small company off Holborn High Street called Blow Up. My boss was a fat Australian who smoked constantly and made bad jokes. He didn't mind that I had no work permit – maybe he didn't either. The set-up felt illicit, down some filthy steps into a windowless basement. People sent us their negatives and we enlarged them into posters 2' × 3' big. My main job was to roll up the posters, insert them in tubes, write the addresses and take them to the post office. Sometimes I had ten tubes tucked under each arm. There was a café on the corner, and I loved everything about it. The chips, the cheese rolls and ham rolls stacked to fill the window, the smoked glass cups of tea. The cheeky waitress called Ginny with backcombed hair and frosted pink lipstick. I wished my name was Ginny. How could anyone called Ginny not be popular?

I liked the boy – I'll call him Graham – who processed the negatives. His hair fell down his back in soft waves, and his eyes were a lovely blue green. Pale and thin, his chest almost concave, he was my first real friend in London. One Friday night I did not go home to Hither Green. I missed the last train and I was so grateful to have a new friend, I slept with him. I climbed into his single bed, even though it was a double bedsit and his roommate was in bed a few yards from us.

'Is he okay with me being here?' I whispered.

'Sure, why not?'

The minute we cuddled, I realised how tense I'd been, for now I felt myself unfurling.

That Monday at work, I asked him: 'Did you have a nice weekend?'

'Yeah. Aside from my girlfriend dumping me.'

He had a cigarette in his mouth, while adjusting a negative in the enlarger. The small space was always full of smoke and Radio 1. 'Hi Ho Silver Lining' was often playing. Radio 1 was like KFRC in San Francisco, but the hits seemed more pop than American pop. Less soul and Motown, certainly. And, weirdly, given the lack of smiles in London, the songs were dumbly happy. Like 'Hi Ho Silver Lining', which was all about seeing the sun shining and not making a fuss. Baby.

'Oh no, what happened?' I asked.

'Oh, not much. She saw me leaving the flat with my arm around another girl on Saturday morning.'

'How could you! That's awful.'

He looked at me.

'Saturday morning,' he said meaningfully.

I moved in with him the next weekend. His bedsit was close to our work and he was going to introduce me to his friends. I needed friends. His friends were all male, but that was all right. As for his eighteen-year-old roommate, I had no idea what he did while we had sex. When we turned out the lights, it was uncannily easy to pretend we were alone. Sometimes the roommate coughed or turned over, and we froze for a second or two. He was shy, but sometimes when he saw me he smiled and sang a few bars of 'American Pie'. I loved that song. Sometimes I'd sing the whole song with him, but we hardly ever talked.

One night the payphone in the hall rang. It was late. I was the only person who got calls, so I jumped out of bed, put on Graham's long black coat (I was naked) and stood shivering in the hall.

'Mom?'

'It is 4pm here. What time is it there?' My mother always asked that first, in her practical but sweet voice. She had the best enunciation of anyone I knew.

'Just past midnight.'

'That's amazing,' she said. 'I have some bad news, I'm afraid.'

The giver of my anticlimactic first kiss was dead. He'd left a note to his mother, who was a friend of my mother. She kept trying to tell me the exact details. Which room in the house, which part of that room, who found him, when the funeral was. She didn't know what the note said. He'd been depressed,

253

troubled, was on medication – but she didn't call the death a suicide. It might have been a note saying he was going out to the store. Finally, she asked:

'When are you coming home?'

'I don't know.'

'I miss you. We all do.'

'I miss you too.'

'Well. Goodbye!'

'Yes, goodbye.'

Then there were a few seconds with us both waiting for the other to hang up. I could hear the refrigerator hum and my father clearing his throat and the dog's toenails clicking down the hall. Home poured into that wordless space, and then she hung up.

'It was my mom,' I whispered, perched on the edge of the bed.

'How is she?' he whispered back.

'Okay. Someone I know died. He was twenty-one,' I whispered back. 'Killed himself, I think.'

'Gorblimey.'

'Oh no!' cried his roommate from the other bed. He sat up in his striped pyjamas. 'That's terrible. Are you all right?'

'Yeah, I guess so. Thank you.'

'I'm so, so sorry.' He touched his chest where his heart was, and sent me a sympathetic sigh. I felt big-sisterly and wanted to go sit on his bed with him, but then Graham pulled me back into bed and slid his skinny arms around me. A cloud of unwashed armpit, feet and groin whooshed out from under the duvet. I kept thinking about the boy who'd died. Depressed? Troubled? But he'd been the star of the neighbourhood.

'People are more fragile than you think, aren't they? And more mysterious.' I said it loud enough to make it clear I was talking to his roommate too.

'I know,' said the roommate with feeling. 'They are.'

*

254

I couldn't connect the boy I remembered with an unbreathing body. I knew it was true because my mother had said so, but the knowledge wouldn't go in. It hovered for days, till one day it altered shape enough to find an entrance, and then I understood he was dead. I locked myself in the communal bathroom down the hall, turned on the tap to muffle my crying. The cistern made a constant gurgling, which reminded me of the bubbles from his water pipe, that time we got high and he kissed me. He'd been the first boy I'd messed around with. Not a great love, nevertheless a colleague in fumbling.

'Oi! Everything all right in there?' Graham called through the door.

'Fine. Out in a minute.'

'Watch the hot water!'

'It's cold water,' I shouted, and wondered how I'd leave him. It felt like it had already happened, I just had to traverse the space between now and then.

When his roommate moved back to his parents' house, we began to use his bed to dump our clothes on. I smoked my first cigarette. Joints always contained tobacco in Britain, so it wasn't a big adjustment. Smoking joints was as habitual as cups of tea, and beyond the usual physical symptoms – pink eyes, dry mouth, increased appetite – was like adjusting the focus on a camera lens. First I'd be worrying whether I had any clean socks to wear tomorrow, and the next I'd be thinking what a clever invention socks were – they were basically gloves for feet, and wasn't that funny? Not really, but it would seem funny, and so would much else. I had a tendency to take myself seriously so it felt good to shift perspective. Things that normally bothered me, ceased to. The downside was lack of energy and motivation. Mostly we sat around in the evenings listening to records, not talking much, rolling joints. It was quarter ounces of hash, not lids of grass, and joints were a more complicated construction than Californian one-skinners. Graham taught me the art of using three rolling papers and a bit of rolled card for a filter, usually from a Shreddies box. I was as proud of my joint-rolling skills as if I'd graduated from UC Berkeley, which I still intended to do one day.

There was a second-hand bookshop near work, on Great Ormond Street, and I took to dallying there on my lunch hours. I got to know the owner, John Chilton. He was like my father, in a way – dry humoured, well-read. I enjoyed his conversation. One day, he asked:

'Fancy coming to hear my band play? It's jazz. You like jazz?'

'Well, sure.'

He was old and bald and married, therefore I didn't consider it a date. The venue was New Merlin's Cave near King's Cross, a dark smoky place with low ceilings and filthy glasses. He sat me at a table near the stage, then disappeared to tune up with the band. He played the trumpet and I wondered how that was tuned up. My father loved jazz, so when the band began, I missed him. I missed talking with him. It was good cuddling with Graham in his single bed, but I had little rapport with him.Impossible to gauge the importance of rapport until it is absent. I sat there alone, smoking and drinking lager, and felt completely fine about being sad. The singer was a squat man with big eyes and huge nose. He was ugly and sexy. He didn't care and was having a good old time.

Afterwards, John introduced us.

'This is George Melly.'

'Nice to meet you, Mr Melly,' I said primly.

He was as old as my father too, and I was raised to address old people by their titles unless invited to do otherwise. I didn't know he was a famous person. I extended my hand, and he shook it after a pause that contained a raised eyebrow. Then he laughed. A big snort of a laugh.

'Christ, John,' he said. 'Where'd you find this one?'

*

One person can be a portal to a whole social world, and I became friends with Graham's friends. I liked some of them better than I liked him – especially the one who dressed like a cowboy. I didn't feel disloyal, but sometimes I wondered what would have happened if I'd met Cowboy first. The most popular man in the group was the one who sold us dope. Mr Cool. Buying was never just a business transaction. We'd knock on his Chiswick flat door at teatime and not leave till after midnight. He'd sit in his armchair and just keep rolling joints.

Early November, we all moved to a squat in Bingfield Street near King's Cross. A three-storey brick mid-terrace building which had been empty a year. The toilet was in a little shed in the back garden with squares of newspaper hanging on a wire. There were six of us, none over twenty-three and half had come from Cork. I was the only girl. We took baths on Saturdays at the Caledonian Bath House, a cavernous place with deep tubs and women who sold us bath salts and called through each door: *More hot?* We boiled water for tea and coffee in a saucepan on the paraffin heater, but we didn't cook. We went down the road and bought doner kebabs dripping with grease, or ate gammon steaks with pineapples and chips in cafés. It was always cold, often wet. I bought my first hot water bottle and considered it a miraculous invention.

At Christmas, we went to Graham's home in Kent. His coal miner father's skin was creamy white – almost blue. He had, I was told, black lung disease, or pneumoconiosis. He smoked Player's anyway, and kept pouring us beer and whisky and port. No wine at the Christmas table, but a lovely turkey stuffed with chestnut and apples. His mother was a slight woman, wrinkled and giggly and chatty. She smoked constantly. I was a smoker now too, but still – I found it hard to breathe in that house. Mostly the talk was about the upcoming three-day week the prime minister had just announced. The coal miners wanted too much money, Heath said, and in addition the recent oil crisis had deepened. Britain needed to use less coal and therefore less electricity. I was too embarrassed to admit I hadn't known electricity could be made from coal. I'd never seen coal till that year.

'They think they can fob us off with a pittance for wage packet, and then act like all this nonsense is our fault. Say we're greedy,' said Graham's father.

'It'll come to grief,' said his mother, nodding grimly. 'No good will come of any of it.'

From 1st January all businesses were to open no more than three days a week, aside from places like schools and hospitals and police stations. Post offices would begin issuing petrol rations. Television would stop broadcasting at 10.30pm. Daily power cut timings would be announced in the newspapers and on the radio. City pubs would close at teatime. Domestic use of electricity was to be conserved continually and rubbish collection would be sporadic.

'There'll be a run on candles, best buy a bunch when you see them,' his mother told me.

'Yeah, and get some tilly lamps too,' wheezed his father.

'Like the war days, eh? Just before you two were born.'

'Remember the candles from the butchers? String dipped in dripping. Oh, the stink in the house burning them things!'

'Hard times, hard times.'

Neither of them seemed dismayed. In fact, they seemed gleeful. I was excited too, braced for hardship in a foreign country. Suburban-bred, I wanted my mettle tested.

In the first week of the new year, I lost my job. My Australian boss blamed it on the three-day week. He couldn't stay in business without losing some staff. I wasn't given notice and had to leave immediately. Graham hugged me quickly in the darkroom.

'You're lucky,' he said. 'Can you pick up some tobacco on the way home? Oh, and more candles.'

I thought it would be fun, like camping, but it was not. Some windows glowed and I spied families playing board games and cards by open fires, but most houses remained dark and cold-looking. Street pavements were shadowy and I stepped on dog shit. Darkened shop windows looked ominous, especially in the late afternoon. We forgot to find out when the day's power cut would be, and we forgot to put the matches in an easy place to find. At least twice, the lights went out and none of us could find a match to light a candle and the batteries in the torches were dead. We stumbled around in the dark, cursing, laughing a little, and then we said goodnight and went to bed even though it was only 7pm.

I was running out of money and had too much time on my hands, so I walked into a temp agency and got a job packing Dunhill lighters in a factory. Calling myself a student, I got an emergency tax code. Jobs were plentiful and no one seemed to care I wasn't legal. Every day I sat in front of a conveyor belt, lifted lighters up, filled them with fluid and packed them in expensive boxes which slid into other expensive boxes. Like putting them each to bed, I thought. The air was sharp with chemicals, making my chest tight. I didn't talk much, but everyone around me was always chattering.

'I don't know how we'll manage, with Harry's pay cut.'

'Oh, and I hear there's worse to come. Edna's Sheila in the police says there's looting in Cannington.'

'Disgusting.'

'Oh, I know. I despair.'

But as with Graham's parents, I detected an edge of excitement in their voices.

Graham was still my boyfriend, and I couldn't figure out how to fix this. I'd been imagining leaving him since Water Pipe Boy died. How did people break up? How did anyone interrupt an ordinary day in order to end a relationship? I realised none of my new friends could help me because they were his friends. If I had a friend in London who was a girl, I could ask her for break-up tips. Then we'd get drunk and laugh, and eventually I'd ask her the more worrying question. Why didn't I want to keep my nice boyfriend? What, in fact, was wrong with me? In 'Hi Ho Silver Lining', the singer tells his restless girlfriend that her sun will shine anywhere she goes, and he'll never make a fuss – and he keeps saying *it's obvious*.

What was obvious? I needed to ask someone.

No Touching His Things!

I told Mom I was going to pack up Dad's closet and take his clothes to the Goodwill. He'd been gone five years and I kept trying to do this. But she got twitchy right away. Her right eyebrow reared up and her left one curled down.

'No! No touching his things. I repeat: No.'

'No?'

'Correct.'

'Why?'

'Are you nuts?' she spluttered. 'Because, because, because . . . those are the things he sees every day. Those are *his things*.' She sounded exasperated.

It was a cruel equation that his clothes remained and he did not. Plus, there was the fact he got very cranky if anyone touched his stuff, and hated it when we helped ourselves to his nail clippers or Scotch tape and didn't replace them. I'd had a habit of borrowing his socks. I couldn't resist the way they nestled in his top drawer, so neat. He wasn't your typical tidy person – he took risks, drove fast, drank, smoked both tobacco and grass – but he was happiest when things at home were organised and calm. The high point to his day was probably martini time – 6pm on the dot. All the ingredients would be in their place – lime, vermouth, green olive, vodka – and all the chores done. Everything where it should be, his dog at his feet, his wife cooking dinner, and us children ranging around the house in our various pursuits.

122 Oak Drive was a comfortable house, I now appreciated. A three-bedroomed bungalow which my parents bought when it was built, back in 1962. The plans were still in my father's desk, well perused – no doubt the original blueprint for daydreams and conversations: . . . *and if we have another baby, it can sleep with a sibling, depending on gender. And if we block up this bit here with shelves, it'll make the living room more private . . . maybe we can turn the garage into a spare room one day?* Everything was a warm shade of brown or beige, the emphasis being on quality. The floors were hardwood and the furniture was either farmhouse-old or Scandinavian-modern. Much of my parents' taste originated in the early sixties, when their icons had been the Kennedys. The sense of kinship with the First Family had been so strong, for a while I thought we were related. That Caroline and John-John were my cousins. Maybe I'd write a story about the morning in fifth grade when Sister Marie Claire told us a bullet had killed John Kennedy. And he'd stayed dead even though a zillion prayers flew in his direction. *Dear Mr President*, mine said. *Don't be dead.*

And then it occurred to me that I owed something as a writer to my Catholic upbringing. The confessional box had been the perfect place to hone a narrative voice. Every Saturday, telling the shameful truth to a stranger who promised not to judge was excellent practice. Only God could judge and he always forgave. Or He forgave. Being a lapsed Catholic means God pronouns get a capital letter sometimes. It was a win-win. And meanwhile I got better and better at framing the truth. Or a truth, because even then it seemed a nebulous entity.

I kept considering the house and tried to see it as if I'd not grown up in it. Even though most things in it were old, it wasn't an old person's house. No clutter, no smell of urine, no depressing floral wallpaper or paisley curtains. Things of beauty and nostalgia were scattered everywhere. Pictures of sailboats Dad had painted, bronze cat bookends from Gump's, framed nautical maps of the San Francisco Bay. Hardbacks from Book of the Month Club, a shelf of Modern Library novels from the fifties and sixties. Jazz records – swing and trad. Even the walls were aesthetically pleasing. Originally covered in dried grass sewn onto paper, they'd been re-covered with redwood panels at an expense so substantial I could still remember the fights about it.

I found myself thinking like Mom: *These were the things Dad saw every day*. He probably felt they'd anchor him to his life forever. How could they not, when they screamed permanence? A life so solidly arranged could never be packed up and dispersed within days by callous offspring. For Christ's sake! *No, no, no*.

Without realising it, I'd embarked on ancestor worship. All along, with every deathbed visit, I'd been squirrelling items away in my suitcase. This was a betrayal to my brother, who'd known I'd be tempted and had made me promise not to. My sister had no such concern. She was taking things too. I suspect Ateca knew I was pilfering, and was prepared to turn me in if she was ever accused of sticky fingers. Already on this visit, I'd taken a small brass bird from my father's desk, an old favourite sweater of my mother's.

My God, I even took a rusty fish-shaped ashtray from the deck. It should've been thrown away decades ago, but now it was sacred because it'd received the butts from a million Dad-smoked Viceroys. All those cigarettes smoked on the deck, sometimes with a black coffee but most often with a glass of wine and some jazz floating through from the open sliding glass door. And not often enough in my company, I now felt. I was always on my way somewhere else, not giving either of my parents much thought. I needed to talk about him to someone who'd known him, and senile or not, Mom was the obvious candidate.

'Mom, do you miss Dad?'

'What?' Frowning.

'Do you think about George?'

We were sitting in the shadowy living room, and outside the midday sun was glaring. She flicked her hands up as if she wanted my words out of the room, as if they hurt. How could I ask something so cruel? But then she laid her hands in her lap and smiled.

'You bet I miss him.' Her tone was – unexpectedly – her old self speaking. Direct, a little hurt maybe, a little defensive, but dignified. 'I miss him every day.'

Maybe the stories I kept telling myself about her were wrong. Dementia messes with memories, not instincts, not natures. Maybe she needed to see Dad's clothes hanging in his closet not because they were imbued with him, but simply to keep seeing what he'd seen as a way of feeling close to him. And then I had another thought. Maybe in a secret corner of her heart – the place that didn't require vocabulary in anyone's heart – she was seeing those suits and ties and shirts *on his behalf*. He couldn't any more, so she was taking that job on. That's what a good wife does: thinks of things to please her husband, and then just darn well does them. And God knows, there wasn't much left for her to do for him any more.

I stole one more item that visit. An un-posed black-and-white photograph of my mother caught mid-laugh in some forgotten afternoon, probably around 1947. She'd yet to meet Dad. The war would have still been fresh, and jobs scarce in Redding. Redwood trees in the background, maybe a picnic at Shasta. She was lifting a too-big log to her shoulder, and someone thought this was funny enough – or sweet enough – to take a photograph. Something about her face gave me a queer feeling of recognition, as if it was my young self I was looking at. But I didn't resemble her, so more likely I was simply remembering the twenty-three-year-old mother I had no conscious memory of. She looked unaware of a photographer. No self-consciousness, just unadorned joy as if she had one thought: *I'm having fun, fun, fun!* She had such capacity for happiness, my mother. I wasn't sure I'd ever properly noticed that before. Maybe it had dissipated by the time I was old enough to value such things. Maybe, partially, I'd been the one to dissipate it.

Magic is Real

Ten years old
California, 1963

A bad man shot a gun at our president, who was riding in a car not doing anything wrong at all. It was Friday. While we were doing arithmetic, he was in one of those cars with no top on, and his pretty wife was with him, and she hadn't done anything wrong either. And now he was in a hospital and lots of doctors were trying to stop him from dying. Our president was fighting for his life and Catholics like us all over the world were already on our knees, praying for him. I knew this because Mrs Connelly in the office always listened to the radio news while she typed and she came and told our teacher, Sister Marie Claire. I sat at the back of my row – there were five rows of ten desks each – so I didn't hear her clearly. At first I thought she said he was fighting with his wife, like my dad did sometimes, and it seemed a silly time to fight – what would it be about? The blood stains? Then I thought she was saying he was fighting with his life, as if his life was a separate thing from himself and had been bad to him. Words had so many meanings and sounded so similar to each other, I was always getting them wrong. Sister Marie Claire kept sniffing. I knew nuns peed and pooed, but I didn't know they cried. I didn't like it.

It was almost morning recess time. I wanted to eat the Hostess apple turnover I'd seen my mom pack in my lunch box, but that would be bad because it was for after my peanut butter and jelly sandwich. I was very fond of my lunch box – it was red tartan metal, with a matching thermos flask for my milk. Sister Marie Claire's face went blurry, then she gave herself a little shake, like my dog did after swimming, and said:

'Pencils down, please, children. President Kennedy has been shot. We're going to pray to the Lord for his recovery. Put your hands together, please, and bow your heads.'

All fifty of us mumbled our way through the Lord's Prayer and then we trooped into the cafeteria with all the other classes and prayed there too, even though Mrs Connelly came in with a wet face and whispered something to Sister Michele, who was the boss of the whole school. Sister Michele's face changed, and I was struck because it was almost like she was a different person for a second. Then she crossed herself and clapped her hands to stop us praying.

'Children, children! I have something very sad to tell you. I am sorry to tell you, President Kennedy, John Kennedy has . . . he has . . . they tried to save him, but he was too hurt . . . and.'

Then Mr Jones the janitor helped her sit down, and Sister Anne from sixth grade told us President Kennedy was in heaven with Jesus.

John Fitzgerald Kennedy was *our* president. We owned him because he was a Catholic and a Democrat like us. I'd understood he was hurt, but it never occurred to me he might die, not with all of our prayers headed his way. Prayers had power. I'd prayed as if he depended on it. Like I would try to stop someone bleeding with whatever came to hand, even if it was my favourite shirt, and even if the bleeding person was my little brother. How could prayers like that from millions of people not work? Nuns were crying in the halls, in the play yard, in the classrooms. When they talked, their voices were terrible to hear. They sounded like I did sometimes, when I had a bad dream and couldn't tell my mom what it was about without feeling the scared feeling all over again. I was not crying. Yes, maybe his heart had stopped, but he couldn't be *dead* dead. There would be a last-minute rescue from an angel and he would be on the morning news again, with that straight-toothed smile. The one he had in the framed picture above our kitchen table. All you had to do was look at that photograph, and you knew everything was going to be okay.

'I can't believe it. I keep thinking about those little kids,' my mother said to my father in the kitchen later. 'John-John and Caroline. How will she tell them?'

I was there but no one noticed me. She was crying and not looking at him. She was straining macaroni into the sink.

'Ah, honey,' he said and put his arms around her from behind. She stopped draining and leaned back into him, her face wet. His face bowed over her shoulder, so their cheeks touched, and his face looked wet too.

And that's how I knew Kennedy was *dead* dead.

That evening after dinner, my whole family went to a special Mass to pray for his soul. Kennedy was going to live forever in Heaven now, and all his earth stuff – his job, his family, all his little habits and worries and preferences and daydreams – was over now. He would get his body back one day, but it wouldn't have any bullet holes in it. Yes, this was true. Lots of things were true that seemed unlikely, Santa Claus being one. Everything I knew about the world argued against the existence of Santa – many of my classmates were disbelievers – but he still came every year. God was magic like Santa, and with magic the normal rules didn't apply. I'd seen the Easter bunny with my own eyes, so I had proof. I'd woken up early in my grandparents' house and seen him bending down to hide eggs in the shrubs by the stone barbecue. Though proof was hardly needed. I was an enthusiastic believer in everything I was told, everything I read, everything I saw and heard. As far as I was concerned, life was one bizarre thing after another. My guardian angel was a personal friend and I lived in a state of perpetual trust. If I overheard anyone claiming there was no proof that God or Santa existed, I just thought to myself: Well! And where's the proof they don't exist?

The Mass for Kennedy was not a normal Mass or a feast day Mass, not even a moveable feast day, like Easter or Good Friday. Nor was it an ordinary time Mass. It was just a Mass – as far as I could make out – because John Kennedy had not been able to keep his soul from flying out of his body. I knew from the nuns that most Masses were called ordinary time Masses. Ordinary time – I loved that phrase. Just an ordinary time, like a Sunday afternoon watching *Lassie* or riding our bikes to school, cars whooshing in and out of the fog like ghost traffic. I preferred ordinary time Masses because you knew what was going to happen, but something else always happened too. A sudden ray of light through a stained-glass window, like a slice of rainbow, making the ugly woman in front of me not so ugly. Or an altar boy dropping the wine and saying *oh shit*. Once a man in front of us farted long and loudly, and me and my brother spent the rest of the Mass giggling even though we knew we'd be in the doghouse later and get a bare-bottom hairbrush spanking from Dad. Ordinary time Masses were never eventless. I had all these thoughts while the priest droned on and on in Latin, presumably sending the words to Kennedy in heaven. Then he spoke in English about Kennedy's family, and we all prayed for John-John and Caroline, who were probably crying right now because Daddy was never going to tickle them again. More Latin, more prayers, and the grown-ups' voices erupted regularly above me with phrases like *Gloria Patri, et Filio, et Spiritui Sancto*. And then the *Amens*, made into beautiful little songs with two words. *A* – high and long. *Men* – low and quivering. Candles near singers went crazy at the *Amens*. They flickered and flared, and some even blew out.

Maybe there was no such thing as ordinary time, I suddenly thought.

I was obsessed with time already. Not just time travel, which was a fantastic concept, but the connection of existence to time itself. My favourite book the year a bullet stopped Kennedy was *Tom's Midnight Garden* by Philippa Pearce. It confirmed my suspicion that time was nebulous, expanding and shrinking continually, sometimes double-backing. Moments of emotional intensity could defy the normal restrictions and last a lifetime, maybe an eternity. Whole other universes shimmered under everything ordinary. Sister Domenica told us some people were saints because they'd bilocated. Appeared in two places simultaneously. Imagine that. Like Hattie in *Tom's Midnight Garden*.

Oh, it was lots of fun being Catholic. Magic and miracles and bilocation and life everlasting. Who wouldn't want to be a Catholic? Not to mention the gold-edged Holy Cards from the mission shop offering routes to wish fulfilment for a mere twenty-five cents. If you had enough money, a whole Mass could be bought and offered for whatever and whoever you liked. The only downside to being Catholic was this: if you had a car accident and died on the way to confession, you were stuck in purgatory forever. Purgatory was a nowhere place. Like waiting in a long line that moved an inch a month, and you couldn't even see the front of the line. It was such a relief when we arrived safely at confession each time – though it seemed unfair that a mere accident could derail me from a life everlasting in heaven. In fact, I was considering editing God's rules. My tailor-made Catholicism would omit hell – bad people could just stay dead – and purgatory and anything to do with devils. They were all too scary. My Catholicism would promote guardian angels. They were even better than holy cards. I also planned to keep the act of confession. What does an innocent-looking ten-year-old whisper in the dark confessional box? Sins, of course. *Bless me,*

Father, for I have sinned. The week before Kennedy was assassinated, I confessed:

'I didn't drink from the same water fountain as Belinda Tassner because no one would, and everyone was saying she had cooties because her glasses are so thick, and also because she smells funny. When some girls pushed her head in the toilet for the royal flush, I didn't tell the nuns, I didn't tell anyone, and Belinda was crying really really hard.'

The priest responded with the soothing words I heard every Saturday, ending with:

'. . . and I absolve you from your sins in the name of the Father, and of the Son, and of the Holy Ghost, amen.'

My penance was twenty Hail Marys and two Our Fathers for the sin of colluding in Belinda Tassner's suffering. I prayed fervently on my knees, clutching my rosary beads. And afterwards? I felt flushed out. Clean and light. Being forgiven was a magic trick.

That year I had my own bedroom for the first and last time in childhood. I was used to my brother breathing in a bed next to mine, and sometimes I crept downstairs to curl up to sleep on his floor. I'd been a little lonely, since moving to Sacramento last summer. I missed our old house in San Rafael, and the higgledy-piggledy road down to the beach, the lumpy island that had become a monster in my nightmare, the chicken farm and the marsh. My dad said we still owned that house and would go back one day, but not for a while. *When?*

'I have no idea,' he said crankily.

I considered that to mean I would never see it again. Sacramento felt different, so flat and hot in summer, but I knew we were happy because my parents kept saying we were. It was our best house yet, and my father had his best job yet. He worked in the capital building for Governor Pat Brown, which was a very exciting and important thing to do. Brown was an Irish Catholic Democrat, like Kennedy. Like us.

And Kennedy kept being dead. Holy Spirit Elementary School closed on the funeral day. Everything was closed. Flags hung at half mast, and we went to Mass for the second time in a week. Me and my brother sat together between our parents. I was wearing a small white veil pinned to my head with bobby pins, and white gloves like my mother. It was hard to see the priest, because all the pews in front of us were packed. I tried to listen but I kept thinking about how it happened. How he'd just been in the car without a top, waving and smiling and trying to be good and do what he should. The bad man watched him from a window somewhere and pulled a trigger. I considered that scene moment by moment because I already knew all past time could be broken up into moments, if you liked, and those could be studied in slow motion, or even frozen and framed. I knew this from the boxing matches on television my grandfather loved to watch. The way a flying punch could be reversed and then played again and again in slow motion. While that bullet left the gun and was whizzing in the air – completely innocent, it was just a bit of metal – Kennedy didn't know about it. He sat there in his car, busy being a president, but I guessed he was also thinking about other stuff. Like what he wanted for lunch. Maybe he liked Hostess apple turnovers too. And then, between one thought and the next, maybe between the moment he began to raise his hand to wave and before his fingers uncurled, that bullet found his flesh and entered it. Quietly, because I imagined a bullet entering a body would make no noise, like a pin going into a marshmallow. And for a further millisecond, no one would know he'd been shot, not even him. Maybe his wife would be the first to notice, and say something like: 'Shit!' or 'Oh gosh!' or just make a frightened noise, like I did when I felt myself begin to fall from my bike. And then, for everyone in that car, time would stop passing like ordinary time. A minute would be an hour.

MAGIC IS REAL

I believed in Santa and angels and people being in two places at once, but I had to accept Kennedy being dead was impossible to fix. No instant rewinds, no replays. Only Jesus had managed that. And boxing referees on television.

Oh, Baloney!

My mother's deathbed had already encompassed half a dozen other deaths, and now it was her sister's turn. My cousin had moved in with her parents when they started to fail a few years ago, and we Jones children had been in awe. We'd been raised to be much more selfish. I guessed that meant I could blame my abdication of daughterly duties on Mom, and I almost did.

My cousin phoned to tell me her mother had died after many weeks of suffering.

'But here's the thing,' she admitted. 'I wanted it to end, but now all I want is for her to still be here!' Then she couldn't talk. I could hear her making little choking sounds and whimpers, followed by wet nose blows. I never knew what to do when people cried. Sometimes I took mental notes, to improve my crying style. Or develop one at all. When I tried to comfort people, mostly they just got embarrassed and said things like *Don't worry, I'm okay*. Which is what she said when she stopped crying.

After I hung up, I told Ateca. She made the sign of the cross and then she cried too. She won the prize for Best Crier Ever. The only crying I'd ever apply the word *keening* to. No hiding her face behind her hands or apologising. She didn't bother to wipe away her tears and snot. She emitted a continuous tuneful howl, which was how I imagined a high-priced professional mourner might sound.

'Guess we need to tell Mom her sister is dead,' I said, when she quietened down.

'No, no. Barbarajones does not need to know this.' This was a command and her face was stern.

'Okay,' I said, feeling spineless but also relieved.

I hadn't had any uncles for five years, and now I was fresh out of aunts too. I knew I was supposed to feel sad, but experience had taught me I wouldn't feel anything for a week or two, maybe a month, maybe never. I cried at movies and sometimes while reading, but real events rarely affected me at the time. I didn't know why my emotional reactions were delayed, but I was used to it. I'd learned to make sad noises at appropriate times so I didn't seem too much of – as my mother would say – an odd duck.

Last Christmas my husband got a new knee. It'd been an intensely weird ellipse of time, coming straight after three weeks at my mother's deathbed. I stayed in a hotel attached to his hospital in Glasgow, and when I considered being an odd duck, that was the first memory that popped up. The odd-duckness of my soul reached a new height during those days. The solitary restaurant meals of salmon followed by French cheeses with quince, while my husband ate mince and tatties in his nearby hospital bed. His drugged and complaining responses to my daily attempts at cheerful conversation. 'Silent Night' piping into the hospital corridors and his attitude affected me so badly I considered delivering him back to his ex-wife. As I remembered our drive home on the A9 in the snowy dark, I recognised a certain tugging sensation in my chest. The tugging, which was also a tilting, was a lifelong affliction. A random thought or image or feeling would float into my mind, and I'd find myself mentally leaning towards it. Leaning away from all the things that deserved my attention, like the pot about to boil over or the question someone just asked. And now, it was as if those days of hospital pathos were exerting a kind of gravity. *Oh, go on*, I told myself. *Write about the damn thing.*

The deathbed days plodded on, each day much the same as the day before it. The weather was consistently beautiful and it was hard to feel anxious. I cleared out the garage. My siblings didn't want any of it, and I couldn't keep anything even if I'd wanted to. Sixty years of camping equipment, tools, dozens of jars and cigar boxes were all neatly labelled with my father's handwriting. A fishing box with hooks and weights in neat little trays. Old sail bags, stiff and yellow. A box of plastic plates and cups for picnics, last used on Point Reyes beach one foggy August day. My mother would have been huddling over a driftwood fire, complaining about the cold and passing out pastrami sandwiches and cups of Kool-Aid.

'It's not cold, honey,' my father would've said, standing above her. 'You've got to move around, that's all.'

'Oh, baloney!' she would have replied.

I took everything to the dump. There's only so many relics even an ancestor worshipper can get excited about, though I still feel guilty about tossing the fishing box.

Some people talk of wishing an aged parent would hurry up and die because it's painful watching them suffer, but I never felt that way about Mom. She didn't seem to be suffering, and besides – being alive suited her. It was her cup of tea. She believed in heaven, but thought death itself was icky. Maybe for her, the afterlife was like the garage, a nearby place her husband had disappeared to regularly. He'd be out of sight, unreachable, but absolutely there. She knew there was no coming back from the garage. Once you stepped out there, that was it. Maybe she was hanging on because she wasn't convinced she'd be crazy about the garage. Did it even have Svenhard's bear claws? *The Sound of Music*?

Silent Night

Sixty-three years old
Scotland, 2016

The huge ships slipping past the window on the Clyde seemed to be in mid-air, floating. The planes taking off and landing, also silent. The thick glass muted the world. I felt sluggish, sedated, as if I was the patient, not my husband. Just beyond and below my room was the hospital where staff glided down long corridors on rubber soles. Some of them would bring food and pills to him, squirrelled away in his cubicle. It occurred to me we had the same view. We might both be looking out at the same time. The image of our two faces staring out identical windows made me feel uneasy. It should have tickled me, but somehow this place forbade humour. At least, it forbade my brand of humour. I reached for it on and off all day, and it had definitely left the house.

The surgeon wore a cashmere pullover, grey slacks and expensive leather shoes. I wanted to ask if those clothes hung in a locker while he severed old body parts and bolted new ones on, or did he wear them under his scrubs? Of course I didn't, even though he had such kindness in his manner I was sure he'd answer. I watched him examine my husband's faulty body part and converse calmly with him. Though his English was perfect, his voice reminded me of hot foreign places, with spicy smells and feral cats and dogs. I imagined a short round mother, stroking his head absent-mindedly while she passed on her way to the kitchen. Brighter colours in that other place, and easy affection. Here, everything must seem muted. Yesterday on Buchanan Street, I only noticed one person who was not wearing grey or black. Out of a couple of hundred, only one. You'd think people would want to add some colour to Glasgow.

I was trying to figure out the uniforms. Blues – all shades of blue – meant nurses of some kind. White means physios, I thought. The green-garbed staff were the cleaners and caterers and porters. They all seemed to be from this neighbourhood – tattoos and Clydebank humour. Rough. *Go to the canteen, you'll no be wanting to pay for your dinner in yon fancy hotel.* They walked with more noise.

All these people, and yet the sense of emptiness was oppressive – as if we were all ghosts. I had to keep reminding myself what I was doing there. My husband was there for a new knee. I was there because we lived two hundred miles north, and our local hospital didn't have enough surgeons with that particular skill. Miraculously we were citizens of a country that paid for our new body parts, ones which were not needed to keep us breathing. Even more miraculously, it paid for a loved one to stay in a nice hotel while it all happened.

After the operation on the second day, I found I was already deeply familiar with the way the carpet in my room flicked up at the edges, as if the carpet layers hadn't quite measured correctly. The journey from my room to my husband's was complicated, and involved two lifts and four long corridors. It was easy to get lost. I timed myself. If I walked quickly it took twelve minutes to get to his room, where he lay sulking. *I wish I'd never had this operation*, he said and made excuses not to exercise, thereby ensuring the operation would not be a success and he'd be correct in regretting it. The operation had been my idea, so it was hard not to take personally. Why did he have to be so negative? My mental archives instantly threw up a dozen similar episodes from the past, when his bad moods had sucked all the joy from life. I made sympathetic noises and wondered if my deep irritation meant marrying him had been a mistake. But this momentary disloyalty was such a familiar sensation, I hardly gave it a perch to rest on. It was gone, and into its place rushed advice from my better self. This was just a phase, I told myself. A rough patch. Then I answered back to myself that life seemed to be one phase after another, and what the hell was that about?

It was three days till Christmas. 'Silent Night' was constantly in the air, broadcast through the hotel corridors and lifts. Usually I couldn't hear those words and feel cynical, but not now. Christmas trees were scattered everywhere – fake, yet tasteful. Who was here to notice them? The good taste seemed wasted and wasteful, which – because of the state of the world – seemed wrong.

It occurred to me that I could go happily insane at any minute. I could stop making the effort to remember the way back to my room. I could stop brushing my hair and teeth. I could stop remembering names and people's birthdays – what a relief that would be! All that mental effort, for what?

I kept reminding myself I was there because my husband was here, but it was still surreal. The place made ordinariness impossible. There I sat in the hotel restaurant, in splendid isolation, with friendly waiters bringing me seabass and white wine and assorted cheeses and quince jelly, while my husband lay in a room at the other end of the building, eating hospital food. I'd ordered a small wine the first night, but now I shamelessly asked for a large, sometimes two, and enjoyed every sip. It should have felt unfair, but I was too busy adjusting to this . . . this . . . what was this? An unasked-for break from my life, which had followed another unasked-for break from my life – fifteen days visiting my dying mother in California. It was tricky remembering what my normal life actually consisted of. Under the layer of hospital weirdness was culture shock, jet lag and deathbed stress. Not to mention Christmas itself, which was its own special cocktail of hell. I'd once stepped off a busy train at the wrong station by accident, and that's how I felt now. I was at the wrong station, on the wrong platform. A well-heated and pleasant place, quiet and remarkable for the absence of anyone I knew. I reminded myself – no small talk here! No obligations! It was suddenly heaven, but after a minute it was back to being too strange. I couldn't relax.

By the third day we were both fully institutionalised. He got restless ten minutes before his next meal was due to arrive, always promptly, always comforting stodge. I'd discovered the cleverest ways to get around, and prided myself on using stairs instead of lifts. My day's high point was entering the restaurant at seven. It opened at six but I made myself wait, otherwise the evening loomed too long. I took my time eating, while reading short stories. One night it was D. H. Lawrence, V. S. Pritchett and Pushkin. I considered how these men wrote perceptively of domestic situations. Their work was still well esteemed, and of course I wondered if anyone would have heard of them had they been born with vaginas instead of penises. What if – I asked myself as I sipped my large red wine – possessing a penis really did endow one with superior insight? What if feminists had got it horribly wrong after all? And what if there really was a God? And what if the climate change deniers were right? These were the kind of crazy thoughts that place made me think.

In the hospital canteen, where I had breakfast (toast and coffee for £2), I read the paper till visiting time. Hours were extremely long and I looked at my watch on and off all day. The table next to mine was full of people in blue medical garb, and they were laughing hysterically. I assumed they'd been working all night and were now succumbing to a cathartic release. I imagined them sharing dire sweaty moments in operating theatres, watching people suffer or even die, and then re-patching bodies and washing wounds. Unlike me, they did things that mattered.

On the day we left the hospital, Christmas Eve, my husband looked terrible. Everyone said he'd get better quicker at home but it still felt dangerous. I wasn't sure I was up to the task of keeping him safe, much less alive. I checked out of the hotel, lugged my bag out to the car, then back to the hospital to fetch him. We'd not fallen out, but still – we were hardly speaking. It was late afternoon, starting to get dark already. I wasn't a confident driver in the dark, and the trip home would take four hours easily. I was tired, but also angry with him for being so moody, and the anger gave me energy. It was one of those times when I seemed to be at a great distance from my life. I kept thinking: *How did I end up here?* It seemed extraordinary I was married to this particular man and was about to drive four hours in the dark in the middle of winter. The Clydebank neighbourhoods frightened me, and with his patched-up body, my husband was either sulking or simply speechless with painkillers. No words aside from occasional directions. *Turn here. Not here. There.* I was fairly certain he didn't notice that I wasn't talking to him and was tempted to tell him: *Just so you know, I'm not talking to you.* Was there any point to an unacknowledged sulk? But that would involve speaking, and I was too committed to silence by now. Then I had an idea. I would phone his ex-wife. We were friends, kind of. I liked her. I could phone her right now. Pull into a lay-by.

Hello, how are you?

Fine, I suppose, she'd say. *And you?*

Yeah, good here. So. Just wondering. Would you like him back?

Finally, near Perth, the familiar A9 stretched out in front of us. I relaxed. At one point I overtook a car, forgetting it was not a dual carriageway any more, and another car almost hit us head-on. I swerved back in the correct lane with a second to spare. Less. We'd come close to dying and he didn't notice. Was he breathing? I checked out of the corner of my eye for his chest lifting. We'd not spoken in hours.

In the beginning, a decade ago, before we'd even kissed, we'd been old friends. No, that wasn't true. We'd been acquaintances and made assumptions of friendship based on seeing each other regularly over twenty years and liking each other's taste in clothes, in books and music. His marriage had ended, he'd needed a place to stay and I'd offered our spare room. It wasn't a long courtship because our illusion of friendship – of *knowing* each other – had created a shortcut to intimacy. We'd trusted it and plunged. How quickly? From our first kiss to the bed took eight minutes. Maybe less. It felt as if a rescue was involved, but I was never sure who was rescuing who. Maybe it was mutual. I'd been confiding in him about dating. About my doubts and disappointments.

'Hey,' he'd said. 'Why can't I be your boyfriend?'

'Huh.' I was stumped. 'We've never even kissed,' I said lamely. 'How do we know anything if we've never kissed?'

At that point, I would have been happy if nothing else happened. But he kissed me, right there in my kitchen. A hard rushed smash of a kiss, almost like an assault. After a second, I kissed him back. Even now, sitting in the car heading north, my lips could remember that kiss.

It had been a busy month, that decade ago. My first husband had, after five years, moved out of our extension. Our divorce was finally underway. From the kitchen window I'd watched him drive off into his new life with nothing but a rubbish bag of clothes and some CDs. It struck me as courageous, and I'd been ambushed by a rush of affection that made me cry. Then my eldest moved out to live with his girlfriend. Just after that, my elder daughter gave birth, developed eclampsia and was moved to the intensive care unit. I was preoccupied with her and the baby, back and forth to the hospital. The baby was always asleep when I visited, but I picked her up and held her each time. Driving home from the hospital one night, on the Kessock Bridge with the moon bright on the firth, I began praying after a lapse of four decades. *Please, please, please, let her live.* Just before the kitchen kiss with the man I would marry, she began to rally. Moved from the intensive care to the high dependency unit, and from there to a normal bed in a ward with other new mothers. She hadn't died – she was a young mother about to come home with her baby. Already, my mind was fretting about all the things she might need or want. I'd almost forgotten the kiss and what followed. I was too distracted to think much at all.

When I was eleven, my father taught me how to sail. I was put into an El Toro alone, pushed out into the lake and directions were shouted to me. *Tack! Pull in your sheet! No, not like that!* It should have been terrifying, but somehow there was no time to be terrified. A gust of wind almost capsized the boat, and these situations – an almost-dying daughter, my first grandchild's birth, an exiting son and husband, kissing an old friend who was technically still married – reminded me of that day sailing. I was holding onto my life for dear life. It was all I could to do to keep afloat.

We passed Aviemore, Kingussie, and made the descent to Inverness and the Kessock Bridge. When we got home, he thanked me, kissed me groggily. Said I was a good driver and that he loved me. I kept thinking about the way I'd let him move in, when I could have – should have probably – explained it could only be a short-term arrangement, we'd need to date a while and then see how the land lay. But if I'd been sensible, would things have turned out better? I thought of Louis MacNeice's poem, 'Entirely'. About the fact no choice is ever entirely right. That life can feel like a mad weir.

'I love you too,' I said. It was such a relief to find I meant it, I said it again with emphasis and hugged him. 'I love you very much.'

My stomach felt it was being tickled from the inside – this is what love is, I told myself. All this time, I was taking bags of dirty clothes from the car into the house, filling a hot water bottle to warm our damp-feeling sheets, drawing the curtains, listening out for my husband in the bathroom in case he fell. I thought about his artificial knee, hidden inside his leg. I supposed it was getting to know the place now, making friends with the locals. The muscles and other bones. New kid on the block by almost seventy years. It wouldn't be easy. No one gave a whippersnapper an easy time, and why should they?

There was, I noticed, a pile of post on the sideboard. The roses I forgot to toss away before we left had all dried, a few petals had fallen on the table. Some droppings dotted the kitchen counter and I imagined the mouse party while we were away. This made me think: *Not a creature was stirring, not even a mouse.* It was, after all, Christmas Eve. Christmas Eve and all through the house, nothing was stirring, aside from two creaky people not ready to call themselves old yet. Outside, inside the darkness, was the Cromarty Firth with all its hidden sea life, and the Black Isle farmhouses and cottages with all their hidden lives. And beyond that, much further, were places where the sun was already shining and people were awake and going about their day. For some it would be Christmas and full of Christmas distractions, but even so – their ordinary worries would still simmer. They might wonder if the turkey would be big enough or defrosted enough. Or if their car's battery would go flat again. Or who they should invite to a New Year's Eve party, or whether they should have a party at all. Some might be hoping to hear from children who'd stopped contacting them for no obvious reason. Or they'd be waiting for test results about some disease of the blood. And beyond all these preoccupied humans was unknowable and indifferent space. Stars, planets, meteorites. Orbs like earth, continually spinning at the same time they were rotating, following gravitational pulls. Not one atom of space cared about Christmas.

These thoughts consoled me. They tweaked the world back to its proper proportions. Things like marriages that occasionally felt empty or spouses who felt like strangers from time to time – these were less than fluff. I went to bed and cuddled up to my drugged husband. He stank of hospital still, a mixture of disinfectant and fear and air that had been recycled too many times. I imagined him feeling pain and numbness in equal measure, and distant from himself. I remembered how he always checked the oil in my car, and bought me presents when it wasn't my birthday. How he mended my clothes and sewed on my buttons. How he sometimes watched television dramas just because he knew I liked to watch them with someone.

'You awake?' I whispered against his beautiful broad back. He sighed. Then he snorted slightly on the next breath in. I waited for the exhale and it didn't come. Three long seconds and no exhale.

'You all right?'

He didn't answer, but he breathed out finally, and his leg began to twitch in a soothingly regular manner. I slipped an arm carefully around his waist. He sighed again, and this time his sigh seemed to be an assent to my arm circling him. A satisfied sound, and my chest filled up. How small can something be and still be enough to keep love afloat? Surprisingly small, I thought.

Joy of Cooking

Early afternoon, late in June. Twenty-two days plus a few hours left of this life for my mother.

Looking back, I'm amazed at the lack of urgency surrounding her final days. The house was calm, still a nice place to be. The clock was ticking, but it had also stopped. Whole minutes dilated into day-lengths, while birds sang and distant cars whooshed down San Pedro as if nothing out of the ordinary was happening. Mom was peaceful enough considering every cell in her body was bowing out. More and more, her days were spent in her hospital bed. The sound from down the hall of her feminine snoring was steady, not remotely like a death rattle. I understood she'd stop snoring soon because she would have stopped breathing, but I didn't believe it for a minute. It reminded me of those fuzzy happy days leading up to the birth of my first child. I would be pregnant forever, and that was fine by me. Did my mother feel like that too? That she'd continue forever, simply because she couldn't imagine not doing so? I'd had an easy birth, maybe my mother would have an easy death. I wondered if Braxton Hicks contractions were the same as the feints at dying my mother had lived through over the last year. Dress rehearsals for the real thing, and the more you had, the easier it would go in the end. Would it be possible to coax Mom through her death throes the way my first husband coaxed me

286

through contractions? Three little breaths, come on! Pant, pant, pant. Now one big deep breath. Breathe! Or . . . *don't breathe.*

Ateca was cleaning the house one-handed while talking on her phone. *Bula-bula bula-bula.* I'd finished my walking, reading and writing, and was standing in the kitchen in a stupefied daze. Was I hungry? Did I want a cold drink, a cup of coffee? I didn't know. Maybe I'd take a nap. Without thinking, I pulled out my mother's *Joy of Cooking* from the shelf next to my father's booze cupboard. How neatly they'd slotted their different selves together over the years, despite the friction. She'd not loved cooking, but she'd loved it on special days like Thanksgiving, or when our adult selves came home for dinner. She always laid out a nice tablecloth, used the silver cutlery and Wedgwood china, put flowers in a vase. She'd insist we say grace, even decades after we'd all stopped going to Mass. *Bless us, our Lord, for these thy gifts, mumble, mumble, mumble.* The television was never on during dinner, though music was allowed. Conversation was compulsory and uncensored, aside from small talk, which was banned. Now I saw that all her efforts, all these rituals, had told me over and over: *Family dinners are important.* I quickly checked with myself. Had I passed on this family dinner tradition to my children? We'd all sat down every night to a meal I'd cooked, and if someone didn't like it, I didn't make them eat it. They were all fussy eaters, and at least one would have Weetabix for dinner instead. I remember lighting candles, filling vases with flowers, not allowing television during meals. *I tried.* But those times weren't always fun or harmonious. They were mostly full of spilled milk, squabbles over favourite chairs or the last piece of pie. Motherhood was such a mishmash. I had a sense it would never end and then, quite abruptly, it ended. I was sadder than I ever imagined I could be. I pined for spilled milk and favourite chair squabbles.

Style-wise, Mom was slapdash in the kitchen and her *Joy of Cooking* was spattered with the juices and greases of ingredients for meals long since eaten. Her fingerprints were everywhere, and the pages with her favourite recipes were stuck together. This book, I told myself, was an artefact. As sacred as any splinter from the holy cross. On the flyleaf pages, she'd scribbled recipes I could taste in memory. New York cheesecake. Teriyaki sauce. Oatmeal cookies. I put the book back on the shelf, mentally marking it as mine.

I drifted from the kitchen back to the desk in my father's office, Mom's snoring still audible down the hall. I was working on a story about how I met my first husband, but it was too hot to think clearly. Also, it was a little embarrassing. Had I really shanghaied that sweet English boy, then cheated on him when I'd got what I wanted? I'd go back to it tomorrow, and hope a more flattering version emerged. Maybe we'd rescued each other. I liked that scenario better. Anyway, I hadn't really cheated, had I? Hardly a fraction more than an illicit kiss, and after the first few seconds, disappointing as heck.

I went back to list-making.

Things I Learned from My Mother:

- If you value family dinners, your children will benefit but also take them for granted.
- If you are struck with a crippling disease in your prime, that's no reason to whine.
- Remember the curative powers of New York cheesecake. Always use Philadelphia cream cheese, not the cheap stuff.
- Doris Day is fun. Ingrid Bergman is classy. Classy beats fun.
- Your family will not always love you as much as you love them, and this doesn't matter.
- Sometimes life isn't fair, but things usually work out.
- God definitely exists. Maybe.

- You can never know what an outcome will be, so choose to believe it will be good.
- If you marry a man who needs lots of attention and love, then stand in the shadows and allow him to absorb all the love going. He needs it more than you.

The day cooled finally. I took another walk to the beach and came home to the spicy smell of Ateca's seafood soup for dinner. Mom was wide awake and sitting at the table in her wheelchair. I reminded myself these endless days were coming to an end. It was now or never to get out the big guns. She had no memories for me to plunder, but maybe she could address something more abstract. I asked her what the secret to life was.

She stopped chewing and seemed to dwell on the question. I wondered if I'd have the time to run and get my phone to video her. My God, I thought. She was at the rock face, maybe she had access to the other side already. *Maybe she knew stuff.* She kept chewing, so I gently prompted her.

'The secret to life, Mom?'

'You live it, silly billy!'

I kissed her for that and kept pushing.

'Is there a God?'

Pause while she had another bite of fish stew.

'I pray every day,' she eventually said.

'So God exists?'

'I. Pray. Every. Day.' Her face was mock-stern, saying this.

Then she giggled her old giggle, the one that said: *Aren't we hilarious, you and me? All of this. You and me, the whole kit and caboodle.*

289

A Long Enough Courtship

Twenty-eight to thirty years old
Britain and Canada, 1981–83

For no reason I can recall, I'd been trusted to open a small news-agents at 6am every day and not steal anything. It was unnerving having so much trust. They must have known I'd help myself to chocolate bars and sneak a look inside the soft porn, but not steal cash. The best part was leaving my sleeping boyfriend in our damp flat, and walking two miles to work in the dark. There were always other people – not many and they mostly walked alone like myself. Now and then I met people who'd not gone to bed yet. Pigeons and gulls far outnumbered us. And some birds I'd just learned were called starlings. They would swoop in a perfect oval shape, and their wings would make a whooshing sound that I stopped walking in order to hear prop-erly. I was never afraid, though I took certain precautions. I wore mannish clothes – a baggy black coat, heavy boots and a navy cap. My handbag was always strapped across my chest, so a purse-snatcher would need to drag my whole body away with it. No matter how tired I'd been when the alarm had gone, walk-ing always woke me. How far could I walk? A million miles, and there was nothing I couldn't figure out or fix.

I'd just moved to Leeds. Though the word *moving* implies intent, and it was an accident. The boyfriend had been a stranger a few weeks ago. He'd given me a lift from the Highlands to Yorkshire, so I could visit a poet in Huddersfield I'd met hitch-hiking. By the time we got to Leeds, it was dark and pouring rain. Huddersfield was a further thirty miles, and the attractions of the poet had waned.

'Here's an idea,' I'd said hopefully.

'What?'

'Well, maybe I could sleep on your sofa? Just for tonight, I mean. Because look at it. It's pouring. And late.'

'Ah. You want to . . . stay the night at my flat?' We were parked on the slip road to the A64. Headlights flashed by, each car spraying us. I was like a stray cat who'd had a taste of warmth, and intended to stay in the dry.

'On your sofa.'

'Ah.'

'You have a sofa, don't you?'

Earlier that day, we'd stopped at a petrol station and I'd bought us both Galaxy ice creams. Not the cheap kind. I was impressed with my extravagance and anticipated much appreciation.

'What's this?' He'd not been smiling. It was a genuine question.

'It's ice cream. Chocolate covered.'

'I see that. But look. It's raining.'

'So?' I began unwrapping mine.

'You can't eat ice cream when it's raining.' He said this very slowly, as if I was a dimwit.

I thought he was kidding. That should have told me all I needed to know about our compatibility – if only I'd paid attention. But I was too busy looking for a man to have a baby with. The overwhelming facts in his favour were that his car didn't need pushing to start and he was a drummer in a new wave band. If I squinted, he looked like a miniature John Lennon, with his wire-rimmed glasses and pencil-straight nose. It was a long lift, and I'd learned much. He'd been the first person in his family to go to university, like my adored father. He was motherless, which stirred my raging maternal instinct. But the deal-breaker was his degree in philosophy. Such had been my glut of book-dumb boyfriends, this fact made my poor suburban heart melt. I might have considered his geekiness a drawback, but being geeky myself, it didn't occur to me. I wasn't sure if he was as aware of his geekiness as I was of mine, but decided that could wait till later. Pity he was short, but I could buy some of those flat black Chinese shoes everyone was wearing.

The day after I stayed on his sofa, he took me to Haworth. We walked around the moors, visited the vicarage, marvelled at the tiny Brontë shoes on display. The tiny-waisted dresses. As we walked back down the cobblestone road, it began to rain again and we held hands. I'm not sure, but I believe he took my hand first. I detected a strong charge travelling between us. Holding hands was tantamount to agreeing to sleep together. Or it was possible only I made that kind of deduction.

Later on, I said:

'So, just wondering how you feel about children.'

We were sitting in his local pub back in Leeds, drinking half pints of Guinness.

'Children? I guess they're all right. I don't actually know any.'

'Good.' I laughed a bit from relief. 'I was worried you didn't want to be a father one day.'

Every other man I'd asked the question of, had responded with various versions of: *Children? Hate the little buggers.*

'Ah! You mean do I want to have children!' He looked startled but interested.

'I just asked you that.'

He paused and I willed him to say yes.

'Well, the answer is,' he said slowly, blinking rapidly. 'I don't know.'

I took that as a positive and proceeded. It had been over twenty-four hours since he'd picked me up. A long enough courtship.

*

A month later, maybe less, my boyfriend announced he'd been offered a job in Toronto.

'That's wonderful,' I said, and waited for him to invite me.

'I know,' he said, and began to make arrangements. Gave notice on his flat. Stored his drum kit and books at his brother's house. I was sad he was going, that we were ending, and I was sad that he seemed not to notice my sadness. I was many layers of sadness – so sad, I sniffed continually behind the till at the newsagents, and my voice was pre-tears squeaky.

'Twenty Silk Cut, please, and excuse me, but . . . are you all right?' asked a customer.

'Yeah, yeah,' I said, blowing my nose. 'Anything else?'

'A *Mail*. You sure you're okay?'

One man wanted to buy me lunch, another came back with some flowers. In the end, I had to tell my boyfriend I was unhappy. How would he know, otherwise?

'You are? Why?' He seemed genuinely startled.

'Because you're going to Canada. I'll miss you. I feel like we've just begun.'

'Oh, well. Yes, yes. I see. We can write.'

'Sure. Or I can come.'

'Come where?'

'To Canada. With you.'

'Ah! I see. Well.'

'Thank you! It'll be much better, so much better that way.'

And so, two months after being picked up by him in Dingwall, Scotland I found myself in Toronto, Canada. There was a weird ellipse of time while we lived in a depressing residential hotel called Mayfair Mansions. Then I found a job handing out flyers on a street corner and we moved to a much more cheerful place, a room in a student house. Everything was improving, but it also felt as if my life was in maddening slow motion. One day when I was offering flyers to the passing current of strangers, the urge to spit became so strong, I fled upstairs to the bathroom. Instead of spitting, I vomited. Sour, the enamel scoured off my teeth. But my stomach felt relieved, and I picked up the pink flyers from the floor and went back to work.

It was an odd job, but no odder than most of the jobs I'd had. I couldn't work legally – my options were limited. If I had any career ambitions stemming from my hard-won English Literature degree, they'd dissipated. Anyway – somehow, someday – all this would all be useful in my writing. At least that was the theory. At the moment, empty-stomached and light-headed, I felt as purpose-less as a windborne seed over the ocean. Random, unconnected. I thought about the appointment I'd made at the clinic for that afternoon. My skirt band felt tight, and if I didn't pace a little, my bare feet in sandals ached. I trawled the pavement, keeping a light smile on my face. I didn't bother with the men, though mostly they sought eye contact, while I sought women's eyes.

I hadn't told my boyfriend. Why worry him if there was no cause? I'd used birth control religiously, so if I was pregnant, it was kind of a miracle. Anyway, he was always busy on his computer. It was an Apple II and the first computer I'd ever seen inside a house. If he wasn't in front of his screen, he was prob-ably thinking about Natasha, the beautiful Russian girl we shared a house with, along with seven others. We were the only couple. We had a double bed but no place to put our clothes, so we kept them in folded stacks on the floor. The kitchen and bathroom were like all communal rooms. If you wanted a dish or pan, you had to wash it first. No one bothered with the bath-room. Some days there was toilet paper, most days not. I'd begun to keep a roll in our room.

At one o'clock, I took the remaining flyers back up the stairs.

'Here you go, Ahmed. Get any customers?'

'Three lady. Two come in and leave. One, she try red dress. End up buying two. One for daughter. What you think? Hot enough today. You want Coke?'

Ahmed was short and fat, with smooth olive skin that glistened. I had no idea what he thought of me. Maybe he didn't judge me at all, had no curiosity. I wondered if he'd heard me retching. I hadn't thought of that before.

'Thanks, Ahmed. Roasting out there, I can hardly breathe. I think I might be getting a bug. My stomach.'

'Oh, you no want sick. Tell it go away. Bug, fly out window.' He smiled, gold teeth glittering.

The lady at the clinic asked if I wanted to wait or not. She could phone me later. No, I wanted to wait. I read the brochures on the table. Alternatives to motherhood abounded. Trips across the border to New York were advertised. Different laws. When was a bundle of cells a human being? Several pamphlets claimed to know. There was no air conditioning, and a slight breeze of exhaust fumes strained through the window screens. While watching a fly that must have come in with someone through the door, the metallic taste re-surged and I closed my eyes to concentrate on my equilibrium. Everything in me was clouded, slow, stupid. My name was called and I was ushered into a small room.

'I'm sorry,' said the nurse, assuming from my ring-less finger it was bad news.

I left the clinic and re-entered the summer day. A long day, one which had already seen me step lightly over boundaries. From lost wanderer to the bearer of important being. Untethered kite to rooted tree. On the bus down Bloor, I crossed my hands over my flat belly and half smiled. Around me, in the air and even through the earth, I could feel a kind of sense emerging where there had been nothing but arbitrariness before. Endless options narrowed down to one unstoppable momentum. There was still the metallic taste in my mouth, but now I knew what caused it, I didn't mind.

*

'But how can we? We don't have money for that, you know,' he said later, kindly not reminding me how little time we'd known each other, how perhaps I was not his choice of mother for his offspring. How much he disliked having to think about people in new ways. We were sitting side by side on our bed, the only place to sit in our room.

I remembered when we'd first arrived. Those long days at Mayfair Mansions when he was at work and I hardly spoke to anyone. Walking the streets or sitting in cafés drinking cappuccinos and eating pastries black with poppy seeds. Scanning the *Star* for jobs that didn't need work permits. It'd been freezing and I'd been cold and pierced with loneliness and boredom. I would watch the clock, and there was always a sense of coming to when he walked through the door. As if I'd been dream-walking through my day.

But the truth was, we didn't know each other. Our conversations were clumsy words tossed on the wind from one island to another, arriving battered and foreign. Only the clear and solid fact of our pull towards each other survived. This didn't seem to require articulation or even thought. But once that attraction passed – didn't all attractions fade? – I didn't know what would happen. When I tried to imagine him without it, all I felt was a washed-out blankness.

'I know this kind of news is supposed to come at a different time,' I told him slowly. 'After much thought and choosing and public celebrations and mortgages and yellow-painted tiny bedrooms with teddy bear borders. All safe and right.'

'Well. Well, yes. Not now, certainly.'

'But does it really matter so much how it starts? The proper timing and reasons, these might be only social niceties. Has a child ever been born who cared about anything but love and warmth and food?' I'd been rehearsing this, was quite proud of my eloquence.

'Not now,' he repeated softly.

A minute passed. I willed him to put his arm around me. He didn't. I scooted in closer to him anyway.

'I need to begin. Begin my life properly,' I whispered, hearing how stupid I sounded.

Then he did a remarkable thing. He smiled. He smiled as if he couldn't help it. As if the pleasure was that sudden. He laid a hand across my stomach, and I covered it with both of my own. I imagined that all the rest of my life, whenever I wondered how anything had come to happen, I would trace events back to this moment. This bed, his smile, our hands. Then he said:

'But I don't want a baby.'

He didn't say it meanly, but neither did he say it sympathetically. He was matter-of-fact, as if he was saying he didn't want hamburger for dinner. Then he took his hand back, got off the bed and left the room.

You Bet

There are physical signs when the time is near. Of course, some people pop off looking one hundred per cent, but most bodies start signalling. My mother's feet and lower legs were becoming a mottled purple because her capillaries were disintegrating. Her bedsores had stopped healing, and for the first time, she expressed pain. Not all the time, but even so. I hated it when she said *ouch*. Her ouch was very feminine, like a child's, which made it even harder to hear.

'This is it,' Ateca told me before Mom woke up. 'Death is here.'

'Really? What about those other times when you said Death was here?'

'Those times were different.'

There was no coming back from mottled legs, apparently. So I kept watch, kept an ear out for her last breath. I wasn't afraid of it. I wanted to be with her. To be of comfort, of course, but more selfishly – and more shamefully – a part of me was curious to see Death close up. I'd never seen anyone die. Never even seen a dead body. I'd booked a long enough visit to encompass death throes, death itself, maybe even the funeral if we got a move on. But Mom held steady, and my return date rolled around.

The last time I saw her, she was sitting in her wheelchair between the desk and the sofa, her box of Kleenex at her side and *The Sound of Music* at the glass summer house scene.

The one in which seventeen-year-old Rolfe knows much more about life, apparently, than sixteen-year-old Liesl. Outside the afternoon sun was blasting down, but in our living room an adolescent crush was being played out in an Austrian garden on a rainy night. Liesl wore a blue dress that floated and her hair floated too, and Rolfe was so blond, so young and masculine. Who wouldn't fall in love with them? Or want to be them? Even knowing they were both doomed in different ways, it was worth it for those intoxicating minutes of innocent flirting.

When the scene moved on, I crouched in front of her wheel-chair and took her hands in mine.

'What is it? Is everything all right?' she asked sweetly.

'Yes, everything's fine, Mom. I have to go now, but I'll be back soon.'

Her face fell, but almost clown-like. As if she was aping regret.

'I don't want you to go.'

'I'll phone you tonight,' I fibbed. I was sure she'd forget, and anyway it felt too complicated to explain I'd be over Greenland tonight and not able to phone till tomorrow.

'I love you,' she said. Lightly, as if she was saying *I like your dress* or *pass the salt*. Or maybe at some uncanny level, she *did* understand. Knew this was the last sight of her firstborn. To save me guilt, she was making it easy for me to go. That's what a gracious loving mother does. Hide the hurt, no strings. *I love you, goodbye.*

'I love you too,' I said.

'I love you more.'

Possibly, I thought.

Back home in Scotland, I phoned her every day. There'd been a time when she'd phoned me daily, and I'd found those calls inconvenient. Often it was just as I was putting dinner on the table. What did the kids want for Christmas, what sizes were they, had I remembered to send a thank-you card to my grand-mother? But mostly she didn't talk long. Just before hanging up, she'd say: *I just wanted to touch base, make sure you're all right.*

Now it was my turn. Whether she was in the mood or not, my voice poured into her ear every morning. Evening for me.

'Mom, it's me. Cynthia. How are you?' I always asked.

'I'm just glad things aren't worse,' she always replied. 'How are you? Is everything all right?'

I was poised to rush back. Waiting for the signal from Ateca, my bag already packed. But the days yawned, and I began to write a story from one of my earliest memories, a vacation we took in the mountains when I was seven. The more I thought about those early days, the more I began to understand what my parents' kind of marriage had taught me about love. About family closeness.

One day I asked my mother how she was as usual, and she said:

'I'm fine,' in a very un-fine voice.

'But you've been better, right?'

'You bet!' she replied energetically, as if I'd finally asked the right question. I perked up because I'd not heard her say *You bet!* for ages. Maybe her younger self was rising to the surface, summoned by the gravity of the situation. *Hold your horses, you're about to do what? Are you insane?*

If I'd known she'd be dead in three weeks, I'd have cancelled that last flight home. Hunkered down for the duration to see her out like a good daughter. I like to think I would have done that.

By Lamp Light

Seven years old
California, 1960

One summer we went to Viola, a small settlement in the foothills thirty miles east of Redding. We stayed in a log cabin without electricity. My grandparents had a cabin too, next to ours. There were about a dozen cabins, scattered along the creek that led to the lake. Blue jays were everywhere, bright against the green pine needles, and so were the yellow jackets that I ran screaming from. The air was full of the squeaky sound of screen doors opening and closing, sometimes slamming. And there were always watermelons cooling in the shallows of the creek, along with netted bags of beer and pop. A very narrow pier – just two or three creaky boards nailed to uprights – extended from the lakeshore. I was fine balancing on the pier until I imagined falling in. The worst part was just before falling. I screamed, but the actual event was fine. The water wasn't deep. After I fell in, my brother jumped in too. It was so hot, we were always running around in our underpants so it wasn't like we were getting our clothes wet. After that, falling off the pier was a game.

My grandfather, whose job was to deliver Coors beer, hunted deer and probably other things as well. He didn't talk much. He drove a pickup and wore a baseball cap, even when he was inside the house. A pack of Trues sat in his shirt pocket, peeking out over the top. When he laughed – which was rare – I never understood why. He was as different from my office-working father as it was possible to be, and slightly scary. He was my grandmother's second husband, and they had a thirteen-year-old son and a daughter so old she didn't have to come. My grandfather and his son both went off early every morning, in their identical checked shirts and hats pulled way down. Sometimes they returned with a dead deer in the pickup, which by some process became jerky by Christmas. I loved jerky. Jerky was meaty gum I could swallow.

Viola was already heaven, and then I made a friend. She was from a cabin three cabins away. We both had grandmas staying at Viola, and we argued about who had the better grandma – but not in a serious way. I didn't know my new friend well enough for that. Anyway, it was obvious I had the better grandma because her grandma was an old lady and mine was young and beautiful. Men stared at my grandma and my mom too. I already understood I came from a tribe of beautiful women and it made me proud. As if beauty was not an accident of birth, but something one could take credit for, like getting an A in arithmetic.

The days were long, and even then, they were not long enough. I didn't like going to bed. I wanted, if I could articulate my wants, to live eternally inside an afternoon by the creek, the dust and pine scent tickling my nose and the pine needle carpet under my bare feet. I did not think of home. I'd forgotten school, friends, the bedspread on my bed, the street we lived on. My parents were there somewhere in the background – reading or playing cards or napping or fishing. My little brother too, never far from my mother. But I was hardly aware of them because I had my new friend to play with.

One night, I slept at her cabin. It was my first time sleeping away and I became homesick. It was a new sensation and I didn't know what it was. Was I sick? My stomach hurt, and my throat felt like it did when I was trying not to cry.

Everything – the smells, the shadows, the sounds – was normal but also utterly wrong. I needed to get back to my family but I was paralysed. I lay there in the wrong sleeping bag and imagined all the things that could go wrong. I might be eaten alive by a grizzly bear. If I wasn't, I might not be able to find my parents' cabin. Or I'd find it, but it would be empty. It would be empty and there'd be no trace of my family having ever been in it. On and on, these dire thoughts pinned me to the bed that smelt and felt wrong. Eventually I ran out of disasters to imagine. I slipped out of my sleeping bag, and with a minimum of creak, opened the screen door and ran back to my own cabin. It was only twenty yards away, but it was dark and I'd forgotten to put my sneakers on.

There was still a light on. I stood a minute on the front porch and looked through the window. I'd come to the wrong cabin. It was just what I'd feared, and so there was no surprise. The man and woman inside were wearing clothes I recognised, but the people were too old to be my parents. I held my breath and watched them sitting at the table in the flickering light of a tilly lamp. I could hear their voices, but not their words. The woman looked empty-faced, while the man leaned towards her and moved his hands in the air. His face looked mean. I couldn't figure out what the woman's face meant. Was she angry? Bored? I could only see part of the man's face. Then suddenly, their features resolved into the faces of my parents. How could I have thought otherwise? There they were, just being the selves they were when I wasn't there. And there was my own copy of *Green Eggs and Ham*, just where I'd left it earlier.

I moved slowly and self-consciously towards them, as if I'd gained weight somehow, or become older during the sprint from my friend's cabin. They looked at me blankly as if they didn't know who I was. Then they seemed almost indifferent. Maybe they'd forgotten I'd gone to bed in another cabin. Maybe they'd forgotten they thought I was amazing.

'It's me,' I said softly.

'Hey,' said my father. 'It's late. You want some milk?'

'Nah.'

'You decided not to stay the night? Did you miss us?' asked my mother.

'Sort of.'

'Well, that's fine, honey. You go on to bed then, and don't wake your brother.'

'Okay. Goodnight.'

And off I went. I was glad to be in my own sleeping bag. I lay listening to the creek make its whooshing sound. It was shallow and when I really listened, I could hear pebbles tumbling along. Then a little wind came up, and the noise in the trees drowned out the pebbles. An owl screeched, but not near, so that was all right. Then I noticed that under everything, my brother was wheezing again. His inhalation was silent, but when he breathed out he made a soft whistling noise, as if the air could hardly get out. Once I heard it, I couldn't go back to not hearing it. I considered telling my mother, but my sleeping bag was cosy and I was enjoying the rightness of everything. My parents were talking again, but not much. Just blunt flat words. Short questions and shorter replies. Probably they were saying the things they always said about this time of night. *Where are my glasses? There. Let's not forget to visit so-and-so tomorrow. I promised we would. All right.*

My stomach felt fine now, and so did my throat.

I slept in. When I woke, my brother was whining because his fire truck ladder wouldn't go up and down any more. It was stuck halfway. My mother was angry that she forgot to pack Kleenex.

'Darn it!' she kept saying. 'Gosh, darn it!'

'Want some of this bacon?' my father asked my mother. 'Have something to eat.'

She didn't want bacon or cereal. Just more coffee. Then she

sat in the only other room and made little noises I recognised. It was the way I cried, not when I hurt myself, but when I was certain I would never get what I wanted. At first I didn't feel worried, just a little fascinated. My father, who was not crying, started out the door.

'Where are you going?'

'Just out. I don't know,' he told my mother.

'All right,' she said, and blew her nose on a T-shirt from the dirty clothes pile. Then she called after him through the screen door:

'We need milk. If you get to the store.'

But he'd gone too far by then and didn't hear her. Or he'd heard her but didn't answer.

Our vacation had three more days, and now this seemed too long. I didn't care about my new friend any more. I began to worry about my mother. I couldn't bear it that my father had not answered her question about the milk. Her unanswered voice had seemed so hopeless, trailing off in the air with nobody's ear to land in. I hung around the cabin all morning till my father returned. I knew he would – of course he would – but I needed to wait anyway, just in case.

When the time came to pack up the car again, I was almost relieved. We did everything we'd done a week ago, only in reverse. Packing, unpacking, packing again. And the drive, too. We'd come all this way on smaller and smaller roads till we were in the middle of the woods by the lake. And now we were rewinding ourselves back to where we started, back to our house near the bay. Like playing with a yo-yo, or winding up a ball of string. Down through the foothills again, as golden and smooth as skin, with occasional clumps of oaks and manzanitas looking cool in the crevices. Black cows, and now and then horses. Through the farm town of Redding where my grandparents lived, down the long valley of apricots, olives, pears, almonds, and eventually – the air fresher now, a tang of the Pacific – the vineyards of Sonoma and Napa.

It was a long drive because the radiator kept overheating. *Goddamn Hillman!* said my father, because that was the name of the car. Finally, mid-afternoon, Mount Tamalpais came into view, deep green with fog creeping around the top. My heart leapt.

'Hello, Mount Tam! I've missed you,' I shouted and meant it, even though I hadn't really missed it. Both these things were true.

My brother was beside me, half-naked and asleep. My parents were talking softly and I could see my father touching my mother's knee as he talked. I was fine now and my family was fine too. Everything was as it should be, but when I closed my eyes I kept seeing my parents through the cabin window. How they'd seemed strangers for a minute, sitting at the table in the lamp light. It reminded me of a page in a book at home, of optical illusions. First it was a picture of a pretty girl, then it was a picture of an old witch and it was almost impossible to see the pretty girl again. I knew my parents, but I didn't *know them* know them. They were always saying they loved me and they loved each other. *I love you, I love you, I love you.* I told them I loved them too. But now I wasn't sure what the phrase meant, aside from a comforting thing to say, like petting the dog and saying 'good boy!' Did it just mean: *I'm here, you're here, everything is okay, we can ignore each other now?* How were you supposed to feel inside when you said it?

When I examined my inarticulate and worried heart, there was only one certainty. Something – something like silly putty – stretched between me and everyone in my family. Sometimes we hurt each other, made each other angry, but that silly putty held tight. We also made each other laugh. Real laughter, the kind you couldn't help doing and only happened if you were connected by silly putty. It was a satisfying explanation, and importantly it didn't rule out my parents loving each other. From then on, everything stemmed from this certainty. Everything.

This is Nuts

Ateca phoned in the middle of the night.

'This is the end. The end,' she repeated hoarsely and dramatically. 'I phoned your brother and sister, but nobody answers.'

'Oh dear. I guess they're working.'

No one attending Mom's final breaths but a paid carer? We were all terrible children. Terrible!

'Yeah. Guess so.' I could hear her sniffing. 'I'll put your mom on the phone. Barbarajones! Barbarajones, it's your daughter on the phone!'

I could hear breathing. Was this the death rattle? It sounded painful. Little grunts in between breaths.

'I, I, I,' Mom kept saying. There was a note of urgency in her voice. I willed her to finish what was possibly her last sentence, but all she kept saying was: 'I, I, I.'

Then Ateca's voice came back on.

'She's trying to say she loves you. But she cannot.'

'Really? She sounds in pain. Have you given her some morphine?'

'No pain.'

What? I had a sudden jolt of doubt. *Who was Ateca?* Maybe she didn't believe in pain relief. Had I even checked her references? No, because she hadn't offered any and I'd so badly wanted to believe she was the simplest solution to the Mom problem. What kind of child trusted their dying mother to a complete stranger?

'She can't hold the phone now,' said Ateca in a hushed tone, breaking into my self-loathing. 'I'll put the phone on her pillow so she can hear you. I'll take a photo with my phone so you can see her talking to you. My darling girl is leaving us!'

There was silence, then I could hear Ateca saying: 'God bless you, Barbarajones!'

This was followed by hysterical crying and receding foot-steps. I pictured her leaving the bedroom and collapsing on the hall floor. My trust in her returned, plumped itself up with a reassuring whoomph. She was not a nurse, not a trained carer, maybe not someone who played by all the rules, but she was a big-hearted honest woman prepared to do what none of us had been prepared to do. Hers was the bigger sacrifice. After Mom died, my life would not change much, but Ateca would be homeless and jobless. Plus, they *loved* each other, Mom and Ateca. I pictured my parents' bedroom, with my mother in her hospital bed facing the window looking out to the bay and Mount Tamalpais. It was late afternoon there – was she seeing the mountain right now? Noticing again how it looked like a pretty woman lying down? I hoped the window was open so she could hear the doves and gulls, feel the fresh air moving, smell the salt.

'Mom, can you hear me?'

'I, I.'

'I love you.'

'I, I, I.'

I was sitting in my dark kitchen in Scotland, shivering, rock-ing myself, tears pouring down my face. A tiny part of me applauded because I was crying like a normal person. On-the-dot tears! Mom loved Christmas, so I sang 'Silent Night'. I was a terrible singer, but she'd never complained before. After 'Silent Night', I went through *The Sound of Music* songs. In between, I talked to her as if she was one of my children who'd woken from a nightmare. I crooned.

'Everything's fine. Everything will be fine. Don't worry.'

'I, I, I.'

After a while, she stopped saying 'I', but I kept up the flow. Finally Ateca came back, sniffing and blowing her nose.

'She sleeps now. I'll phone again when there's change.'

After I hung up, I looked at my phone and there was the picture Ateca had sent. My beautiful mother, a phone on her pillow, presumably with my voice in it. Her expression was not loving or accepting. Her mouth was stretched wide and her eyes had a look I recognised. Urgent and cranky. I knew exactly what she was thinking:

Get me out of here! This is nuts!

Ave Maria

Once she was dead, Mom really came into her own. When Dad died, he likewise grew in stature for a while, and we children couldn't remember a single bad thing about him. But Mom had pushed him off the stage and it was her we idealised now. The woman I'd thought boring most of my life was suddenly fascinating. *Mother, Mom, Mommy!*

Me and my siblings were close, but we grieved separately. I didn't cry in front of my husband either, but in stolen private moments. In the bath, in the car parked in lay-bys, in the woods with the dog. The week before my mother's funeral, I was back in San Rafael, sitting in a 4th Street café alone and reading. It was a good book. My eyes began stinging, burning. Then to my alarm, tears washed down my face. Was I crying in public? It appeared so. My tear ducts had stopped waiting for permission from my self-conscious brain, and just gone for it. As in so many things, I was an amateur. An amateur and an onlooker in my own life.

The funeral was to be in Mission San Rafael, a small and very old adobe church in town. My brother had given our father's eulogy, I was giving our mother's, and our sister would give our eulogies, I guessed. I'd begun writing it while waiting for my connection in Terminal Five. Already I was six pages over the limit, but how could any life be summed up in 1,200 words? The priest had been firm on word count. Ensconced back in my parents' house in San Rafael, I kept whittling away, each time deleting more and more until it was the required length. It was, I felt, concise to the point of dullness.

It wasn't strange being in the house without Mom dying down the hall. I kept waiting for it to feel oppressive or spooky or weird, but the house felt like it always did. An easy place to sit around and daydream or read. I spent a lot of time considering what was going on with Mom now, if anything. Forget the party room full of dead people drinking cocktails, I decided. That was a nice place for Dad to hang out, but Mom would be happier waking up in a normal day from her past. No company, just her family around. One of the countless days that left no memory because nothing unusual happened. And being dead and that normal day now stretching to eternity, she'd understand this was happiness. No one knows the truth about time and the afterlife, which meant this scenario was possible. I deleted half of my skeletal eulogy and wrote about wishing her a normal day instead:

It's a perfect fall day, with green coming back to the hills. She can walk now, run, dance, whatever she wants. And her Brownie box camera has a new roll of film. Near to her, are us – not sulky teenagers, and not exhausting babies either. Maybe we're all about seven. None of us have runny noses and we're not fighting. Dad is about to walk in the door after work, his briefcase swinging, and she's checking her watch. Checking her reflection in the bedroom mirror, putting on some red lipstick.

'I'm home, honey!'

From down the hall, not seeing him yet, she tells a big fib.

'Good. Dinner's almost ready.'

His face lights up when he sees her, because he's forgotten again, just in the course of his day, how lovely she is. She admits her fib and he says:

'Hey, I'm not that hungry yet anyway. Let's have a beer.'

'Okay,' she says, even though she isn't crazy about beer.

And before she knows it, the evening's over and they're putting the house to bed – lights, locks, heating, teeth, dog. She gets into bed, making a mental note to change the sheets tomorrow, and that's it. Just a house full of children safe in their beds, and for a sweet eternity, a husband who enjoyed her macaroni and cheese again as if it was steak and caviar.

Like most funerals of old people, everyone was in a good mood. Their best, kindest selves. I was wearing a black dress my husband – who'd remained in Scotland because he was the kind of teacher who never took time off – had bought me for the occasion. My siblings were dressed tastefully too. Mom and Dad would be proud, we assured ourselves. We sat in the front pew. In front of us on the altar were the three vases of sunflowers I'd bought that morning at United Markets, my mother in a brass urn, and a giant cardboard photo of her face. It had been taken when she was about thirty-six, probably at the Marin Yacht Club because her smile was the smile of a person in her favourite place. Most likely she was looking at her husband, because her eyes had that I-know-you-inside-out look. It was a great photo, but I couldn't help but think Mom would hate it being on display. She'd say: *Get it out of here!* Or would she? Maybe she'd flinch initially, but then she might notice Dad's affronted face, and dead or not, he'd definitely be put out. He'd be thinking: *What the hell? I'm supposed to be the centre of attention!* That would make her giggle, and from there a whole new dynamic might be born. Posthumously Mom would spread her wings, tell her husband to fuck off, then run away to live with the man she loved the most. Her son.

I waited for the show to begin. I was nervous, but also looking forward to reading my revised eulogy. I hoped I made at least one person cry. Father Andrew invited us to stand and sing a hymn, then we sat down again and he mumbled some words. Very soon he stopped talking and indicated with a nod it was my turn. It seemed a little early for the eulogy, but I stood and walked to the pulpit, full of solemn purpose. I was important today. I took a moment to breathe and look at the audience, because that is what published authors do. The congregation, I kept having to remind myself, not the audience. I loved reading to a large group, damnit. Their faces were gratifyingly rapt, and I began.

'. . . our grandmother was a teenager when my mother was born, sixteen or seventeen, her own family recent arrivals from Domodossola in Italy. My mother's father was a teenager too. He jumped on a freight train when she was three and she never saw . . .'

The priest was standing very close to me suddenly, which seemed rude, but I blocked him and carried on. Any professional reader would.

'. . . but she never said anything negative. *He was young, it was the depression*, she would say and shrug. There are stories of her jumping for fun into the Sacramento River off a very high . . .'

The priest moved closer, moved in front of me and removed my eulogy notes. I hadn't even begun my description of her eternal day and I was a little peeved. If a throat could be cleared kindly, that is what he did next.

'What are you doing?' I whispered.

He didn't reply, just pointed to the pulpit shelf in front of me. There lay a sheet of paper with a reading from Job. My name was at the top, along with the words *First Reading*.

'Oh, Christ.' I was so proud for not saying *shit*.

A tiny smile from the priest, his head slanted as if to say: *No sweat*.

I'd known my siblings were giving Bible readings, but me too? I tried to make sense of the words on the page, but mirth began bubbling up. Mirth like a liquid, like the stage in the cycle of carsickness when I knew I was about to throw up. Oh, silly, silly me, imagining a funeral Mass could begin with a eulogy. If I wasn't me, I'd kill myself laughing at me, I was so funny. I let one bark escape, in the hope that it would decrease the pressure building up.

'Book of Job 19,' I finally croaked, and then heard myself mispronounce Job to rhyme with sob. I said Job again, this time correctly, to rhyme with robe. But then I couldn't continue speaking. Oh! Giggling in church was a sin. Worse – giggling in church at a funeral. *Causing* the giggling at your own mother's funeral in a church! I could hardly breathe.

'Sorry for the false start,' I told the congregation finally, choking, tears running down my face. 'I'll start again. This is a reading from The Book of Job 19.

'Oh, that my words were written!
Oh, that they were inscribed in a book!
That they were engraved on a rock
With an iron pen and lead forever!
For I know that my Redeemer lives.'

The reading choice was a cosmic joke. I don't recall how I made it back to my pew, but I remember how happy I felt. And no wonder – my body was thumping with endorphins. If church-giggling could be bottled and sold, who'd bother with drugs or alcohol? Or sex, for that matter. I settled back to enjoy the Mass. There were more hymns, and the Lord's Prayer, readings from my siblings, and a sermon about God's gift to us: our own lives. Of a promised eternity, if we loved – not just Him, but everybody. It sounded fair to me, but that might have been because I was high on church-giggling. There was Holy Communion, and we were first at the altar. We stuck our tongues out like the lapsed Catholics we were, not realising that for the majority, the tongue ritual had stopped thirty years ago. Then it was eulogy time. The priest nodded at me, gently smiled – I liked him suddenly, very much – and I took to the stage again. Pulpit.

'. . . and she was always taking photographs of us with her Brownie box camera. Later, as cameras became more complex, she'd say to Dad: *George! Quick! Get the camera!* Take a *picture!* One day I noticed his camera had no film in it, he was just clicking away to keep her happy and . . .'

I looked at the congregation a lot, took my time. Then the chapel doors opened and a man walked up the aisle towards me. He was Hispanic, middle-aged, and by the smell and state of his clothes, probably one of the 578 homeless in San Rafael. I paused because he was making mumbling noises as he approached, then I kept reading because I was a professional reader.

'. . . a few months ago, when she was asked if she and her husband had built their house, she'd answered: *Yes, when we were alive, we built this house . . .*'

Homeless Man came on the altar. No one did or said anything. I glanced behind me at the priest, but he seemed unconcerned. Homeless Man was smelling the sunflowers, stroking the petals and humming happily. Then he sat down on the floor in front of my mother's giant photo, gestured to her like an old friend, and began talking softly and warmly in Spanish. I raised my voice slightly and read the bit with Mom's eternal day. Then I stopped looking at my notes and said:

'If Mom was here right now, she'd say: *Well, look at you all! You all look beautiful! Now, off you go. Don't mind me, I'll be fine. Go on! Scoot! Take lots of pictures! Three kisses! I love you, goodbye!*'

Only my siblings understood when she said I love you, good-bye, she meant *Go away, you're making me cranky.* It was the only in-joke in the eulogy. I sat down. Homeless Man clapped his hands furiously and the priest shushed him in a nice way. Then he put his hands together and announced we were fortun-ate today, because we had a soloist to sing 'Ave Maria' for us.

'A surprise appearance,' he added.

A beautiful young Hispanic woman walked up to the altar and, unaccompanied, sang. Sunlight poured through the windows and I thought of the line in Joni Mitchell's 'Chelsea Morning', about the sun sticking to all her senses. Shafts of light on the sunflowers and my cardboard mother and the upturned face of Homeless Man. The words of 'Ave Maria' rose and fell through the yellow light. It was unbearably wonderful. 'Ave Maria' might do the conversion trick, I was thinking. Then it was over. The priest blessed us and people were shaking hands, hugging each other. Homeless Man began distributing sunflowers to everyone. I stood a moment, reluctant to move, to let the next moments in my life commence. My sister had married here, my father's funeral had been here, and my parents had married here. 'Ave Maria' had been sung on that day too, no doubt by another beautiful young woman. On this very same altar, my mother and father had looked at each other, aged twenty-two and twenty-four, and on cue pressed their lips together. I imagined them turning around to face everybody and smiling goofily, because true happiness is an involuntary thing. I knew those sudden goofy smiles. I'd seen them every time I'd come home.

'Wah!'

'What?' asked my brother.

'Nothing,' I said.

'Come on, we better get home before everyone else does,' said my sister.

So we went home and got drunk. The house was heaving. My parents' friends, cousins I'd not seen in years, cousins I'd never met, neighbours I'd known since I was five. Much laughter and no tears. Ateca, who was the true mistress of our house, announced she and her Fijian friends were about to sing a song for Barbara Jones. We all hushed and watched. The women were splendid in long brightly coloured dresses, and the men were in their suits. The singing was weak at first, the six voices wavering, discordant, and I determined to clap extra loudly when they ended. Then the singing became something else. Something cohesive, substantial, mounting emotionally. People began looking for tissues, sniffing. My mother's name was part of the song, but all else was in Fijian. In the end, it was just Ateca's voice, plaintive, repetitive, heart-wringing. Her face was wet, her eyes soft and dark. When it ended, no one clapped for a moment, then everyone did.

'It is what we do in Fiji,' she explained to us, after her bow. 'When someone is dead, we call to them one more time. Summon them, so we can say goodbye. Barbarajones came. She was right here and I said to her, I said: I love you and goodbye.'

This was not the same as Mom's *I love you, goodbye.*

Ateca put us to shame. All the Fijians did. What was wrong with us, in our casual clothes, laughing and getting drunk and not feeling sad? For a full minute I felt bad, but I couldn't keep it up. It was the last party in my parents' house. They'd loved giving parties – loud, drunken, late-night parties with off-key singing, cigarette burns on the rug, rowdy arguments about football teams, Billie Holiday and Duke Ellington on the record player. I wanted to keep having fun.

Stop Worrying about the Fish

In the beginning, time was all around me – a seeming infinity, like the sky or the sea. I'd begun leaking time already, but it hadn't felt like it. The memories from childhood were few but indestructible, as if they'd been stored in the black box of a burning airplane. Memories from the rest of my life, by comparison, were corrupted things. I suppose as I got older, I began to edit events to suit how I wanted to see myself that particular day. Victim, hero, misunderstood genius, the choices were endless. Writing about my past and imagining an audience, I kept wishing my memories were more flattering. That they made more sense as a whole. But then, what would be the point of that? Real life isn't a novel – it's a mixed bag, as Dad liked to say.

'I'm having a baby,' I'd announced.

'Huh.'

'Aren't you pleased?'

'Sure, but I've got to warn you,' he'd said, with an expression I'd take decades to realise was protective, not critical. 'It's a mixed bag.'

In any case, what audience was going to be interested in the life of an American nobody? I wasn't a celebrity. I hadn't survived a tsunami, or sailed single-handedly across the Atlantic, or overcome heroin addiction, poverty or racism. I hadn't had an abusive father. Damnit, I hadn't even had cancer! I was just a middle-class, middle-aged white woman from an American suburb, and by global standards, utterly spoiled. I used to have an enthusiastic audience of one, but now she was dead and she'd taken the best version of me with her.

A few months after the funeral, something odd happened. It was the middle of winter and I'd been in a deep sludge of a sleep, with no dreams I could recall. Earlier, I'd taken Night Nurse so I'd sleep without coughing. I was dragged out of this deep dark sleep by a frightening commotion in the kitchen. It wasn't one voice calling out for help, it was a solid mass – a howling entreaty for help. *Emergency! Wake up! Catastrophe is happening!* I didn't respond to this plea heroically. I found it terrifying, as if some injured convict was loose in our house, wreaking havoc in his misery. As I opened my eyes – slowly, due to depth of sludge-sleep and Night Nurse – the ruckus abated until there was just one clear noise. The sound of a kitchen cupboard shutting quietly. My first thought was to turn to my husband and tell him someone had broken into the house – but then, he must have heard the noise too and therefore also be awake. It was pitch dark, but I could feel his body next to me, his broad back, and he was still asleep. This fact seemed proof that I'd imagined the commotion. It had been, in fact, a bad dream which had somehow sneaked over the boundary into wakefulness.

But later in the day, I began to think of it again. If the noise had been a dream, why had it been so place-specific? Dreams weren't logical and scenes could happen anywhere – why the ordinary kitchen? I then placed the fact, on top of this, that I'd spent much of the previous day unpacking my dead parents' belongings in the kitchen. Nothing had broken, despite the fact they'd been at sea for eight weeks, wedged into a wooden container. They'd travelled further than I'd ever managed. Ningbo and the Panama Canal, Hong Kong and Mombasa, finally ending up here in my kitchen in Scotland. The wooden fruit bowl Mom used for bananas and apples for sixty years.

The chair my father sat in for meals every day, the only one with arms, the one my mother called the king's chair. The bedroom mirror they'd both looked in daily and which had witnessed both their deaths. Some of their ashes were secreted away here too. Dad was in the wooden container he'd used to keep keys in. Mom was in her own vanity case, the one she'd bought for her honeymoon. Was it possible things were not hunky-dory in the afterlife, and what I'd witnessed in the middle of the night had been a kind of spiritual temper tantrum? A maelstrom of frustration? A *what the hell is going on with my things?* Maybe my parents – now out of life's loop – were not happy campers. It didn't happen again the next night, which I took as a good sign. There's probably an adjustment period for people after they die, I told myself.

But was I adjusting? As time went on, I couldn't shake the feeling I was still at my mother's deathbed. There she lay, down the hall in her hospital bed, and in a sense it felt as if she'd always been there, would always be there, dying slowly and gracefully, *classy as hell*. I could be in Tesco, deciding whether or not to buy chilled fish already battered, or to buy fresh fish and batter it myself – when whoosh! There was my mother, right there, lying in her hospital bed and insisting: *I'm great! How are you? Can you please tell me the time?* My father was there too sometimes, but never lying down. He hadn't occupied a deathbed long enough and he was always standing up. *Come on*, he said when he got my attention. *Stop worrying about the fish. You take life so seriously! Let's go out for lunch.*

But my mother never mocked me. She smiled as if I was three and had just figured out the shape sorter toy. *You clever girl – the wooden squares go in that hole!*

I'm sorry, I told her.

She smiled and shrugged her c'est la vie shrug. Turned slightly and said: *Did you hear that, George? She's sorry.*

What for?

321

I have no idea.

Then she looked back at me, frowned as if I was nine now, with a scrape on my knee from falling off my bike.

Are you all right?

I'm not all right, I said.

Oh, good gravy, she said, not missing a beat. *Don't worry, no one's all right. Not a single person.*

This was good news, albeit bewildering. Could I apply it to my fish dilemma? I opened my mouth to ask, but instead – just like that – out popped my mother's *Wah!*

Epigraph and
Acknowledgements

Some of this book is drawn straight from memory, without embellishments or omissions. The rest is only loosely based on memory. I have created dialogue, compressed or expanded events, rearranged time, deleted people, combined people, made up names – all to serve the greater purpose of making a readable book. Most of the people mentioned have kindly agreed to be included, and for this generosity I am grateful. I was unable to locate some people, and if this includes you, please accept my apology. For those of you who have been disappointed to *not* find yourself in these stories, again – my apology. I'm working on another book, for what it's worth.

Thanks to Carolyn Jones, Michael Jones, Claire Aitcheson, Anne MacLeod, Laura Hird, Zoe MacKenzie, Nic Halloways, Linda Engbrenghof, Maggie MacDonald, Molly Heatherwick, Isla Dewar, Nicky Guthrie, Kate Ashton, Martin Russell, James Robertson and Michel Faber for their corrections and viewpoints. It was impossible to be objective and their input was invaluable.

Thanks to Moira and Bob at Sandstone for giving me another whirl. And to their editor Nicola Torch for her wisdom and perseverance.

Finally, an immense thank you to my husband Peter Whiteley, for still liking me at the end of reading this book. Or pretending to, which is good enough.

www.sandstonepress.com

Subscribe to our weekly newsletter for events
information, author news, paperback and e-book
deals, and the occasional photo of authors' pets!
bit.ly/SandstonePress

 facebook.com/SandstonePress/

@SandstonePress